Interventions in Political Economy

An Explorative Observations

Interventions in Political Economy

An Explorative Observations

Essays in Honour of
Prof.Manjappa.D.Hosamane

Edited by
Prof. Muzaffar H Assadi

KALPAZ

First Published, 2017

Published by

Kalpaz Publications
C-30, Satyawati Nagar,
Delhi – 110052
E-mail: kalpaz@hotmail.com
Ph.: 9212142040

Printed at: G. Print Process, Delhi

Cataloging in Publication Data—DK
Courtesy: D.K. Agencies (P) Ltd. <docinfo@dkagencies.com>

Interventions in political economy : an explorative observations : essays in honour of Prof. Manjappa D. Hosamane / edited by Prof. Muzaffar H Assadi.
pages cm
Contributed articles.
Includes bibliographical references.
ISBN 9789351282815

1. India—Economic conditions. 2. India—Economic policy. 3. Finance—India. 4. Economics. I. Hosamane, Manjappa D., honouree. II. Assadi, Muzaffar H., editor.

LCC HC435.I58 2017 | DDC 330.954 23

Contents

List of Figures

List of Tables

List of Contributors

- **Kishore G.Kulkarni, Ph.D**
  Distinguished Professor of Economics & Editor IJEB
  Campus Box 77, P.O.Box 173362
  Metropolitan State University Denver, Denver, CO 80217-3362, USA
  E-mail: kulkarnk@msudenver.edu

- **Dr. Younos Vakil Alroaia**
  Assistant Professor and chairman, DOS in Management,
  Islamic Azad University, Semnan Branch, Semnan, Iran,
  E-mail: younos.vakil@gmail.com

- **Selva Kumar. D**
  Ph.D Scholar, School of Management
  National Institute of Technology, Rourkela
  E-mail: 512sm2007@nitrkl.ac.in

- **Dr. Dinabandhu Bag**
  Associate Professor, School of Management
  National Institute of Technology, Rourkela
  E-mail: dinabandhu.bag@gmail.com

- **Dr. Vinay M R**
  Practice Lead Data Scientist
  Analytics Business Unit, Infosys Ltd.

- **Mr. Prakash K**
  Consultant, Infosys Ltd.

- **Dr. Niranjan.R**
  Assistant Professor
  Department of Studies & Research in Economics
  Vijayanagara Sri Krishnadevaraya University
  Ballari, Karnataka. E-mail: nijannr@gmail.com

- **Prof. D.S.Leelavathi**
  Professor of Economics
  Department of Studies in Economics & Co-operation
  Manasagangothri, University of Mysore, Mysore, Karnataka
  E-mail: prof_leelavathi@yahoo.co.in

- **Prof.S.Mahendra Kumar**
  Professor of Co-operation
  Department of Studies in Economics & Co-operation
  Manasagangothri, University of Mysore, Mysore, Karnataka

- **Mr. Seyed Mehdi Pourkiaei**
  Research Scholar
  Department of Studies in Economics and Co-operation
  University of Mysore,
  Mysore, Karnataka

- **Prof. Shri Prakash**
  Professor of Eminence
  Birla Institute of Management and Technology (BIMTECH)
  Greater Noida. E-mail: shri.prakash@bimtech.ac.in

- **Mr. Sudhi Sharma**
  Senior Project Associate
  Birla Institute of Management and Technology (BIMTECH)
  Greater Noida. E-mail: sudhi.sharma@bimtech.ac.in

- **Prof. Muzaffar H Assadi**
  Professor of Political Science
  Department of Political Science
  Manasagangothri, University of Mysore
  Mysore, Karnataka
  E-mail: muzaffar.assadi@gmail.com

- **Prof. S Rajendran**
  Professor of Economics
  Department of Economics,
  Gandhigram Rural Institute- Deemed University,
  Dindigul District, Tamil Nadu
  E-mail: myrajendran@gmail.com

- **Prof. D.V.Gopalappa**
  Professor of Economics
  Department of Studies in Economics and Cooperation
  University of Mysore,
  Mysore, Karnataka
  E-mail: gopalappa666@rediffmail.com

- **Prof. Dr. H.R.Uma**
  Professor of Economics
  Department of Studies in Economics and Co-operation
  University of Mysore,
  Mysore, Karnataka
  E-mail: umahr30mahesh@gmail.com

- **Mr. Madhu.S**
  Research Scholar
  Department of Studies in Economics and Co-operation
  University of Mysore,
  Mysore, Karnataka

Preface

In this slim volume, in honour of Dr.Manjappa.D.Hosamane, a student of mine has articulated a scheme of intervention which he hopes is invariant to any interference by other policies. This is quite an important aspect of intervention, basically referring to "correcting" the imbalances, if any, in the intervention of political economy. It concerns both politics and economics, which are invariant to any other influences of policy measures, taken either by the government or corporate sector. This looks quite surprising, but Dr. Manjappa Hosmane has emphatically rejected the view and sticks to his interventionalist approach.

Dr. Manjappa Hosamane has trained a band of his students to articulate further his invariance thesis. The various papers in the volume testify it. The scope of the paper cover a wide range of issues: from Iranian small scale industries to the industries of Mysore, from voluntary retirement schemes to fallacies in IS-MP curve model to climate change. It is a bold attempt where other narratives if any, will not make any difference to the way he viewed it.

The book makes significant departure from the beaten track. It represents a refreshingly creative and useful contribution to political economy. In the liberal tradition, it shows how political economy may be treated without bogging down in the trivialities. This is how teachers should groom students and extract from them their vision in a substantial manner. This is a teacher's work, as well as the pupil's support.

Basically the volume is a tribute to Dr. Hosamane by his students. It tells about their teacher his commitment to teaching and scholarship. He has been very successful in bringing out the talents of the pupils in a concise manner. Turning to the coverage in general, the scope is very wide and makes an interesting reading. I wish Dr. Hosamane the best of luck. Bon Aperitif!

Prof. Ranganath Bharadwaj
Honorary Visiting Professor
Institute for Social and Economic Change (ISEC) Bangalore
&
President of All India Input-Output Research Association.

A concise profile of Prof. Manjappa.D.Hosamane

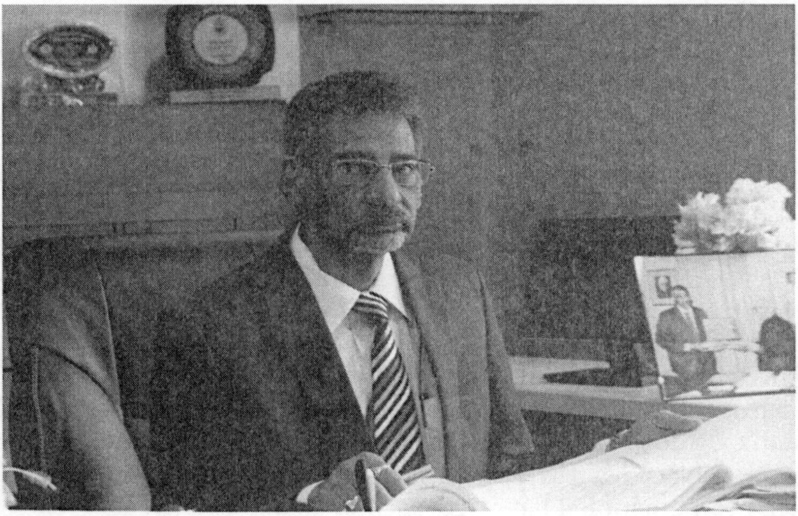

Prof. Manjappa D Hosamane is an eminent professor, econometrician, scholar, administrator and more over a gifted humble down to earth simple person. Prof. Manjappa.D.Hosamane needs no introduction in contemporary academics in India. He has established himself as a genuine academician and as a proficient administrator. Professor is born in an agricultural family, in the village called Nisarani, located in Sorab Taluk of Shivamogga District, Karnataka. He did his early education up to S. S. L. C in Government Primary School, Nisarani and Secondary Education in Vidya Vardhaka Sangha High School at Nisarani. For higher studies he moved to Mysore and joined the Maharaja's college for Pre-University and continued his Bachelor Degree in the same college. He did is Post-Graduation at Department of Studies in Economics and Cooperation, Manasagangothri, University of Mysore. After completing Master Degree in 1978, he was given Guest Faculty position in University of Mysore and posted to Mangalore Campus. Further in 1982 he was selected as an Economic Officer in Dena Bank and posted in Bombay. Along with his service in 1984 he has registered for Ph.D. in Bombay University under the supervision of well know Econometrician, Prof Ranganath Bharadwaj and completed the Doctorate in International Economics with specialization in Applied Econometrics in 1989.

With plenteous practical banking experience, he entered academics as Associate Professor to Karnatak University, Dharwad. In the year 1997-98, he has been awarded Commonwealth Fellowship as a visiting Fellow for the University of Essex, Colchester, United Kingdom. With his academic excellence, in 1999, he joined as Professor to University of Mysore. Prof. Manjappa.D.Hosomane had a lengthy teaching carrier spanning for more than three decades. The Professor has put up his direct service to a number of universities such as Mangalore University, Karnatak University, University of Mysore and Vijayanagara Sri Krishnadevaraya University. Also rendered his indirect academic and administrative service to numerous universities in Karnataka and elsewhere. In this lengthy academic career, he has to his credit over 100 research papers published in reputed international and national journals and over dozen research projects and he has visited numerous foreign universities. His published papers were translated in to different international languages such as Japanese, German, French, and Arabic. He has groomed 20 young bright students in realizing their dream of obtaining Ph.D degree and guided over 50 M.Phil students. He is a source of inspiration for his students.

In recognizing his academic service to the student community and society in large, he has been awarded with Shiksha Rattan Puraskar and Certificate of Excellence by India International Friendship Society in 2007.

Prof. Manjappa.D.Hosamane, being a distinguished academician also an efficient and experienced administrator. He served as an economist in a commercial bank for ten years, in the Department of Economic Research & Project Evaluation, undertook evaluation work of different development projects implemented through NABARD. Also served as first Vice-Chancellor of Vijayanagara Sri Krishnadevaraya University, Ballari and put all his innovative thoughts and decades of academic and administrative experience, for the growth and development of the new university. He is also a member of Karnataka State Higher Education Council (KSHEC).

Prof. Manjappa.D.Hosamane is associated with University of Mysore till his retirement in April 2016 and also served as Chairman of the Department of Studies in Economics and Cooperation in University of Mysore.

1

INTRODUCTION

Professor Muzaffar H. Assadi

Last couple of years has seen the intensification of debates centreing on the issues of political-economy, both as theoretical construct as well as empirical reality. These debates centred around the following: will political economy approach solve the problems afflicting the people? Will it come out with uniform prescription that can be adopted universally? How to conceptualise the transformation taking place both in the economy as well as in politics? How political economy is linked to and over-lapped with the issues of freedom, liberty, rights and, at the same time how it is linked to the larger issues of governance, economic development as well as well-being of the citizens. All these doesn't mean that political economy is simply revolved around one single school or approach, particularly liberal school, rather the Marxian critique which include dependency theory too, which has further strengthened and enlarged the scope of political economy approach/perspective over the decades.

Uptil the arrival of Mill's Principles of Political Economy, for one hundred years, Adam Smith's text, The Wealth of Nation dominated the discourse on political economy. That doesn't mean that both treated the issues on an equal footing-the difference lies in the fact that Adam Smith analysed and comprehended the newly emerging industrial economy/market and advocated laissez-faire as prescription. On the contrary, Mill advocated utilitarianism. Adam Smith believed that economy works most effectively and efficiently in the midst of a free market, and in the midst of least interference by the State.

Paradoxically his theory continues to help in extending debate to the issues of appropriate boundaries between free market economies on the one hand and the strong or weak state on the other. Incidentally, Neo-liberalism is trying to reclaim his thoughts to justify the dismantling of state structure, opening up the market for global capital, privatise the economy. Adam Smith continues to influence successive political economist such as Ricardo, Marx John Maynard Keynes, and of late Milton Friedman.

This does not mean that there were no other philosophers who would focus on political economy: Jean-Jacques Rousseau, Anne-Robert-Jacques Turgot or Francois Quesnay, Jeremy Bentham, Immanuel Kant or Edmund Burke, David Hume are some names. Their treatment of political economy was not the same. Rousseau argues in his *A Discourse on Political Economy* written in 1755 that "The word Economy, or Economy, is derived from oikos, a house, and nomos, law, and meant originally only the wise and legitimate government of the house for the common good of the whole family. The meaning of the term was then extended to the government of that great family, the State. To distinguish these two senses of the word, the latter is called general or political economy, and the former domestic or particular economy". It is in this text that he introduced the concept of general will. He argued that there are three maxim on which virtuous state stands on; '(1) Following general will in every action; (2) see that every particular will is in conformity with general will and finally all the public needs must be satisfied'.

Anne-Robert-Jacques Turgot (1727-1781) was a major political and intellectual figure in pre-revolutionary France. Initially he was treated as physiocrate, particularly in his book *Reflections on the Formation and Distribution of Wealth* (1766) wherein he argued that land is the only source of wealth. He became the defender of liberalism, as he advocated complete freedom for commerce and industry.

Francois Quesnay was another French economist who again believed in the theory of physiocrates-believing that agriculture was the only productive sector and treated industry as "sterile". His argument in favour of political economy was apparent in his *Tableau économique* (1758). He was the first to advocate economic equilibrium and was first to use the term laissez-faire and, advocated policy against government interference in trade. His major argument centred around the issues of capital-the latter being avances-looking at capital as a stock of wealth which needs to be accumulated in advance for the purpose of production. He argues about the presence of two forms of capital-one, fixed and another, circulating and advocated deregulated trade and reduced taxes.

Jeremy Bentham, a British economist, in fact started as Smithian but attached to laissez-faire. Incidentally, he belongs to utilitarian tradition who converted this tradition into a secular and systematic form. At the same time he made the utilitarian tradition a part of moral and legal philosophy. In his Manual of Political Economy Jeremy Bentham argues that" the principle of utility in every branch of the art of legislation, the object or end in view should be the production of the maximum of happiness in a given time in the community in question' (p.1).

Immanuel Kant, although is known as moral philosopher, however cannot be ruled from writings on political economy. His readings on property law, public sphere or history were his response to economic conditions/treatments. He was a champion of freedom. He believed that freedom is the basis of any state. Hence he argues in Critique of Practical Reason that "Any action is right if it can coexist with everyone's freedom in accordance with a universal law, or if on its maxim the freedom of choice of each can coexist with everyone's freedom in accordance with a universal law". In other words everything such as happiness and others co-exist only with freedom (p. 230).

Edmund Burke, best known as British conservative but also equally known for political economy perspectives. At the same time he is known as ardent supporter of Market – for him Market is the meeting point of consumers and producers. The argument in favour of least interference is quite obvious in his argument that, "What the State ought to take upon itself to direct by the public wisdom, and what it ought to leave, with as little interference as possible, to individual discretion. "(*The Writings and Speeches of Edmund Burke*, ed. Paul Langford *et al.* (Oxford: Clarendon Press, 1981, 133)

David Hume, a Scottish scholar, was a contemporary of Adam Smith who countered the arguments of British mercantilist. He is better known as political economist. He made two major contributions to political economy. One is in the sphere of monetary quantity theory and the second was in the sphere of advocating economic freedom, in the latter case he argued that economic freedom is the necessary condition for political freedom. In fact, he was credited with floating the ideas of inflation, foreign trade, and private property. He was the first to develop the economic model on "Balance of Trade".

There are others too, who had also contributed to the study of political economy. They include such political economist as Francis Hutcheson, Bernard de Mandeville, David Ricardo,

Henry Thornton, John Ramsay McCulloch, James Maitland, Jean Charles Léonard de Sismondi, Nassau William Senior, Edward Gibbon Wakefield. These are better known either as classical liberals or conservatives. They stressed too much on Market, believing that Market tends move a position of equilibrium. Interestingly it was Chydenius, a Finnish priest was the one who advocated economic liberalism much earlier to Adam Smith. He stressed on democracy, freedom and equality for the larger human happiness. Interestingly his name has not been referred to as the precursor to Adam Smith. This is where academic amnesia is operating.

Economic liberalism came under sever contestation under Marx, the latter completely changed the perspective on political economy. While making a departure from liberal discourse on political economy, he tried to give radical perspective. Paradoxically his analysis would touch liberal economist who contributed considerably to the study of classical political economy. This includes Adam Smith, Ricardo and Malthus etc. However, 'his notion about the modern state fundamentally altered traditional notion about the state. He had multiple opinions, although traditionally it is argued that he had only one opinion about the state-it is an instrument of ruling class. But in fact he would view the state interims of its changing nature. For him state is not only the instrument of ruling class, but also he advocated 'abdication theory of the state', wherein the ruling class abdicate the power in favour of another class. His argument about structure or base and super structure – explain the fact that economic structure finally determines or decide the governmental machinery such as government, police, army etc.

Interestingly Marx would view capitalism as not only dominant/principal mode but it would become universal mode. This does not mean that he advocated uniform mode of production, which is also called as progressive and systematic-that each country would undergo – classical/ancient, feudal, and capitalist. In fact, his argument about Asiatic mode of production in the context of India and China seems to be a different mode specific to the Asian conditions. However, one thing is true every economy finally has to reach capitalist mode one or the other day for the transformative politics. Marx view that discovery of new colonies and subsequent colonial exploitation constitute the capitalist growth in colonised country, and that primitive accumulation constitute industrial growth, brought a paradigm shift in the analysis of political economy. In fact, one can call Marx as the first systematic theorist to foresee the arrival of globalisation in recent past.

A lot of Marxist scholars carried forward the arguments of Marx who are either called as "neo-Marxist", "Post-Marxist" or "Radical Marxist". They represented Marxian tradition. There were orthodox Marxist including revisionist as well. Lenin, Mao followed orthodox tradition, changed some of the notions about linkage between politics and economics depending upon the specific conditions available in their respective countries. Lenin's work on "Capitalist Development in Russia", "Imperialism: the highest stage of capitalism", Mao's 'on contradictions' are some of the works in this direction.

Neo-Marxist tradition is basically a loose group of Marxist who were the product of World War I and also post-colonial present. In fact, these Neo-Marxists also not averse to using such theories as critical theories, existentialism etc. They were not averse to use Weberian understanding either. There are Marxian sociologist, Marxian critical theorist who were not averse to be very close to linguistic philosophy, or sociology.

In the first case we have scholars such as Adorno, Luckas, Horkheimer Hebarmas etc. They belonged to what is called Frankfurt school. They combined critical theories vis-à-vis the Marxian one. Hebarmas went to the extent of advocating "network" as opposed to party. Herbert Marcuse went further to critique the consumer society. Adorno critiqued effect of mass culture and fascism on the European world. The period 1970s and 1980s saw the growth of another streams of neo-Marxist who came largely from the journal called *Monthly Review*. Herbert Marcues, Baran, Sweezy, Kalecki represented this tradition. Maurice Dobb, a known orthodox Marxist also followed the Neo-Marxism.

Interestingly these Neo-Marxists, particularly those who are closely observing growth and development in European world believed in integrating "bourgeoisie' argument to understand the nature of capitalism in industrialised world. In fact, they believed that in industrialised world capitalism, more than becoming competitive, as argued once by Marx has become Monopolistic in nature. For the Neo-Marxist State has either become "soft", "hard relatively autonomous" or "autonomous".

The third stream of Neo-Marxist are closely associated with what is called "Dependency Theory" or what is called World System, theory. They were the post-colonial theorist as well who emerged countering the modernisation theories. A.G. Frank, Wallerstein, Samir Amin, Walden Bello, Walter Rodney, Keith Giffin, Sunkel etc. Majority of them focussed on Latin America except Samir Amin. These theorists believed that the resources flow from "periphery" of poor countries to the core makes the latter rich. The poor countries by virtue of the fact that they provide natural resources, cheap labour and market to the rich countries. On the contrary, the rich try to control the periphery through a set of strategies such as economics, banking, education, media, culture etc. In fact, the underdevelopment of the periphery is the result of continued linkage with the core countries even after the termination of colonial rule. This is the reason why political economists such as Andre Gunder Frank calling for "delinkage" with the core by the periphery.

However, there are other political economist too who followed Marxism: Bernice Shoul-US political economist, David Yaffe-a British political economist and John Hobson-a great theorist of Imperialism etc. In fact, Hobson is known as centrist rather than critical political economist.

The collapse of Soviet Union, unification of Germany and disappearance of communist countries necessitated the need for relook into Marxist understanding about the linkage between ideology, economy and politics. During all these days questions were raised as to: Why Soviet Union collapsed even though it declared that it had already reached the stage of socialism? What went wrong with Soviet State? Did its economy fail to reach out to every citizen or is it merely the reflections of its defeat, beginning with the period of collectivisation, are some of the questions often raised. It is in this context one cannot deny the fact that at present Marxism is in deep crisis-to survive as a distinctive ideology. This is the reason why Marxism is now increasingly focussing on such issues as identity, ecology, social movements. In fact, it is now increasingly transforming its discourse from class politics to identity politics, however without giving up the claim on "class politics".

Incidentally, globalisation of twentieth century has given rise to two streams of political economist, sometime blurred categories as such. Political economist such as Amartya Sen represented such overlapping-he is liberal as well as critical. He is critical of globalisation but at the same time he is the defender of "rights and freedom" in a liberalised economy. Stiglitz is another name who started off as a defender of globalisation but in the course he became one of its bitter critiques. They became critical for the simple reason that globalisation, more than becoming solution is increasingly becoming problem -it has increased inequality across the world, the number of poor has multiplied, number of farmers committing suicide has crossed beyond two million, number of people displaced due to the development agenda has crossed few millions. They can be called critical political economist. Incidentally they came from liberal tradition as well. But there are other critical political economists who came from Marxian tradition. Home grown Prabhat Patnaik, Utsa Patnaik represents such tradition.

Bhagawathi on the contrary who views in globalisation, a 'panacea' represents neo-liberalism. This trend began with Austria by Hayak who questioned the validity of central planning. This was followed by Chicago school, among them Milton Freedman is important. Milton pushed the idea of Market competition and economic liberty as the most important component for the economic problem of Latin America. He along with other economist including the international institutes such as World Bank, IMF and WTO pushed globalisation for the simple reason that it would solve all the problems afflicting the developing world. But they proved wrong. Their theories of structural adjustment, or liberalisation proved that globalisation while pushing capitalism has created two forms of capitalist path of development: aggressive path of capitalist development and non-aggressive path of development. The capitalism is pushed at the cost of human rights, freedom and liberty. It has created large number of depoliticised categories on the one hand, politicised and vibrant civil society on the other. This is where the theories of political economy and prescription provided by the political economist are facing the problem. In other words political economy theories are under crisis. Neither they could solve the problem nor could they come out with a universal theory to solve the problems afflicting different social categories.

It is in this deep crisis we need to look at the contribution made by different scholars to this edited volume brought out in honour of Prof Manjappa Hosamane, former Vice-Chancellor of Vijayanagara Sri Krishnadevaraya University and Professor of Economics of University of Mysore. Prof Manjappa represented the liberal tradition but at the same time he is also a part of critical.

In other words he combines 'liberal as well as critical tradition"-this is not an ambiguity rather reflecting the independent scholarship.

Preview

Most of the articles contributed to this volume represent the liberal tradition. Even, they reflected the larger concern of scholars afflicting the communities or the social categories in around their localities. They are also concerned about the way the public policies are dislocating the local communities, including the fact that they are concerned about how migration has become a major phenomenon in recent past. Contributions also reflected the debates emerging in the discipline of economics in the western world. Each contribution is unique as they try to address diverse issues from their perspective.

Kishore G. Kulkarni's article on Fallacies in IS-MP Curve Model to explain Monetary Policy effects with special reference to Federal Reserve' deals with an interesting debate on intermediate macroeconomics textbook which dealt on IS-LM Curve model. This model was used to interpret the consequences of changes in money supply of an economy-shift would bring in general equilibrium point which will move to the situation where interest rate is lower and GDP is higher. This has been questioned over the past twenty years with the help of monetary policy curve (MP). This replacement was supported by the argument that shift in interest rate done by Federal Reserve MP Curve become an useful tool to find out the effect on real GDP. It, therefore, becomes a common place to treat the interest rate as an active policy tool for monetary policy. The famous Taylor rule in fact came up with so-called efficient formula by which the interest rate will be changed monetary policies not only in USA, but also in other capitalistic countries.

Younos Vakil Alroaia's article makes an interesting reading. His article on export decision-making in Small-Scale Industries of Iran focuses on the preference of industrial export in Iran's-Small-scale industries. He argues that economic success of any nation now depends upon the ability of industries to compete with global this calls for two things: effective export assistance is to improve their competitiveness in the global market, secondly, help in overcoming the obstacle or bottlenecks in the globalised economy.

Another interesting article is on the issue of Mysore Brand by Selva Kumar, D, and Dinabandhu Bag argues in their paper on "Ance or Backwaters : The case of Mysore Industries" that the legacy of Mysore which represented host of State-Owned Enterprises (SOEs) namely, Mysore Lamp Works Ltd; Mysore Paper Mills Ltd; Mysore Cements Ltd. and Mysore Petrochemicals Ltd are no more represent flourishing empire of "MYSORE ESTATE" in recent past. The authors argues that this could be due to excessive state interference in the affairs of these enterprises, declining rate of capital formation; declining margins; rising cost of goods sold; stagnant and falling market share and the inability to achieve scale economies. Further, investment in fixed assets; product development; brands; network of branches; skill improvement of employees; newer technology; role of unions towards business goals are also some of the pre-dominant issues affected the Mysore brand. The legacy unfortunately no more continued.

Vinay, M R and Prakash, K in their article "Innovative Business Solutions Using Big Data Analytics -An Empirical Analysis on Retail Customer Behaviour" that the retail industry is experiencing major challenges in recent past mainly due to changes in market structure, change in customer behaviour, product differentiation and price discrimination. It is in this context one of the major question is how to understand customer behaviour and cope up with business challenges. At the same time the challenges is how to enhance the growth, productivity, revenue and increase in customer base of the firms. Interestingly, the authors tried to develop business solutions based on Customer Behaviour Analytics which emphasise on focussing on purchase pattern, trend, profiling, segmentation, attrition and loyalty.

Niranjan, R's article on financial integration and dynamics of industrial growth in India focuses on the debate on the dynamics of industrial growth and financial integration in India. Article assesses this link for a panel of selected major fifteen manufacturing industries (classified under NIC 2004) for the period from 1990 to 2007. Further article tries to investigate the effects of financial integration on industrial growth by focusing on industry's external financial dependence and domestic financial development interacted with financial integration. He argues that the integration of financial systems has its trickledown effect-promotes growth of all industries regardless of their characteristics. At the same time article argues that financial integration has marginal influence on sectors which are dependent on external finance. Finally article argues that more financial integration coupled with financial development to have direct effect on industrial growth.

D.S. Leelavathi's article on voluntary retirement scheme is one more interesting piece of scholarship. Her article, Voluntary Retirement Scheme in Public Sector Banks: critical issues start with globalisation which aims at integrating Indian economy with the rest of the world. As a consequence of this, a series of changes in the form of reforms have been introduced in various sectors of the economy, including the banking sector. Apart from introducing reforms in the banking sector as suggested by Narasimham Committee, though of late, it has also embarked upon the employee restructuring mechanisms of which Voluntary Retirement Scheme (VRS) is the most widely debated as well as practiced unlike in other sectors. VRS is the most human technique to provide overall reduction in the existing strength of employees. It is a common method for trimming the excess employees. It is a generous tax-free severance payment to persuade the employees to voluntarily retire from the company. Has it been able to increase the efficiency is one moot quest that the article tries to address.

Shri Prakash, and Sudhi Sharma's article Focus on Gaps and limitations of official statistical system of India: A Note" focus on gaps and limitations of data gathered by different agencies of Government of India in general and CSO in particular. Further the article concentrates on data limitations and gaps relating to input output modelling and employment of human resources in Indian economy. It argues further that the major gaps in data base of input output modelling relate to (i) total absence of such data for the compilation of capital coefficients matrix of Indian economy; (ii) absence of data relating to inter and intra-state trade along with price differentials among the economies of the states; (iii) absence of I-O matrix with uniform classification since 1973 without which inter-temporal comparative study is not possible. Change in technology is also difficult to be averred without such tables; (iv) Both inter-state and intra-state growth differentials warrant that each input output table has an inter-regional transaction matrix as its supplement; (v) No data relating to transactions that take place between rural and urban establishments and people within a district and among the districts of a state are available; (vi) Sector-wise data relating to employment with education-occupation profile and corresponding wage/salary rates are not available at all. Data relating to non-formal and unorganised sector are not available. This makes it extremely difficult to examine changing factor endowment of Indian economy during the course of development.

S. Rajendran in his article, Economy, environment and sustainable development: concept and concerns" argues that development planners and policy-makers have often emphasised the need for Sustainable Development in the long run. Any development programme should sustain shocks, though larger sometime, and ultimately deliver the goods in a judicious manner. The concept, Sustainable Development is more and closely related to resource use as the resource has to be meticulously used for attaining Sustainable Development. Unfortunately due to increasing wants such resources-mainly non-renewable-are non-judiciously used.

D.V. Gopalappa makes quite interesting observation in his article, "Economic viability of rain fed sericulture vis-à-vis the competing crops -an economic analysis". He argues that sericulture activity was introduced, in India, as one of the income-employment enhancing poverty alleviation programmes during the sixth plan as it suits and sustain regular income to the subsistence marginal and small categories of farmers. However, the recent trend is quite disturbing for the development of sericulture as most of the farmers have been uprooting mulberry plants and shifting towards horticulture and other commercial crops, which resulted in the reduction of the area under mulberry to the extent of about 60 per cent. Despite this a large number of marginal and small farmers in India (especially in Karnataka state) continued to earn their livelihood through rain fed sericulture under the support of whatever little rain that was available. However, the policy-makers are not in favour of these categories of farmers as they think that only irrigated sericulture gives better returns. The article based on both secondary and primary data analysis, reveals that rain fed sericulture is still profitable compared to the competing crops in the study regions and therefore, it is one of the major livelihood systems for the downtrodden. Hence, rain fed sericulture is an option in India to compete with China, in silk production, as China has been the potential threat to India as it is trying to destroy the silk industry in India and dominate the world silk market.

H.R. Uma and Madhu, in their article on "International Labour Migration and India" argues that Migration is a global phenomenon but at the same time it is a multi-faceted experience that encompasses opportunities for personal, social and economic development and also includes risks of violence, abuses and exploitation for men and women alike. Globalisation has opened up national boundaries for human mobility across borders, even though it includes all strategies to let capital and commodities flows across them. Globalisation and post-reform play an important role in international migration and they are responsible for an increase in the international flow from developing countries. They are not only driven international labour flow but also considered as an important consequences of this. There is deep divergence in demographic trends in developed and developing countries leading to a high demand for labourers in developed countries and supply of labourers in developing countries along with this changing trends in consumerism, advancement in transport and telecommunication are become the key factors to stimulate large scale labour migration.

Seyed Mehdi Pourkiaei and S. Mahendra Kumar in their article, "Financial Analysis of Public, Private and Foreign Banks in India" argues that the banking sector has played a major role in the augmentation of Indian economy, given the fact that they supplement the required credit, stabilises the prices or inflation, including the fact that they advocate financial inclusiveness of the social categories as well as regions. However, the question quite often asked is which sector among banking sector are performing better and also play a key role in the economic development. Over the years it has been said and argued that the public sector did play a major role when compared to private sector. Interestingly in recent past foreign banks start entering Indian economy. Authors have argued that foreign banks are performing better as compared to private and public sector banks.

Finally is the article by Muzaffar Assadi. His article, "Political Economy of Climate Change: Debates, Contestations, and Issues in India/Karnataka" fundamentally tries to look at the issues from the critical political economy perspective. He argues that climate change is not simply an issue of relationship between science and society but it needs to be seen in the larger context of commodification of nature, capitalist exploitation and the marketisation of economy. In India, except Karnataka no other state has prepared themselves for the larger consequences of climate change. In fact, there is great danger looming large over different parts of India including Karnataka due to climate change. This is why he argues that "States as well as societies will not survive unless and until capitalism is not disciplined, commoditisation of environment is not contained, and consumption is not restricted.

However, what is required is deep critical political economy perspective to address the issues. Incidentally, political economy perspective has its own weakness too-we cannot just gloss over it. Many a time it is wrapped up in ideological moorings, or polemical debates or even used as means for subversion. It is in this context political economy needs to be retrieved from such subversions and from polemical debates.

PART–I

INDUSTRY, FINANCE AND BANKING

2

Fallacies in IS-MP Curve Model to Explain Monetary Policy Effects With Special Reference to Federal Reserve

Professor Kishore G. Kulkarni

I. Introduction:

Main aim of this paper is to summarise the fallacies of the newly developed but often used IS-LM model while teaching the monetary policy effects in a closed economy. It is also pointed out that the old IS-LM framework did a more remarkable job and was not deserving of discard from intermediate macroeconomics textbook. The above assertions are greater important when seen in the light of monetary policy-making since the financial crisis (2009) in case of US with special reference to the Federal Open Market Committee (FOMC) behaviour. While the IS-LM model treats interest rate as the policy variable actively used by the monetary policy in reality it is not used even once in last seven to eight years. Given these special circumstances, this paper goes further to prove he irrelevance of the famous "Taylor Rule", which also uses interest as the only policy variable. This task is accomplished by dividing the paper into three sections. Section 1 shows the IS-LM model's derivation as well as its so called effective use on a theoretical level. Section 2 shows the derivation of old IS-LM model which treats money supply (M1 or M2) as the main policy variable for the monetary policy. Section 3 uses the data of last 10 years for US economy and shows that hanks to recent QE attempts, money supply is much more used to active the monetary policy than the interest rate change. In the light of this long experience, it is concluded that IS-LM model has a whole lot more explanatory power than the IS-LM model and therefore the former model needs to be rough back in the intermediate macro textbooks to offer a meaningful theoretical explanation to the students.

Section II: What is the (Big Deal of) IS-LM Model?

Traditionally, the students of intermediate and advanced macroeconomics are used to IS-LM model that was widely used in almost all textbooks. A short survey of all macroeconomics textbooks reveals that some textbooks are still using the same model for explaining the policy effects. In 1990s, however, some of the famous intermediate macroeconomics textbooks (see Blanced, Hubard-Obrein-Rafferty, Gorden and Hoover) introduce the IS-LM model to analyse the effects of expansionary policies, especially fiscal and monetary. The main reason to move this "advanced" theoretical tool was the observation that in 1990s, (especially after 1992) FOMC was changing discount rate roughly seven times/year. Naturally, the interest rate (discount rate in case of USA) was seen as the major policy tool affects the money supply. Because interest rate is changed exogenously (some time arbitrarily) monetary policy curve (MP curve) was drawn as the horizontal straight line in Fig. 2. Hence any action of changing discount rate was supposed to shift the curve up (or down) depending upon how the interest rate is changed. In IS-LM model, the IS curve was seen, as usual, as the locus of combinations of real GDP and interest rate at which commodity market is in equilibrium. The equilibrium of the commodity (sometimes called good markets, or product market) needs an equality of total expenditure (C + I + G + X - M) and total income (C + S + Tx).

Where:

C = Consumer expenditure, I = Private domestic investment, G = Government expenditure,

X = Total export of goods and services, and M = Total imports of goods and services,

S = Savings, Tx = Tax revenues.

Hence, commodity market equilibrium condition requires that

$$C + I + G + X - M + C + S + Tx$$

Given the usual upward sloping from left to right consumption function and interest (I), Government expenditure (G), Export (X) assumed to be autonomous (independent) of GDP, and Import (M) to be determined by import function which shows that import is directly related to GDP, the total expenditure line is shown as the TE line in following figure (The derivation is pretty standard, those who need more information on this can refer to any principles of macroeconomics textbook.) the 45 degree angle line Fig. 2.1 is an imaginary line with slope = 1 and at all its points, the level of total expenditure is equal to the level of total income. At the intersection point, point E, the commodity markets equilibrium is defined and the equilibrium level of GDP is Y1.

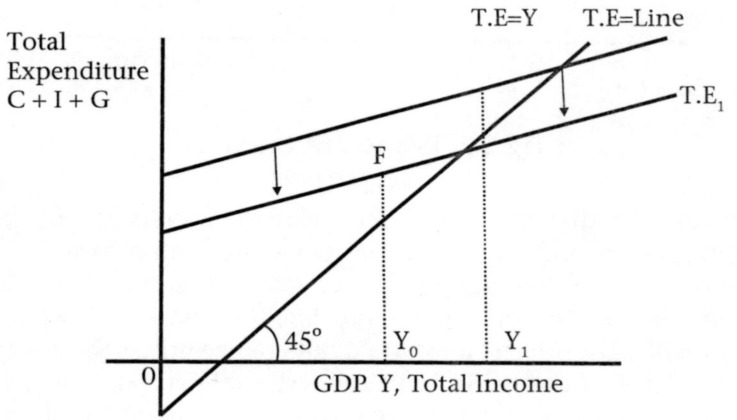

Fig 2.1:Commodity Market Equilibrium.

Recall, that any changes in interest rate will make a changes in real investment (I) in an inverse fashion. This is because increase in real interest rate would discourage business sector from carrying out investment activities. In that case an increase in interest rate would shift the total expenditure line 1 to lower level, say to TE 1 level. This would make the commodity market equilibrium point to move to point F. Thus, increase in interest is responsible a lower GDP that would keep commodity market in equilibrium hence if we want to show the relationship between interest rate and (commodity market) equilibrium GDP as in Fig. 2.2, the IS curve would be sloping downward from left to right.

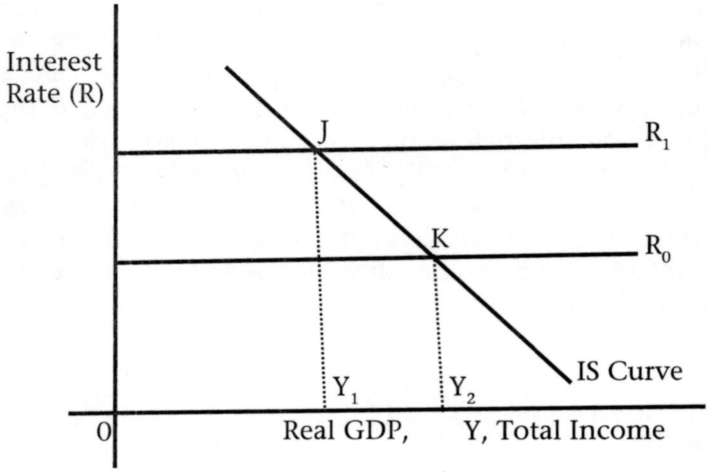

Fig 2.2: IS and MP Curves.

Now consider that monetary policy can always change interest rate in series of announcements (as per some central bank) or as a response to the data analysis (as per Federal Reserve). If interest rate in taken as the controllable variable, then no matter what is the level of GDP, interest rate would not change unless the policy-maker decide to change it. Hence, interest rate is assumed to be constant and a policy determined exogenous variable as shown by the horizontal straight line. There are varied interpretations of the X-axis variable in the above graph too. While some textbook authors have turned that into the rate of growth in real GDP variable, thinking that they would be able to point out the potential real GDP growth rate at certain level and then define the deviations of actual real GDP growth from this (imaginary) potential real GDP growth rate. This arrangement, however, has complicated the things. They (such as Blanchard and Hubbard, O' Brien and Rafferty in the reference list) have still labelled IS curve same way as before. Actually it is anything, but IS curve.

Some other authors, have plotted the absolute real GDP values on X-axis, just like it should be and have called the curved is IS curve. In any case, as the gap between actual real GDP and the potential real GDP widens, the monetary policy is supported to have lowered the interest rate, (shifting MP curve downwards) and increase the real GDP. So, we thought we found a new tool to analyse the policy changes and shown their effect on the real HDP and the macro-economy. In fact, as it is famous by now, John Taylor proposed a nice little rule in which the response of monetary policy by changing the interest rate was seen in the equation for targeted interest rate (Federal Funds Rate, the rate charged by one Financial Institution (FI) for is loan other FI) by the Federal Reserve. This equation has come to be known as the "Taylor Rule" of monetary policy. In its classical form summarised as:

$$1)\quad i_t = r_{t+}\pi + \frac{1}{2}(\pi_t - \pi_t^*) + \frac{1}{2}(y_t - y^\wedge_t)$$

where i_t is a short-term nominal interest rate such as the Federal Funds rate, r_t is the real interest rate, π_t is the inflation rate target, y is the log of real GDP, and $y^\wedge_t$ is the potential output. In short, Taylor rule in its classic form extends Fisher's equation by adding two correctors when is disequilibrium in the form of inflation or output gaps.

Unfortunately, however, the practice in USA as well abroad, has been anything but consistent with these arguments. In last nine years there has been no change in interest rate (discount rate) by Federal Reserve which stayed close to 0.25 per cent for all these years). This unchanged interest rate in there despite the real GDP gaps and a moderate inflation gaps that have occurred since 2007. (See Table 2.1) Hence the Taylor rule is irrelevant and as proposed by Sawhney, Kulkarni and Cachanosky (2016) it has been irrelevant in India as well. Moreover, the IS-LM model is not an acceptable or sufficient way to explain the monetary policy effect. In fact, the GDP has done a cyclical fluctuation in these years which means the GDP gaps have in fact been significant. So Taylor rule adoption by Federal Reserve would have predicted a wide change in interest rate. Table 2.1 also shows the gyrations of inflation rates in the last 20 years as well as the US unemployment, national debt and federal budget deficit. Fluctuations in none of these variables have promoted Federal Reserve to change any amount of interest rate. It is therefore quite questionable if Federal Reserve and (FOMC members) make policy changes based on changes in any of these variables. What in not questionable however, is the fact that FOMC does not hesitate making changes in money supply directly when they see these changes are warranted. Take a look at change in M1 (and even M2) money supply from 2006 ($1352 billion) to 2014 ($2981.5 billion). This is more than 120 per cent increase in less than eight years. So our theoretical model should assess the change in money supply more aptly than changes in interest rate.

Table 2.1: USA Macroeconomic Data

Variables:						
Production		***Money Supply***				***Price Level***
NGDP Billions	*RGDP (2005)*	*Prime Interest Rate*	*M1 Billions*	*M2 Billions*	*Exchange (SDR)*	*Inflations*
$7,664	$9,360	8.5	1145.9	3491	0.68791	2.71%
$8,100	$9,715	8.5	1130.5	3646	0.673944	2.94%
$8,609	$10,151	8.25	1079.6	3822	0.694374	2.34%
$9,089	$10,609	8.5	1080.9	4044.4	0.74452	1.55%
$9,661	$11,099	7.75	1107.1	4388.1	0.708771	2.19%
$10,285	$11,553	8.5	1137.2	4648.8	0.726696	3.37%
$10,622	$11,666	9	1086.9	4952.6	0.763938	2.82%
$10,978	$11,874	4.75	1190.3	5417.8	0.795716	1.60%
$11,511	$12,208	4.25	1215.6	5757.9	0.736561	2.30%
$12,275	$12,670	5.25	1302.8	6023.6	0.673049	2.67%
$13,094	$13,094	7.26	1384.3	6369.7	0.648207	3.37%
$13,856	$13,443	8.25	1375.5	6672.3	0.700111	3.22%
$14,478	$13,682	6.98	1362.1	7061.8	0.662789	2.87%
$14,719	$13,642	3.25	1370.7	7466.7	0.633525	3.82%
$14,419	$13,263	3.25	1638	8240.6	0.650992	-0.32%
$14,964	$13,599	3.25	1718	8429.3	0.538176	1.64%
$15,518	$13,817	3.25	1858.6	8814.2	0.646907	3.14%
$16,155	$14,138	3.25	2205.5	9724.4	0.648119	2.08%
$16,633	$14,452	3.25	2456.9	10468	0.649263	1.46%
$17,348	$14,797	3.25	2660.6	11059	0.650475	1.61%
$18,125*	N/A	3.25	2931.5	N/A	0.697589	0.10%

Source: Department of Commerce, 2015.

			Government Spending			
CPI (2010)	*Unemployment*	*Budget Deficit % NGDP*	*Defict (Surplus) in Billions*	*National Debt % NGDP*	*Debt in Billions*	*Year*
69.9	5.70%	3.1	$237.59	66.1	$5,065.97	1994
71.93	5.50%	2	$162.00	66.3	$5,370.43	1995
73.61	5.00%	0.9	$77.48	64.7	$5,569.70	1996
74.76	4.60%	-0.3	($27.27)	62.2	$5,653.48	1997
76.39	4.30%	-0.8	($77.28)	60.1	$5,806.02	1998
78.97	4.10%	-1.8	($185.13)	55.9	$5,749.20	1999
81.20	4.80%	-0.30	($31.87)	57.3	$6,086.29	2000
82.49	5.90%	3	$329.33	59.5	$6,531.61	2001
84.36	6.10%	5.2	$598.56	61.3	$7056.06	2002
86.62	5.60%	4.8	$589.20	62.7	$7,696.36	2003
89.56	5.20%	3.5	$458.28	63.3	$8,288.31	2004
92.45	4.70%	2.6	$362.25	63.9	$8,853.92	2005
95.09	4.70%	2.1	$304.03	64.8	$9,381.18	2006
98.74	5.90%	4.8	$706.49	76	$11,186.14	2007
98.39	9.40%	12.1	$1,744.65	87.1	$12,558.60	2008
100.00	9.70%	10.7	$1,601.19	95.2	$14,246.11	2009
103.16	9.00%	10.1	$1,567.31	99.4	$15,424.79	2010
105.29	8.20%	8.5	$1,373.20	100.83	$16,289.39	2011
106.83	7.40%	4.1	$681.96	101.17	$16,827.81	2012
108.57	6.20%	2.8	$485.75	102.98	$17,865.07	2013
N/A	N/A	N/A	N/A	N/A	N/A	2014

So, What is the Acceptable Alternative?

The best alternative for all macro textbooks is that we need to go back to the old model of IS-LM curves. In old LM curve the monetary policy change was analysed be changes in money supply rather than changes in interest rates which is more relevant and realistic is US environment. One such new book edition that has moves back to IS-LM model is Abel, Bernanke and Croushore (2016). One can find in their chapter 9 the same old analysis as under IS-LM framework which works as follows: While he IS curve has same shape slope and the same derivation as we saw in earlier part of this paper the LM curve derivation needs money markets equilibrium situation as shown in the following Fig 2.3.

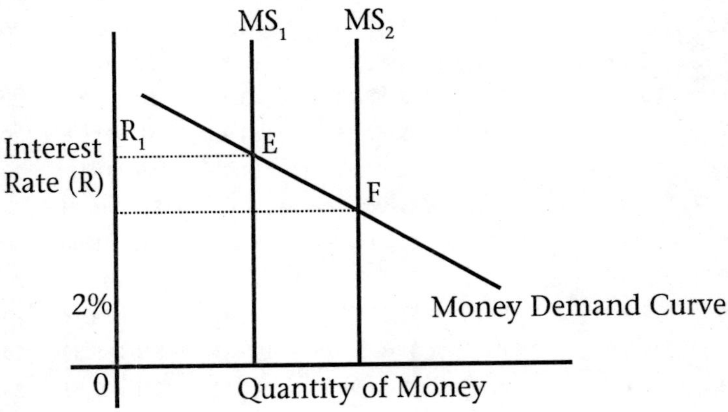

Fig 2.3:Money Market Equilibrium.

In the money market, as the conventional monetary theory wisdom goes, two forces operate, demand for money and money supply which together determine the "price" of money, the interest rate. Consider the demand for money curve as the down sloping curve in Fig 2.3 because as the interest rate goes up, ceteris paribus, people will hold less cash (liquidity preference is lower when interest rate is high). Moreover, the quantity of money demanded by the public is positively related to real GDP as countries with higher GDP would tend to hold higher cash. Money supply (MS) curve is a vertical straight line because we can (safely) assume that the money supply changes are determined by the monetary policy, whose action undertaken autonomously. When the quantity of money demanded is equal to the quantity of money supplied, we determine the equilibrium of money market as at point E. As the money supply is increased, the new money market equilibrium is at point F with lower interest rate.

Moreover, if real GDP goes up, there is a rightward shift in the demand for money curve leading to higher interest rate which will keep the money market in equilibrium. This gives us the LM curve which is the locus of all combination of real GDP and interest rate at which money market is in equilibrium. LM curve is upward sloping because as in Fig 2.4, higher real GDP would need a higher interest rate for money market equilibrium. The shifts in money supply curve occur due to monetary policy action. A higher money supply would shift the MS curve to the right and lower equilibrium interest rate. So, interest rate is seen as the reaction to the change in money supply in this model as against the instrument of policy change in IS-MP model of the last section. In fact, as the typical explanation of the famous Keynesian liquidity trap goes, at a very low interest rate the demand for money curved is a horizontal straight line creating same shape for the LM curve. In that only fiscal policy can make the change in GDP and the monetary policy is completely ineffective. As in Fig 2.4, in this case the interest rate has already reached to the lowest possible level.

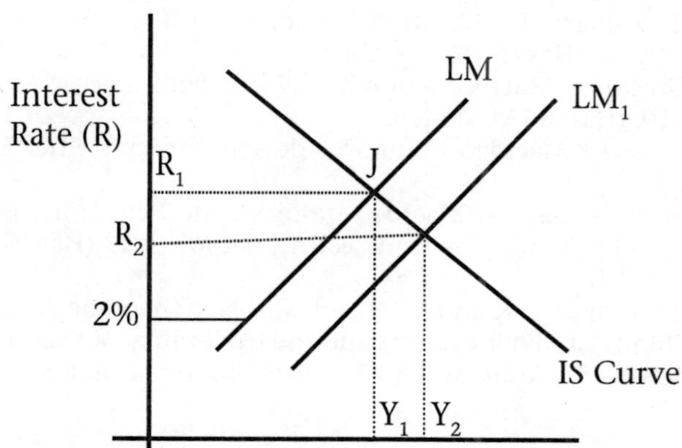

Fig 2.4:IS-LM Model: Old (was) is Gold.

IV. Summary and Conclusion

We, in this paper have seen that the recent US economy's macro situation is better explained by old IS-LM model rather than by IS-LM model and the Taylor rule. Policy effectiveness is better explained when interest rate is treated as the reflection of money supply change rather than as an instrument to make the change in money supply. The behaviour of Federal Reserve (as well as that many other policies around the world) is more consistent with old Keynesian explanation of liquidity trap rather than IS-LM model which assumes interest rate to be a controllable variable. Even if granted that liquidity trap was an extreme case, the very low level of discount rate has fact rendered Federal Reserve to be an ineffective policy institution.

References

1. Abel, A., Bernanke,B.,Crushore, D., "Macroeconomics", Pearson Edition Inc., 9th Edition, 2016, Chapter 9. (Has IS-LM Model).
2. Barro, Robert, "Intermediate Macro", First Edition, Cengage Learning, New York, 2007. (Has neither IS-LM nor IS-MP Model).
3. Blanchard, James, "Macroeconomics", Fifth edition, Prentice Hall Publishing, New Jersey, 2008. (Has IS-MP model).
4. Dornbush, R., Fischer, S and Startz, R, "Macroeconomics", 12th Edition, McGraw Hill Education, 2014, Chapters 11 and 12. (Has IS-LM Model).
5. Hubbard, G., O'Brien., T., Rafferty, M., "Macroeconomics", 2nd Edition, Pearson Education Inc, Boston, 2014. (Has IS-LM Model).
6. Hoover, Kevin, "Applied Intermediate Macroeconomics", Cambridge University Press, 2015, Chapter 13, (Has IS-LM Model).
7. Kulkarni, Kishore, "Principles of Macro-monetary Economics", Kendall-Hunt Publishing Company, Fifth Edition, 2009, pp. 1-425.
8. McEachern, William A, "Macroeconomics", Southwestern College Publishing, 2011, (Has IS-LM Model).
9. Mankiw, Gregory, "Macroeconomics", Worth Publishers, Seventh Edition, 2010, (Has IS-LM Model).
10. Parkins, Michael, "Macroeconomics", Addison Wesley Higher Education, 2009.
11. Romer, David, "Advanced Macroeconomics", McGraw Hill Global Education Holdings Inc., New York, Fourth Edition 2013 (Has IS-LM nor IS-MP Model).
12. Sawhney, B., Kulkarni, K and Chachanosky, N, "Theoretical Explanations of Monetary Policy Effects and the Irrelevancy of the Taylor Rule Application in India and USA", unpublished working paper, February 2016.

3

Export Decision-Making by Small-Scale Industries in Iran: A Preference Order Approach

Dr Younos Vakil Alroaia

I. Introduction

The promotion and development of small-scale industries (SSIs) has been acknowledged in various articles and multi-lateral agency reports as being important for achieving diverse social and economic objectives (Asia Development Bank, 1990; Birch, 1988; Flannery and Shapiro, 1992; Heshmati, 2001; UNCTAD, 1998; Weaver *et al.* 1998; World Bank, 1991). The nations face in international markets, with increasing trade deficits and other economic problems, have forced to refocus their attention on the search for strategies and design of policies and assistance programmes aimed at the promotion, development and enhancement of the export capabilities of industrial product.

One area that has received much attention is the use of export decision-making by firms to internationalise their business activities (Leonidou and Katiskeas, 1996). Decision-making process in internationalise is particularly needed to small and medium sized firms that are resource constrained. Small-scale industries (SSIs) export strategy research has examined a myriad of issues from the stage theory of export-development; export and non-exporter differences; export decision-making; export performance predictors; to export attitudes and consequent behaviours in SSIs (Young *et al.*, 1986).

International trade has emerged as a separate and important branch of for decision-makers. There has been a rapid increase in the growth and complex nature of problems posed by international trade, and today it has transcended the traditional exports of goods, to various types of commercial services, capital development, investment, transfer of technologies, intellectual property rights, e-commerce, and so on. These in turn give rise to new and unique problems to be solved by the decision makers.

This is further complicated by policies adopted by the various governments to further their trade efforts (Balogopal, 2006). This programme is also important in SSI in a globalised era.

In the current context of a liberalising economy that is attempting to industrialise within the spaces provided by a world capitalists system, export of manufactured goods is the key to industrial transformation and oil economy like Iran. Iran gradually focused its attention on investment in the industrial sector; new rivals emerged in the market share of SSIs. Iran's manufactured products, especially in such fields as petrochemicals mining and decorative stones, have already found their way into the world market.

A number of empirical studies have been carried out on the subject of export or the internationalisation of SSIs[1]. These studies have revealed that both external and internal factors have influenced for explaining the export decision-making of entrepreneurship. However, constituting the internal factors are firm-specific and decision-maker characteristics that have been found to be correlated to the firm's ability to identify and appropriate export opportunities and to participate successfully in exporting. The commonly studied firm-specific variables are firm size, years in business, competitiveness of products, international experience, foreign market coverage and ownership structure of the firm. Managerial characteristics that have been studied include education and age of the manager, foreign language skills, international orientation and international travel. Amongst the external factors are stimuli (e.g. customers, economic integration and market opportunities) and government assistance programmes.

While a significant amount of research has been conducted in the area of exporting, and the drivers of export decision-making, a review of the literature reveals several shortcomings that have limited our understanding of these issues. First, Morgan *et al*. (2004) note that although much research has been conducted on export activities, there are few strong theoretical frameworks for researching marketing aspects of export activity. Rather, they noted that the majority of studies are descriptive, are largely a theoretic, or draw upon divergent theoretical perspectives, thus making it difficult to integrate findings from prior work. Given the lack of theory in this area, they argue that the field is at a standstill. Responding to this call, we adopt an

[1] e.g. Axinn, 1989; Kaynak and Kothari, 1984; Louter et al., 1991; Naidu and Rao, 1993; Phillip, 1998; Obben and Magagula, 2003; Craig, 2003; Timothy and Wolff, 2003.

organisational learning approach to better understand the theoretical aspect of managerial decisions driving export marketing strategy and export decision-making. Second, previous studies have been conducted at the overall firm level. As a result, the determinants of export decision-making were conceptualised as firm-specific characteristics. An underlying theoretical justification for internal and external levels studies are the theory of internalisation (Beamish and Banks, 1987; Buckley and Casson, 1985; Rugman, 1981), which argues that in imperfect markets, firms should internalise the firm-specific advantages, both tangible and intangible, to extract maximum rent. Because firm-specific advantages are derived not only from the development and marketing of a particular product but also from the total learning process of the firm, export decision-making should be investigated at the internal and external levels. Third, a synthesis on prior research on marketing strategy within the exporting literature suggests that the main purpose of marketing activity is learning about local environments and the development of capabilities that facilitate adaption (Diskson, 1992). Given this focus, the majority of the marketing strategy export literature has focused on the issue of marketing strategy adaption/standardisation. However, as Ryans, Giffith, and Withe (2003) conclude, with rare exception the majority of this research has been without a strong theoretical foundation. The introduction of organisational learning theory to the export decision-making literature provides a theoretical foundation for the seminal issue in the field of international marketing. Specifically, the organisational literature reveals the importance of learning about a firm's environment as a basis to develop internal capabilities that facilities adaptation.[2] Under this perspective, industries are theorised to develop core competencies that allow them to learn at least the same baseline rate as that at which environment change (Stata, 1992). Therefore, we offer a more comprehensive, theoretically found, understanding of the simultaneous links internal and external market forces of the firm, marketing strategy adaption, and past and current export decision-making.

In sum up, the importance of small-scale industries in Iran economy has been increasingly recognised. It is observed that the economy can grow faster in twenty first century depends on expansion and improvement of SSIs function. Because SSIs play a vital role in job creation and innovation, the development of modern SSIs has been one of the most significant and characteristic features

[2] Diskson, 1992; lord and Ranft, 2000; Ozsomer and Gencturk, 2003.

of industrial development (Iran Small industries and Industrial Park, 2003). Of course, increase in the number, production, employment and export of SSIs over a period of time could be common adjudge the role played by small enterprises in the country. In the small sector a comparison between 2004 and 2005 indicates a growth of 23 per cent of the total export, 20 per cent of output of the manufacturing sector, 35 per cent indirect investment, 18.4 per cent value added and 4 per cent for creating employment. In addition, the SSIs have merged as the most dynamic sector of Iran industrial economy accounting for over 80 per cent of industrial sector. Hence, expansion of SSIs activities and measures to increase products of this sector of the country's economy would soon open new horizons for the export of SSIs products (MIM, 2007).

In Iran, although the rise in the price of oil has increased the country's revenues, however, there are still other issues such as employment, investment for setting up new establishments, renovation of industrial machinery, improvement of industries export and implementation of economic projects in different parts of the country in an effort.

Therefore, the aim of this study is to find out empirically the best alternatives of export decision-making in small-scale industries in Iran. In this case, in the section II explain the methodology used in measuring export decision-making. Section III to find out the decision-making processing small-scale industries in Iran. The last section is the conclusion.

II. Methodology

Population and Sample

The population for this research consisted of 12836 small firms in Iran. The sample consisted of Iran industries involved in exporting a product or service to one or more countries. The firms that had 50 employees or less were included in the sample. The 10 most active provinces in industry activities were selected. These provinces represented 78.6 per cent of total SSIs, 74.3 per cent of total value added, 69.2 per cent of total investment, and 77.2 per cent of employment in the SSIs in 2004 (Iran statistical centre, 2005).

The questionnaire was mailed to the selected 210 companies. One hundred and eighty responded to the questionnaire. Therefore, the study is based on information provided by 86 per cent organisation for the analysis of export decision-making in Iranian small-scale industries.

Technique Used in This Paper

In this section, we briefly review the technique that we make in our study to identify the best alternatives of export decision-making in Iranian small scale industries.

Measurement Scale

After generating a group of overall objectives and sub objectives or attributes, a next logical step is to select a unit of measurement of physical performance for each lowest-level attribute on the groups. The purpose of selecting physical performance measures is to give concrete, physical interpretations to their related lowest-level attributes.

There are three kinds of scales of measurement that can be employed for the measurement of quantities: ordinal, interval, and ratio (Stevens, 1959 and Torgerson, 1958). Selecting physical performance measures must be done judgmentally. Hence, we used the general method for judgment values via internal scale that is using the bipolar scale of interval.

Topsis

In this paper we use the Technique for Order Preference by Similarity to an Ideal Solution (TOPSIS) method was developed by Hwang and Yoon (1981) for solving Multiple-Attribute Decision Making (MADM) problems with a finite number of solutions. Fig 3.1 exemplifies show TOPSIS works.

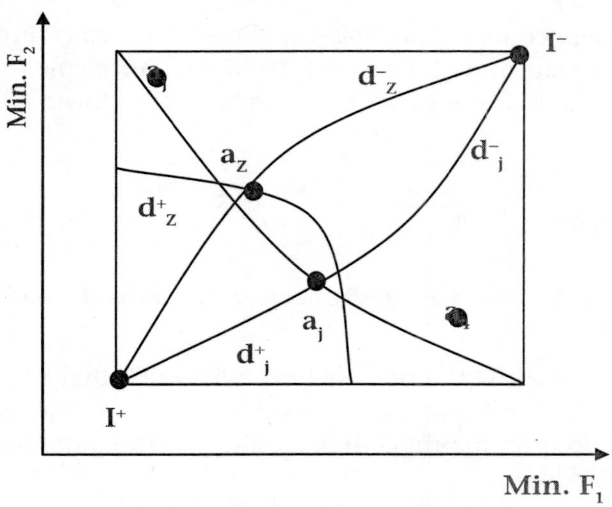

Figure 3.1: TOPSIS Distance.

The basic concept of the TOPSIS method is that the rank of the alternative selected as the best from a set of different alternatives, should have the shortest distance from the ideal solution and the farthest distance from the negative-ideal solution in a geometrical (i.e., Euclidean or City Block distance) sense.

In order to the TOPSIS method evaluates the following decision matrix, which refers to alternatives that are evaluated in terms of criteria / attributes.

Attribute / ***Alternatives***		x_1	x_2	x_3	...	x_n
	A_1	r_{11}	r_{12}	r_{13}	...	r_{1n}
	A_2	r_{21}	r_{22}	r_{23}	...	r_{2n}
D =	A_3	r_{31}	r_{32}	r_{33}	...	r_{3n}
	:	:	:	:		:
	A_m	r_{m1}	r_{m2}	r_{m3}	...	r_{mn}

where A_1, A_2... A_m is m alternative x_1, x_2... x_n is n attribute, and r_{ij} is the performance measure of the i_{th} alternative in terms of the j_{th} attribute. Hence, in order to different alternatives solution, the following steps are performed:

Step 1: Construct the normalised decision matrix

This step converts the various dimensional measures of performance into non-dimensional attributes. An element r_{ij} of the normalised decision matrix D is calculated as follows;

$$r_{ij} = \frac{r_{ij}}{\sqrt{\sum_{i=1}^{m} r_{ij}^2}} \quad \text{... (1)}$$

Step 2: Construct the weighted normalised decision matrix

A set of weights W = (W1, W2, ..., Wn) (such that Swj = 1), specified by the decision-maker, is used in conjunction with the normalised decision matrix D to determine weighted normalised matrix V defined by :

Weighted normalised matrix $V = N_D.W_{n.n} = \begin{bmatrix} v_{11},\ldots,v_{1j},\ldots v_{1n} \\ . \quad . \quad . \\ . \quad . \quad . \\ v_{m1},\ldots,v_{mj},\ldots,v_{mn} \end{bmatrix}$ ...(2)

Step 3: Determine the ideal and the negative-ideal solutions

The ideal (A+) and the negative-ideal (A^-) solutions are defined as follows:

A+ = {(max Vij | jεJ), (min Vij|jε)| i=1, 2, ..., m} ...(3)

$= \{V_1+, V_2+, \ldots.., V_j+, \ldots.., V_n+\}$

A^- = {(min Vij|jεJ), (max Vij|jε)| i=1, 2, ..., m} ...(4)

$= \{V_i^-, V_2^-, \ldots V_j^-, \ldots.., V_n^-\}$

Step 4: Calculate the separation distances

In this step, the concept of the n-dimensional Euclidean distance is used to measure the separation distances of the rank of each alternative from the ideal solution and the negative-ideal solution. The corresponding formulae are:

$$d_{i+} = \{\sum_{j=1}^{n}(V_{ij} - V_j^+)^2\}^{1/2}; \qquad i = 1, 2, \ldots., m \qquad \ldots(5)$$

where d_i+ is the separation of the rank of alternative i from the ideal solution,

$$d_{i-} = \{\sum_{j=1}^{n}(V_{ij} - V_j^-)^2\}^{1/2}; \qquad i = 1, 2, \ldots., m \qquad \ldots(6)$$

where d_{i-} is the separation of the rank of alternative i from the negative ideal solution.

Step 5: Calculate the relative closeness coefficient

The relative closeness coefficient for alternative Ai with respect to the ideal solution A+ is defined as follows:

$$C_{i+} = \frac{d_{i-}}{(d_{i+} - d_{i-})}; 0 < C_{i+} < 1; i = 1, 2, \ldots, m \qquad \ldots(7)$$

Step 6: From the preference order

The best alternative can now be decided according to preference order of C_i+. It is the one with the rank has the shortest distance to the ideal solution.

Determination of Alternatives

In this section, we present our approach to select alternatives of export decision-making in SSIs. Five questions, C_1, C_2, C_3, C_4, and C_5 are considered for evaluation.

(1) Phase I of the approach to select the best alternative

We consider the following sets of criteria for the five groups, for evaluating each of the questions.

1.1 EXPANSION OF EXPORT

A_1 Improve the terms export package credit

A_2 Provide more export related credit

A_3 Lower import duties on raw material

A_4 Reduce export formalities

A_5 Provide marketing support

A_6 Arrange fairs, exhibitions

A_7 Reduce delays in port and customs clearance

A_8 Improve shipping frequencies

A_9 Improve physical infrastructure

A_{10} Lower excise duties on output

1.2 REQUIREMENT OF ASSISTANT

A_1 Export management training

A_2 Trade contact

A_3 Procurement of raw material

A_4 Product improvement

A_5 Product design

A_6 Market information

A_7 Packaging

A_8 Export incentives

A_9 Marketing mission

A_{10} Market studies

A_{11} Export finance

A_{12} Quality control

A_{13} Government policies

1.3 GOVERNMENT MAJOR IMPEDIMENT

A_1 Government foreign policies problems

A_2 Lack of establishment of monetary and finance policies

A_3 Low limitations and lack of low support

A_4 Tax

A_5 Lack of establishment of economics (stagflation, inflation ...)

1.4 WHAT NEED TO BE DONE

A_1 Lower costs

A_2 Improve quality

A_3 Invest to increase sale of output

A_4 Tie up with foreign groups

A_5 Improve packaging

A_6 Tie up with export houses

A_7 Shorten delivery schedules

A_8 Introduce foreign specifications

1.5 MAJOR CONSTRAINTS AFFECTING ON EXPORT

A_1 High shipping cost

A_2 Restrictive import regulations

A_3 Lack of market demand

A_4 High quality requirements

A_5 Inadequate shipping services

A_6 Lake of tread contact

A_7 Payment problems

A_8 Lengthy export procedures

A_9 Low prices

A_{10} Lack of market information

A_{11} Heavy duties

III. Empirical Result

Since the main objective of this study is to select the best alternatives of export decision-making in small-scale industries in Iran, Expansion of export, Requirement of assistant, Government major impediment, what need to do, and major constraints affecting of export represented SSIs export improvement have been taken. Hence, the result and findings of the TOPSIS method of each question addressed in this study are presented in the following phase II.

Phase II. The C_1, C_2, C_3, C_4, and C_5 values of the illustrative export decision-making with the different separation measures are given in Tables 1, 3, 5, 7, and 9 are shown as the steps 4 (Separation distance) and 5 (The relative closeness coefficient). Tables 2, 4, 6, 8, and 10, also, show the step 6 (Rank the preference order) can be decided for the best alternative. It is one with the rank has the shortest distance to the ideal solution.

Table 3.1: Separation distance, relative closeness coefficient calculated by expansion for export improvement

d+	*d–*	*c**
$d_{1}+_{=}$ .147867	$d_{1-=}$ 14696	$c_{1=}$ .498462
$d_{2}+_{=}$ .146092	$d_{2-=}$ .83875	$c_{2=}$ .364425
$d_{3}+_{=}$ .157460	$d_{3-=}$ .076668	$c_{3=}$ .327461
$d_{4}+_{=.}$ 193180	$d_{4-=}$ .047791	$c_{4=}$ .198329
$d_{5}+_{=}$ .144506	$d_{5-=}$ .161811	$c_{5=}$ .528246
$d_{6}+_{=}$ .150835	$d_{6-=}$ .094861	$c_{6=}$ .386091
$d_{7}+_{=}$ .170086	$d_{7-=}$ .055059	$c_{7=}$ .244548
$d_{8}+_{=}$ .210373	$d_{8-=}$ .026773	$c_{8=}$ .112898
$d_{9}+_{=}$ .166239	$d_{9-=.}$ 095329	$c_{9=}$ .364452
$d_{10}+_{=}$ .164307	$d_{10-=}$ .086549	$c_{10=.}$ 345006

The best alternative for the expansion of export in Iranian SSIs is A_5. The preference orders are (A_5, A_1, A_6, A_2, A_9, A_{10}, A_3, A_7, A_4, and A_8) as shown in Table 3.2.

Table 3.2: Rank the preference order for expansion of export

Rank	*Expansion of Export*	*Alternative*
1	Provide marketing support	A_5
2	Improve the terms export package credit	A_1
3	Arrange fairs, exhibitions	A_6
4	Provide more export related credit	A_2
5	Improve physical infrastructure	A_9
6	Lower excise duties on output	A_{10}
7	Lower import duties on raw material	A_3
8	Reduce delays in port and customs clearance	A_7
9	Reduce export formalities	A_4
10	Improve shipping frequencies	A_8

Since the best alternative is the one with the highest relative closeness coefficient, the preference order for the expansion of export, as shown in Table 3.2, are $A_{5,}$ $A_{1,}$ and A_6. That means, provide marketing support, improve the terms export package credit, and arrange fairs, exhibition are the best of expansion of export as could government to do.

Table 3.3: Separation distance, relative closeness coefficient calculated by requirement of assistant for export improvement

d+	*d–*	*c**
$d_1+_=$ .111366	$d_{1-=}$ .049840	$c_{1=}$ .309171
$d_2+_=$ .115387	$d_{2-=}$ .048628	$c_{2=}$ .296484
$d_3+_=$ .102410	$d_{3-=}$ .057469	$c_{3=}$ .3594548
$d_4+_=$ 984432	$d_{4-=}$ .060119	$c_{4=}$ .379150
$d_5+_=$ .101246	$d_{5-=}$ .062427	$c_{5=}$ .381411
$d_6+_=$ .106960	$d_{6-=}$ .070490	$c_{6=}$ .397240
$d_7+_=$ .108257	$d_{7-=}$ .077976	$c_{7=}$ .418700
$d_8+_=$ .119712	$d_{8-=}$ .048348	$c_{8=}$ .287685
$d_9+_=$. 112780	$d_{9-=}$ .057625	$c_{9=}$ .338165
$d_{10}+_=$ 121335	$d_{10-=}$ .048766	$c_{10=}$ .286690
$d_{11}+_=$ .068392	$d_{11-=}$ .103946	$c_{11=}$ .603152
$d_{12}+_=$ .098038	$d_{12-=}$ .08090	$c_{12=}$ .452124
$d_{13}+_=$ .093342	$d_{13-=}$ .108243	$c_{13=}$ .536958

The best alternative for the requirement of assistant in Iranian SSIs is A_{11}. The preference orders are (A_{11}, A_{13}, A_{12}, A_7, A_6, A_5, A_4, A_3, A_9, A_1, A_2, A_8, and A_{10}) as shown in Table 3.4.

Table 3.4: Rank the preference order for Requirement of assistant

Rank	*Requirement of assistant*	*Alternative*
1	Export finance	A_{11}
2	Government policies	A_{13}
3	Quality control	A_{12}
4	Packaging	A_7
5	Market information	A_6
6	Product design	A_5
7	Product improvement	A_4
8	Procurement of raw material	A_3
9	Marketing mission	A_9
10	Export management training	A_1
11	Trade contact	A_2
12	Export incentives	A_8
13	Market studies	A_{10}

As shown in Table 3.4 the preference order for requirement of assistant, above all, are A_{11}, A_{13}, A_{12}, and A_7. That means export finance needs, government policies, product quality, and packaging are the best of requirement of assistant as improve export performance.

Table 3.5: Separation distance, relative closeness coefficient calculated by government major impediment for export improvement

d+	*d–*	*c**
$d_1+_=$ 362852	$d_{1-=}$.150583	$c_{1=}$ .293285
$d_2+_=$ .491800	$d_{2-=}$ .102277	$c_{2=}$ .172161
$d_3+_=$ .491842	$d_{3-=}$ .080549	$c_{3=}$ .140719
$d_4+_=$ .474785	$d_{4-=}$. 092550	$c_{4=}$ .163132
$d_5+_=$ .123306	$d_{5-=}$ .488093	$c_{5=}$.798322

The best alternative for the government major impediment in Iranian SSIs is A_5. The preference orders are (A_5, A_1, A_2, A_4, and A_3) as shown in Table 3.6.

Table 3.6: Rank the preference order for the government major impediment

Rank	*Government major impediment*	*Alternative*
1	Lack of establishment of economics (stagflation, inflation ...)	A_5
2	Government foreign policies problems	A_1
3	Lack of establishment of monetary and finance policies	A_2
4	Tax	A_4
5	Low limitations and lack of low support	A_3

Table 3.5 exhibits the government major impediment in these decision-making. At the present major impediment of government are A_5 and A_1. That means establishment of economics and improvement of government foreign policies are most of all, for government impediment as government barrier policies.

Table 3.7: Separation distance, relative closeness coefficient calculated by what need to do for export improvement

d+	*d–*	*c**
$d_1+_=$ .112188	$d_1-_=$ .194769	$c_{1=}$ .634548
$d_2+_=$ .119505	$d_2-_=$ .169611	$c_{2=}$ .586653
$d_3+_=$ .182838	$d_3-_=$ .056950	$c_{3=}$ .237501

d_4+= .192141	d_4– = .089281	$c_{4=}$ .317249
d_5+= .156692	d_5– = .120381	$c_{5=}$.434474
d_6+= .208182	d_6– = 053541	$c_{6=}$ .204572
d_7+= .167384	d_7– = .0794474	$c_{7=}$ .321941
d_8+= .159501	d_8–.= .084758	$c_{8=}$ .347

The best alternative for what need to do in Iranian SSIs is A_1. The preference orders are (, A_1, A_2, A_5, A_8, A_7, A_4, A_3, and A_6) as shown in Table 3.8.

Table 3.8: Rank the preference order for what need to do

Rank	*What need to do*	*Alternative*
1	Lower costs	A_1
2	Improve quality	A_2
3	Improve packaging	A_5
4	Introduce foreign specifications	A_8
5	Shorten delivery schedules	A_7
6	Tie up with foreign groups	A_4
7	Invest to increase sale of output	A_3
8	Tie up with export houses	A_6

Table 3.8 reveals that the best preference orders for what need to do are A_1, A_2, and A_5.That means invest decrease of product cost, improve quality, and improve packaging.

Table 3.9: Separation distance, relative closeness coefficient calculated by major contractions affecting on export for export improvement

d+	*d-*	*c**
d_1+= .134604	d_{1-}= .188073	$c_{1=}$ .582852
d_2+= .14	d_{2-}= .15249	$c_{2=}$ .521350
d_3+= .123802	d_{3-}= .150028	$c_{3=}$ .547881
d_4+= .120591	d_{4-}= .161313	$c_{4=}$ .572227
d_5+= . 117664	d_{5-}= .215052	$c_{5=}$.646344
d_6+= .140047	d_{6-}= .100001	$c_{6=}$ .416588
d_7+= .132815	d_{7-}= .16567	$c_{7=}$ .555036
d_8+= .127202	d_{8-}= .222456	$c_{8=}$ .63621
d_9+= .111395	d_{9-}= .251213	$c_{9=}$ .692794
d_{10}+= .120101	d_{10-}= .157518	$c_{10=}$ .56739
d_{11}+=.125984	d_{11-}= .13439	$C_{11=}$ .516144

The best alternative for the major constraints of export in Iranian SSIs is A_9. The preference orders are (A_9, A_5, A_8, A_1, A_4, A_{10}, A_7, A_3, A_2, A_{11}, and A_6) as shown in Table 3.10.

Table 3.10: Rank the preference order for the major constraints on export

Rank	*Major constraints on export*	*Alternative*
1	Low prices	A_9
2	Inadequate shipping services	A_5
3	Lengthy export procedures	A_8
4	High shipping cost	A_1
5	High quality requirements	A_4
6	Lack of market information	A_{10}
7	Payment problems	A_7
8	Lack of market demand	A_3
9	Restrictive import regulations	A_2
10	Heavy duties	A_{11}
11	Lack of tread contact	A_6

Table 3.10 indicates that the preference order for major constraints effecting on export are A_9, A_5, A_8, and A_1. That means low prices for existence of competition, weakness of services, lengthy export procedures, and high shipping cost.

Conclusion

In this paper, we proposed a five-question multi-criteria group approach to selecting the best alternatives of export decision-making. In the attributes of the approach, we identified important criteria for evaluation of the alternatives (expansion of export, government major impediment, requirement of assistant, what need to do, and major constraints affecting of export) represented small-scale industries export decision-making. Then, we used TOPSIS method (Technique for Order Preference by Similarity to Idea Solution) to find the success potential of each alternative, as evaluated by the group.

In summary, selection of preference order taken varied SSIs and had different influences on industrial export intensity and export growth. The preceding analysis has demonstrated amply that the Iranian SSIs path to internationalisation is not trouble free but is beset by many obstacles of variable severity and significance. Some of these obstacles are associated with internal weakness (for example, government and finance policies), while others related to external factors (as in the case foreign policies and market information).

Therefore, public decision-makers should assist companies in reducing the inhibiting effect of these problems, since exports can increase foreign exchange reserves, can reduce unemployment levels, and can improve standards of living in the country.

References

Asgharpour, M.J. (2002). *Multiple criteria decision making.* Tehran, University of Tehran.

Asia Development Bank, (1990). *The role of small and medium-scale manufacturing industries and industrial development.* Manila, Asia Development Bank.

Axinn, C. (1988). *Export performance: Do managerial perceptions make a difference?* International Marketing Review 5(2), 61-71.

Axinn, Caherin, N. Ron Savitt, James M. and Sharon Thach, (1994). *Export intention, beliefs, and behaviors in smaller industrial firms.* Journal of Business Research, 32(1) 49-55.

Baird, S. Majorie A. L., and Orris, J. B. (1994). *The choice of international strategies by small business.* Journal of Small Business Management 32(1), 48-59.

Balagopal, T.A. (2006). *Export management.* 8th Edition, Himalaya Publishing House.

Beamish, W. and Banks, C. (1987). *Equity joint ventures and the theory of the multinational enterprise.* Journal of International Business Studies 18(2), 1-16.

Birch, D.I. (1988). *The new economy: Trading places.* Inc. 42-3.

Buckley, J. and Casson, M. (1985). *The economic theory of the multinational enterprise.* New York: St. Martin's Press.

Calof, J. L. (1993). *The impact of size on internationalization.* Journal of Small Business Management, 31(October), 60-69.

Craig, C. Julian, (2003). *Export marketing performance: A study of Thailand firms.* Journal of Small Business Management 49(2), 213-21.

Dichtl, E. M., Leibold, H., Koglmayr, H. and Muller, S. (1982). *The export decision of small and medium-sized firms: A review.* Management international Review, 42(2), 49-60.

Dickson, P.R. (1992). *Toward a general theory of competitive rationality.* Journal of Marketing, 59(1), 69-83.

Flannery, R. and Shapiro, D. (1992). *Taiwan: Taipei's brave new world.* Asian Business 28(12): 34-48.

Heshmati, A. (2001). *On the growth of micro and small firm: Evidence from Sweden.* Small Business Economics 17(3): 213-28.

Hwang, C.L. and Yoon, K. (1981). *Multiple attribute decision making method and application.* Springer-Verlag, New York.

Kaynak, E. and Kothari, V. (1984). *Export behavior of small and medium-sized manufacturers: Some policy guidelines for international marketers'.* Management International Review 24(2), 61-9.

Leonidou, L. and Constantine, S. (1996). *The export development process: An integrative review of empirical models.* Journal of International Business Studies 27(30, 517-551.

Lord, M.D., and Ranft, A. (2000). *Organization learning about new international markets: Exploring the internal transfer of local market knowledge.* Journal of International Business Studies 31(4), 573-589.

Louter, P.K., Ouwerkerk, C. and Bakker, B. A. (1991). *An inquiry into successful exporting.* European Journal of Marketing 25(6), 7-23.

Ministry of Industries and Mines of Iran, (2007): www.mim.org.ir

Morgan, R.M., and Hunt, S.D. (1994). The commitment-trust theory of relationship marketing. *Journal of Marketing,* 58(3), 20-38.

Naidu, G. M. and Kanti, V. (1994). *Predictors of export strategy and performance of small firms.* Journal of Business Research 31(2), 107-115.

Naidu, G.M. and Rao, T.R. (1993). *Public sector promotion of exports: A needs-based approach.* Journal of Business Research 27(1), 85-101.

Obben, J. and Magagula, P. (2003). *Firm and managerial determinates of the export propensity of small and medium-sized enterprises in Swaziland.* International Small Business Journal 21(1), 73-91.

Ozsomer, A. and Gencturk, E. (2003). *A resource-based model of market learning in the subsidiary: The capabilities of exploration and exploitation.* Journal of International Marketing, 11(3), 1-29.

Philp, N.E. (1998). *The export propensity of the very small enterprise (VSE).* International Small Business Journal 16(4), 79-93.

Rugman, M. (1981). *A new theory of the multinational enterprise: Internationalization versus internalization.* Columbia Journal of World Business (Spring), 23-29.

Ryans, J.K., Griffith, D. and White, D.S. (2003). *Standardization/adaptation of international marketing strategy: Necessary conditions for the advancement of knowledge.* International Marketing Review, 20(6), 588-603.

Stata, R. (1992). *Management innovation.* Executive Excellence, 9(6), 8-9.

Steven, S.S. (1959). *Measurement, psychophysics, and utility: Definitions and theories.* Churechman and Ratoosh (eds), pp.18-63.

Timothy, L. and Wolff, A. (2003). *Firm characteristics and managerial perceptions of NAFTA: An assessment of export implication for U.S.* Journal of Small Business Management 41(2), 117-32.

Torgerson, W.S. (1958). *Theory and method of scaling.* Wiley, New York.

UNCTAD, (1998). *Handbook on foreign direct investment by small and medium-size enterprises: Lessons from Asia.* Geneva: United Nations Organization.

Weaver, K. M., Berkowitz, D. and Davies, L. (1998). *Increasing the efficiency of national export promotion program: The case of Norwegian exporter.* Journal of Small Business Management, 36(4) 1-11.

World Bank, (1991). *World development report 1991: The challenge of development.* Washington, DC: World Bank.

Yoon, K. (1980). *System selection by multiple attribute decision making.* PhD. Dissertation, Kansas State, University Manhattan, Kansas.

4

Renaissance or Backwaters: The Case of Mysore Industries

Selva Kumar, D, and Dr Dinabandhu Bag

"Public Enterprises without a plan can achieve something, but a plan without enterprises is likely to remain in the papers only". - Hanson (1959)

1. Introduction

State-Owned Enterprises (SOEs): Reminiscence

The "MYSORE" Industries brand affirms the array of State-Owned Enterprises (hereafter, SOEs) of Karnataka classified under State-Government Company, Non-Government Company, and Subsidiary of Foreign Company. The case distinguishes both listed SOEs (namely, Mysore Paper Mills Ltd. (MPML); Mysore Cements Ltd. (MCL); and Mysore Petrochemicals Ltd. (MPL) which are currently active and also an unlisted SOE, Mysore Lamp Works Ltd. (MLWL) which is currently under liquidation (See, Table 4.1). We narrate the reminiscence laying sufficient repercussions on the progress of Central Public Sector Enterprises (CPSEs) and their impeding remarks headed for SOEs. The pre-ponderous of Public Enterprises aimed to achieve socio-economic goals such as health, education, employment and infrastructure that required fresh capital issues in curbing fiscal deficits and borrowings. Highly dependent on debt SOEs censure the slick of equity as witnessed by CPSEs. They utilise the local resources to augment the industrial growth providing a supportive strand to CPSEs. As a result, the firm size does matter with an overall investment of ₹ 100 crores (SOEs) against a whopping ₹ 1000 crores (CPSEs). Due to these constraints, investment decisions also get politicised as there is no governing board to process the investment proposals and neither are the bureaucrats professionalised to effectively manage the enterprise. This has led them to be biased in introducing economic reforms as various political parties in power do not approve the nature and extent of reforms to be undertaken. In response, the central government between 1990-91 to 2000-01 have rather curbed SOEs in isolation against the ambit of National Renewal Fund (NRF). As Mishra and Navin (2002), elicit SOEs are restricted from appointing Chairman-cum-Managing Director, Executive Directors, and Non-Official Members appointed through the Public Enterprise Selection Board (PESB). They also mention, the S.V.S. Raghavan Committee Report on SOEs in Tamil Nadu, put forth recommendation to setup Disinvestment Commission. Disinvestment became a popular phenomenon due to its effective functioning in United Kingdom under Margaret Thatcher as several developing economies laid impetus for economic growth.

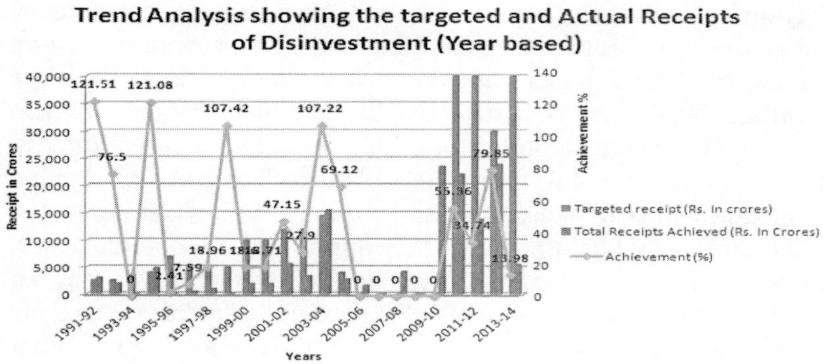

Fig. 4.1: Trends of Disinvestment.

Note. Retrieved from *"Disinvestment Dilemma: An Empirical Study"*, by Kumar and Bag (2015), Chapter 22, Trends of Disinvestment, pp. 316.

In a transient economy like India, Disinvestment was put forth as an alarming signal to nullify licensing, political intervention, bureaucratic practices, trade barriers, and regulatory compliances. Whereby in 1996, Disinvestment Commission led by Mr G.V. Ramakrishna was set up to support public enterprises and provide explicit remedies on disinvestment issues. Department of Disinvestment became a separate department in May 2004, to cater the disinvestment proceeds of public enterprises. These artefacts can be used for expansion, capital expenditure, discharge of liabilities, dividend payments, working capital requirements, corporate governance, and social sector initiatives. As such, Disinvestment has bi-directional views from both government and potential investoRs In case of former, disinvestment refers to public enterprise selling off a portion of its assets to raise capital that ultimately reduces stakes of sovereign owner. For the latter, disinvestment is a gradual attempt to withdraw their portion of ownership claims due to inefficiencies of the enterprise in satisfying stakeholder's needs. In case of CPSEs, the funds obtained through disinvestment are credited to National Investment Fund (NIF) which meets their recapitalization needs. Impressively, SOEs support the public enterprises to handle competition, mergers and acquisitions, takeovers and credit rationing. As Kumar and Bag (2015) extend assessment of disinvestment decisions can consider earnings capability, historical achievements, customer concentration, knowledge base, technology, human capital and their contribution to society. Therefore, the planning commission stepped forward to provide the requisite information relating to investments, turnover, capacity utilisation, contribution to state economy, sectoral composition, employment generation, and nature of operations. The economic well-being of a state can be examined through SOEs to create employment opportunities, support large scale investments, control monopoly and improve standard of living. A well-defined Disinvestment policy succumb fiscal consolidation, wider utilisation of resources, public private participation, operational efficiency, market discipline and corporate governance. Interestingly, Nagaraj (2005) argues disinvestment of SOEs may not affect the economic performance as the state presumes majority shareholding such that their likelihood to influence share prices are minimal in nature. Subsequently, Som (2013) examines performance and corporate governance practices of SOEs against OECD guidelines based on transparency, accountability and full disclosure. They acclaim disinvestment mechanisms include initial public offerings (IPOs), closed auctions, asset sales, strategic sales, share buybacks, employee buyouts, spin-off and cross sales. The case justifies potent deterrence of SOEs that have led to their demise of nightmare such as declining margins and rate of capital formation; rising cost of goods sold; stagnant and falling market share; and inabilities to achieve scale economies. Further, to be specific, product development; brands; network of branches; skill improvement of employees; newer technology; role of unions towards business goals are the predominant issues raised for discussion. The next section highlights State Government's Intervention in the affairs of enterprises.

SOEs and the Emerging Markets: An Altruistic Outlook

Prior literature on SOEs evident lacunas and their aftermath from the realm of sustainable economic development. Most often, state's political interference have a decisive influence on capital formation; higher minimum support prices of raw materials; skill development of employees; and also investment in fixed assets. To elucidate, Shleifer and Vishny (1998) report that state-owned entities are affected by government intervention which impede both political objectives and corporate decisions curtailing firm value. They mention political objectives adhere to retain employment milieu for the prime aim of social stability and economic growth. Likewise Guariglia and Poncet (2008) argue state-government interventions in Chinese state-owned firms are an important engine of economic growth and development. Further, Guariglia, Liu, and Song (2011) connote Chinese state-entities innately depend on promoters having major chunk of total assets and rather are unaffected by cash flows. They conclude, interference of state-ownership in both allocation and disbursement of capital plays a vital role in obtaining access to external financing (investing activities). Similarly, the case of Indian public enterprises paves a milestone in rejuvenating sick enterprises from brisk of hallucination. In India, the need to set up Sick Industrial Companies Act (SICA, 1985), was the initial step to care of entities under severe financial distress with respect to their tracing, viability, and rehabilitation initiatives. Succinctly, Board for Industrial and Financial Reconstruction (BIFR) a prime body was established to examine financial distress issues. Prior literature on Indian context such as [Anant, Gangopadhayay, and Goswami (1992); Goswami (1996); Falk (2005); Gopalan and Xie (2011); Komera and Lukose (2014)] provide prime impetus on institutional malaises that augment financial distress. They affirm both external causes (government policies, shortage of raw-materials, and product market competition) and internal causes (inefficient management, employee grievances, under-utilisation of plant capacity, and cost control) are the lacunas to be mitigated. Likewise, Anant, Gangopadhayay, and Goswami (1992) studied 455 companies from 1987-1990 on manufacturing industries; and report two years prior to their filing bankruptcy protection cause financial distress. Accordingly, Wohlschlegel (2002) noted that consecutive governments in Indian perspective have provided sufficient budgetary support to both distressed and unproductive firms for rehabilitation. He argues about the pre-dominance of local politicians with their electoral interest rather impedes soft-budget constraints. Hence, firm managers most often take sub-optimal decisions and are postulated to forego opportunity cost of capital and deploy their resources in sub-optimal projects. Likewise, Komera and Lukose (2014) examine 1185 firms between 1992 and 2009 that filed for bankruptcy and found firm-specific and industry-specific factors are prime constraints (augment 42 per cent cash flow shortfalls) of financial distress. The next section substantiates dilemma of financial distress.

Post Liberalisation Disinvestment avenues

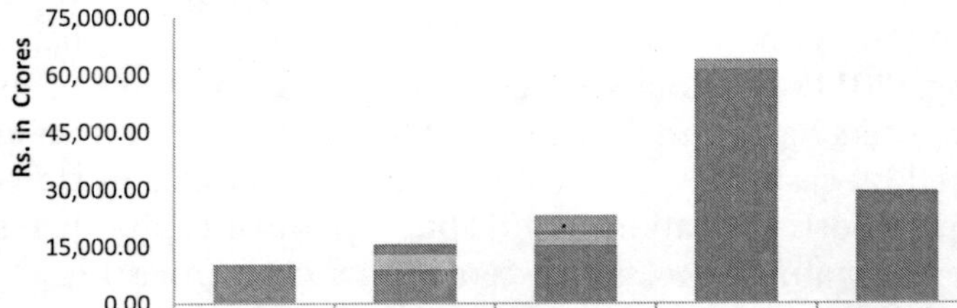

	Eighth FYP	Ninth FYP	Tenth FYP	Eleventh FYP	Twelfth FYP
Residual Shareholding			4,031.33	2,366.94	
Related Transactions		2,843.02	1162.15		
Strategic Sales		3,749.57	2,594.78		
Majority Shareholding		1,317.23			
Minority Shareholding	10,341.50	7,760.38	15,441.68	61,405.64	29,547.25

Fig 4.2: Five Year Plans of Growth (Disinvestment).

Note. Retrieved from "Disinvestment Dilemma: An Empirical Study", by Kumar and Bag (2015), Chapter 22, Five Year Plans Pattern of Growth, pp. 314.

II. REVIEW OF LITERATURE

Financial Distress: A Bird's eye view

Several researchers have contributed swashbuckling rudiments on the term financial distress. For example, [Ohlson (1980); Altman (1993); Shumway (2001)] probability of failure; Zmijewski (1984) filing a bankruptcy petition; Pursell (1990) secondary sickness; Andrade and Kaplan (1998) high interest expenses; Kam, Citron, and Muradoglu (2005) economic distress; [Kornai, Maskin, and Roland (2003); Komera and Lukose (2014)] soft-budget constraints and so on. The pioneer work of Beaver (1966) defines "Failure" as "the inability of a firm to pay its financial obligations as they mature" (p. 71). Succinctly, Altman E. (1968) terms Bankruptcy as firms that are granted the right to reorganise, and/ or either placed in receivership. Zmijewski (1984) defines financial distress as "the act of filing a petition of bankruptcy" (p. 63). Wruck (1990) elicits financial distress as a situation where in the present cash flows realised are unable to meet current financial obligations of the entity. Chan and Chen (1991) confine marginal (distressed) firms that "have lost market value because of poor performance, they are inefficient producers, and they are likely to have high financial leverage and cash flow problems. They are marginal in the sense that their prices tend to be more sensitive to changes in the economy, and they are less likely to survive adverse economic conditions" (p. 1468). In addition, Kaplan and Stein (1993) describe higher levels of debt impede higher risks in terms of bankruptcy rates and financial distress affecting both promoters and public shareholders curtailing corporate value. Subsequently, Christidis and Gregory (2010) term financial distress when a firm officially defaults its financial obligations (suspended status; liquidation; deferral of quotes for more than three years; both firm and/or administrative receivership; and withdrawal). Subsequently, Bae (2012) describes financial distress as the situation whereby the enterprise is unable to fulfil promises to its creditors The financial distress costs augments inefficiencies in management, transfer of corporate value from creditors to shareholders, increase in borrowing cost of capital, and difficulties in obtaining additional financing (external sources). Similarly, financial failure asserts high leverage posing higher interest payments. From an Accounting perspective, Falk (2005) studies 4,400 firms from 1988-1999 and reports that the prime reason for industrial sickness as futile pre-reform efficiency at a higher extent. He confines distressed firms if, the overall accumulated losses entails net worth for consecutive five years and also reported net profits (RNPs) are negative for continuously two years Thereafter Pindado, Rodrigues, and Torre (2008) put forward two main conditions for financial distress i.e. EBITDA (operating profits) less than financial expenses (financial obligations); and simultaneously two years losses in the market value (operational deficit).

Financial Distress: A Holistic Perspective

Gutierrez, Olalla, and Olmo (2009) highlight the significant bankruptcy codes prevalent in the European nations laying emphasis on bankruptcy law of the country and also factors that affect market value of distressed firms. Several laws were enforced for example, in case of Germany [Scheme of Arrangement code

(1935), and Insolvency statute (1994)]; Spain [Suspension of payments law (2002), and Bankruptcy law (2003)]; France [Law relating to the Judicial Reconstruction and Compulsory Liquidation of Business (1985)]; and United Kingdom [Insolvency Act (1986), and Enterprise Act (2002)] respectively. They infer economic implications of bankruptcy laws enlist three stages namely, declaration process; firm's control; and restructuring plan. Further, the amicable actions include examining solvency requirements, level of control rights and time limits. Succintly, financial implications adhere to improve probability of survival, reduce information asymmetries and avoid credit rationing. Campbell, Hilscher, and Szilagyi (2008) mention financially distressed firms in United States file bankruptcy compliances under Chapter 7 (Liquidation) or Chapter 11 (Reorganisation); and delist themselves for performance related nuances; but do not completely exit from the business. Consequently, Caplan, Dutta, and Marcinko (2012) exemplify business model of Lehman Brothers amid the brink of bankruptcy. This impedes how quick firms are resilient to aggressively move their tables during bankruptcy debacle and look for alternatives through reorganisation and liquidation procedures with fresh-start accounting and financial statements. Similarly, Bellovary, Giacomino, and Akers (2007) confine distressed firms in US adhere to Chapter 7 and Chapter 11 which elicit distressed firms as entities unable to service their debt capacity and fail to meet their financial obligations. Further, Balcaen and Ooghe (2004) report financially distressed firms do not change their legal status of bankruptcy filing practices. In this context, Radono, Velarde, and Tarantino (2016) study bankruptcy procedures such as reorganisation and liquidation in lieu, with the borrower's settlement phenomenon. They argue reorganisation measures can effectively strengthen borrower's repayment ability to re-negotiate outstanding financial agreement that increase the cost of obtaining bank loans and reduces their investment. Similarly, liquidation measures fortify creditor rights reducing cost of bank funds and stimulate investment.

Statement of the Problem

"The success of State-Owned Enterprises (SOEs) are impeded by political interventions; stakeholders obscure stances; maladministration; firm-specific deterrence and market competition which ambit their survival".

Research Questions

1. What role(s) do the prime stakeholder's play that affect the success of SOEs?
2. What are the inherent constraints that affect the performance of SOEs?
3. What are the rehabilitation efforts to be considered to protect SOEs?

Research Objectives

The case aims to answer potent hindrances such as declining margins and capital formation; stagnant and falling market share; rising cost of goods sold; and the inability to achieve scale economies. The pre-dominant issues for debate targets investment in fixed assets; product development; brands; network of branches; skill improvement of employees; newer technology; and the role of unions towards business goals.

Hypotheses

H1: *The stances held by the stakeholders affect the success of SOE.*

H2: *Both internal and external constraints affect the performance of SOEs.*

III. THE MILIEU OF MYSORE INDUSTRIES

We begin our anecdotes by providing due emphasis on each of the selected SOEs under "MYSORE" brand. The first anecdote entails Mysore Lamp Works Limited (MLWL) incorporated in 1936 profoundly known as the "State's Pride", a pioneer in production and sale of electric lamps. It is an unlisted enterprise categorised under the non-government company with its current status being under liquidation. The Board for Industrial and Financial Reconstruction (BIFR) case was registered in 1996 (Case No. 605/1996) with its last order dated 18th July, 2000 recommended for winding up. The firm age spans over 79 years that had an authorised capital of ₹ 150,000,000 with a paid-up capital of ₹ 118,102,328 respectively. The last Annual General Meeting (AGM) was held on 12th September 2013 with the final balance sheet dated 31st March 2013. This anecdote reports stakeholder's insights from the view of State Government, High Court of Karnataka, Trade Union, Bureaucrats, BIFR recommendations, MLWL's stance and others respectively.

Anecdote One: Mysore Lamp Works Limited

H1: *The stances held by the stakeholders affect the success of SOE.*

Mysore Lamp Works Limited (hereafter MLWL) was established in 1936 at Bengaluru with government shareholding of 91 per cent. The 78-year-old pioneer with state of the art facilities in electric bulbs segment has suffered a whopping loss of around ₹ 90 crores between 1993-2002. The decision to shut down MLWL was taken in early 2002, when it was enjoying a market share of 20 per cent in Karnataka and 3 per cent nation-wide. MLWL enjoyed golden reign over several decades in terms of profitability, employment, production capacity, operational efficiency and effective management. According to India notes (2016), MLWL aligned a collaboration agreement with General Electric Co., New York during 1962-63. Over 63,052 equity shares of ₹ 10 each, with a whopping 49 per cent were allotted at the rate of ₹ 35.07 per share. In 1977, General Electric Co. decided to sell its shareholding (94,578 equity shares) and eventually from 1979, it became a SOE. In 1989-90, MLWL jointly with M/s Premier Electrical Industries Pvt. Ltd., Kathmandu, collaborated towards technology transfer to manufacture GLS lamps under the 'Mysore' brand in Nepal. Further, MLWL provided right issues in 1992 at a ratio of 1:2 with the ex right dated 18th Dec 1991 evidences last investor returns. At last, MLWL was unable to meet shareholders requirements and failed to provide dividend between 1999-2009. The case of MLWL extended over 12 years from various facets and therefore, financial descriptive are nullified as it was closed long back (See, Table 4.2). Hence, we narrate interesting facets of MLWL that provides fresh insights on how different stakeholders opine on the state's pride.

BIFR Stance

The Board of Industrial and Financial Reconstruction (hereafter, BIFR) in case no. 605/96 implies that MLWL was unable to decompose its accumulated losses within stipulated time; failed to meet all financial obligations and hence suggested to be wound up u/s 20(1) of the Sick Industrial Companies Act (SICA, 1985). The case was registered in 1996 and heard on 27th Jan 1997, wherein the Industrial Development Bank of India (IDBI) was nominated as Operating Agency (OA) u/s 17(3) of the Companies Act. Giving ample opportunities to revamp, BIFR noticed there was no concrete proposal for change of management nor sought privatisation.

MLWL submitted a company petition 231/2000 proposal to the OA for induction of ₹ 11.13 crores by state-government besides mobilisation and/ or ₹ 14.22 crores from sale of surplus land. BIFR observed state-government neither attempted to provide funds for its revival, while the co-promoter M/s Tremac India (P) Ltd. could hardly establish its credentials over which the bench expressed serious doubts. Looking into these intricacies, BIFR noticed the petition was pending since 1996 and no effective steps were taken by the state-government to revive MLWL; while the Drafting of Rehabilitation Scheme (DRS) prepared by OA (COP 231/2000) was also scuttled on plea of privatisation. In this context, BIFR u/s 20(1) after considering all relevant facts and circumstances and after hearing the parties concerned, opined that no scheme can be of no use to MLWL which could not be rehabilitated and seeks closure and recommended for winding up. Being referred to BIFR, approval to rehabilitate MLWL required a whopping ₹ 19.91 crores. The setbacks administered also include both banks and financial institutions who expressed their inability to provide additional term loans, thus reducing cost of rehabilitation.

State Government's Stance

The dilemma that often quests the functioning of SOE ensemble devising revival plans and their implementation. No doubt, advent of Globalisation, Privatisation and Liberalisation have relished substantial markets amid, there are potent hindrances. The newspaper article "Mysore Lamps will be closed down" dated 7.7.2007 presumed Industries Minister Mr Katta Subramanya Naidu who connoted state government wished to develop factory land and rent it to private agencies. Unfortunately, Bengaluru Development Authority (BDA) Commissioner Mr Bharath Lal Meena rather refused to carry on the project due to insufficiency of funds. Interestingly, Pattanashetti (2014) states remarks of Energy Minister Mr D.K. Shivakumar which lays new repurcusions. The state government intended to buy nearly one lakh transformers and had made an initial advancement of ₹ 20 crores to state-run electrical enterprises namely, New Government Electrical Factory (NGEF) and Karnataka Vidyuth Karkhane for purchase. To the demise, both MLWL and NGEF are unable to operate in an efficient manner. The Corporate Bureau of Indian Express in their article highlight NGEF divested its 28.75 per cent stakes in MLWL with the earlier investment of ₹ 13.29 lakhs out of the total capital of ₹ 1.36 crores receiving consent of state government for divestment. Similarly, the newspaper article "Mysore Lamps up for sale" dated Dec 14, 2000 connotes Minister of State for Information and Publicity, Mr B.K. Chandrasheker reported failure to attract investors to invest in MLWL, would eventually lead to winding-up thereby revamp compensation structure to employees. Amid these nuances, Badrinath (2004) noted the brand "Mysore" has been leased out by state-government for a mere ₹ 75,000 to an association of ancillaries (suppliers) while their office term. The state government in lieu to directives of Justice Mr Ram Mohan Reddy, on 23.7.2013 Principal Secretary, Mr P.M. Mahishi, announced that an integrated technology park would be proposed which would provide employment opportunities to over 5,000 persons in the 22 acres land. Yet again, state government's stance neither attempted to forego the management, mal-administration and intense competition in electric bulbs division thereby failed to sought revival plans raises a sad demise.

High Court's Stance

Krishnaprasad (2014) opines judgement affirmed by Justice Mr Ram Mohan Reddy on 18th July 2000 extended time-span to rejuvenate MLWL and directed state government to devise revival plans and its implementation. Further, on 23rd Jan 2014 he recommended state-government to float a global tender and invite bids for rejuvenation through the manufacture of LEDs which can reap fruits for both public and private sector. Nonetheless, state government was provided liberty to impose terms and conditions duely compliable while inviting tendeRs Thereafter, on 28th July 2014, company petition no. 231/2000 between BIFR (Petitioner) and M/s The Mysore Lamp Works Ltd. (Respondent) referring to BIFR case no. 605/96 ensembles winding up of the enterprise. In this respect, the Justice deferred proceedings whereby State Government was recommended to actually merge MLWL with Mysore Minerals; thereafter manufacture LEDs and pave way for absorption of employees as a final chance to rejuvenate.

Employees and Union Stance

With immediate effect on 4th Jan 2002, state-government issued official orders to wind-up MLWL operations without considering rehabilitation strategies neither looking into the consensus of around 1,556 workmen (1,419 opted for VRS; 33 absorbed in other state-owned entities and the remaining 104 enticed to work in the undertaking). As Badrinath (2004) elicits, the illuminators of Taj Mahal, Mysore Palace, Vidhana Soudha, Qutub Minar, Agra Fort and Fatehpur Sikri had to plead Energy Minister Shobha Karandlaje for their work to make electric lamps such as CFLs and LEDs for the state's Belaku project. Thereafter, the state government announced its plan to replace all light bulbs in its buildings with LED lamps, for which it decided to buy lights from Hyderabad and Kolkata. Nevertheless, MLWL was neither rejuvenated which could have provided employment to the workforce alongside to produce lights at a much lower rate was under milieu.

Film Association Stance

Interestingly, Shyam Prasad (2014) elicits the state's pride MLWL had also attracted the film association of Karnataka to begin an official film studio. In her remarks Smt Tara (Actress and Member of Legislative Council) invoked state government to provide the premises for film industry. With over 250 films having been shooted in MLWL, the sheds, and godowns have reproached an unofficial studio.

Bureaucrat's Stance

Having been transferred over six times in a short span of six months, Mr M.N. Vijaykumar, a senior IAS officer, was appointed as the Managing Director of MLWL. Ironically, Mr Vijaykumar had no salary, supporting staff, neither official car as he headed a sick enterprise. Notwithstanding, he suggested the state-government to consider MLWL while implementing both Bhagyajyothi and Kuteerajyothi projects to provide electricity to all households in promoting use of LEDs and CFL lamps. At the same time, providing contract to MLWL for supply of LEDs would revive towards directed goals. The Annual General Meeting held on 12th Sept 2013 execrate material allegations that confer "To make the company borrow more and make it incur loss"; excuse of technical collaboration and distribution networks revamps the facets of MLWL.

From first anecdote MLWL, we reported the aftermath that eventually went under liquidation. In this case, we highlight the presently active SOEs such as Mysore Paper Mills Ltd; Mysore Cements Ltd; and Mysore Petro Chemicals Ltd. The second anecdote envisages Mysore Paper Mills Ltd. (hereafter, MPML) a leading pioneer in production of newsprint. The enterprise is listed in BSE (scrip id: 502405), a state government company specialised in paper and paper products. The firm age spans over 79 years that has an authorised capital of ₹ 1,500,000,000 with a paid-up capital of ₹ 1,188,934,270 respectively. The last AGM was held on 30th December 2014 with the recent balance sheet dated 31st March 2014. The BIFR case was registered in 2012 (Case No. 601/2012) with its last order dated 26th September, 2000 and its BIFR status propose pending determination of sickness. The third anecdote evident Mysore Cements Limited (at present, Heidelberg Cement India Limited), a well-known enterprise in production and sale of cement in both North and South India. The enterprise is listed in BSE (scrip id: 500292), a subsidiary of foreign company specialised in manufacture of non-metallic mineral products n.e.c. The firm age lasts over 57 years that has an authorised capital of ₹ 2,800,000,000 with a paid-up capital of ₹ 2,266,131,200 respectively. The last AGM was held on 7th August 2015 with recent balance sheet dated 31st March 2015. The final anecdote describes the artefacts of Mysore Petro Chemicals Limited. The enterprise is listed in BSE (scrip id: 506734), a non-government company specialised in Commodity Chemicals. The firm age spans over 47 years that has an authorised capital of ₹ 150,000,000 with a paid-up capital of ₹ 65,834,880 respectively. The last AGM was held on 24th August 2015 with recent balance sheet dated 31st March 2015. These three anecdotes provide useful financial insights on their financial and operating performance. This section portrays the following anecdotes.

H2: *Both internal and external constraints affect the performance of SOEs.*

Anecdote Two: Mysore Paper Mills Limited

Mysore Paper Mills Limited (hereafter, MPML) was established by Krishnaraja Wodeyar during 1937 under Mysore Companies Regulation, VIII of 1917. Under sec 617 of the Companies Act 1956, it became a government company in 1977. The share capital of MPML reports an Authorised capital (₹ 150 crs) enriching a paid-up capital (₹ 120 crs) respectively. The state holds nearly 65 per cent of stakes; financial institutions about 18 per cent; and public concentration of 17 per cent respectively. It is a BSE listed enterprise located at Bhadravathi, in Shimoga district of Karnataka. The company has over 3,380 employees, which also includes nearly

1,150 contract workers In recent years, the total accumulated loss of MPML stands at ₹ 475 crores. As (Veerendera, 2015) reports Mr M.J.Appaji, Member of Legislative Assembly (Bhadravathi) had urged state government to release grants for modernising MPML. The undertaking also runs a sugar factory and a paper mill. The prime reason for the loss attributes to antiquated production methods and requires a sum of ₹ 1,000 crores to modernise and make it profitable. Due to accumulated losses, Smt K. Ratna Prabha, the Additional Chief Secretary and Director of MPML recommended a management lease-contract, whereby routine affairs would be controlled by private sector and discretionary powers remain under the ambit of state government. Over 15,000 families of cane growers supply sugarcane to MPML and are directly dependent; and have contributed a whopping ₹ 200 crores per annum to exchequer. MPML has been ISO 14001 certified that covers manufacture of newsprint, printing and packaging paper, writing and manufacture of plantation white sugar. The (Economic Times, 2016) bureau states as on 30-Sep-2015, the enterprise realised sales of ₹ 39.16 crs For the quarter ended 30-Sep-2015, MPML asserts a total of 118,893,432 outstanding shares.

Anecdote Three: Mysore Cements Limited (Heidelberg Cement India Ltd.)

Mysore Cements Limited (Mycem) is a public enterprise set up in 1958-59 by Mr Sarangapani Mudaliar in collaboration with US based firm KaiseRs The enterprise was taken over by Mr G.D. Birla in 1962 under the control of Birlas whereby, in 1983 Mr S.K. Birla chaired the enterprise. At present, the operational activities are carried out in four states namely, Karnataka, Madhya Pradesh, Maharashtra, and Uttar Pradesh respectively. The plant locations are Ammasandra, Damoh, Dolvi and Jhansi. Mysore Cements Limited (hereafter, MCL) operates in three different segments such as cement, sponge iron and others Between 1990s–2006, MCL gained prominence under Mr Nandalal Hamirwasia (Managing Director) and Mr. Nirbhaya Lodha (Executive Director) who paved the benchmark in the production of cement in South India. Since 1980s, the Ammasandra unit began to produce Clinker; thereby two products such as Portland slag cement and Portland pozzolana cement have been produced. Nearly 3,500- 4,000 real time employees work on daily shift basis in this unit. MCL in terms of Infrastructure and Development provided its employees with Hospital facilities,

Insurance, School and College, recreation facilities and residential quarters Similarly, Damoh unit was modernised in 1989 with an investment of ₹ 800 million to increase the operational efficiency and productivity. Likewise, at Jhansi an investment of ₹ 590 million was utilised for Diamond cement, with a green field 500,000 tpa grinding capacity being raised. The enterprise also appointed Andersen Consulting Group to re-look cost reduction strategies and to advice in certain areas for improvement. The Ammasandra unit faced certain internal issues and conflicts between employees and management in 2002, due to salaries and wages, that led to closure of school (for 15 days) and other essential requisites. In 2006, MCL was taken over by Heidelberg AG, Germany and has been renamed on 16th April 2009 as Heidelberg Cement India Limited (hereafter, HCIL). HCIL is listed under the BSE scrip id MYSORECEM controlled by Heidelberg Cement group, having its operations in more than 50 countries. Recently, it acquired Indorama Cement to strengthen its operations. At present, Heidelberg Cement owns around 54 per cent stake in Mysore Cement and has acquired 100 per cent in Indorama. Post-merger, it has obtained around 69 per cent stakes in the merged enterprise. Heidelberg acquired 50 per cent stakes in Indorama in 2006 and the remaining 50 per cent stake was acquired thereafter. The consolidation between Heidelberg Cement and Indorama Cement has improved the managerial efficiency. The acquisition cost Heidelberg Cement paid ranges ₹ 436.82 crore ($95.53 million) with an enterprise value of $117 per tonne.

Anecdote Four: Mysore Petrochemicals Limited

As per the Economic Times bureau (2016), Mysore Petrochemicals Limited (hereafter, MPL) was incorporated in 1969. The (NDTV.Profit, 2016) sources mention MPCL, formerly Premier Petro Chemicals was renamed on 3.9.1970. It had two technology collaboration agreements with Chemicsche Farbrik Von-Heyden (GmbH) and Lurgir Mineraloeltechnik (GmbH), West Germany in 1969 to manufacture phlathic anhydride and special equipment supplies (battery limits). The enterprise is presently operating in Organic chemicals segment with a market capitalisation of ₹ 28.54 crs (as of 31.3.2015). MPL, a mid-cap entity is specialised in the manufacture and sale of chemicals such as plasticizers, maleic anhydride and phthalic anhydride realising ₹ 36.96 crs in 2015. Its two plants are located at Raichur (Karnataka) and Taloja (Maharashtra) with installation capacity of 12,000 MTPA (for phthalic anhydride) and 7,000 MTPA (for maleic anhydride) respectively. The products manufactured are used in plasticizers, dyes and pigments, paints, polyvinyl compounds, polyester resins and alkyd resins. MPCL stakes are actively traded in both BSE (scrip id: 506734) and NSE (code: MYSORPETRO) respectively. The enterprise is led by Mr M.M. Dhanuka Group, a major promoter of IG Petrochemicals (wholly owned subsidiary) with total outstanding shares of 6,583,488 as on 31.12.2015. According to (Dion global solutions limited, 2016), MPCL approved dividend or ₹ 1.50 per share value of ₹ 10 each in 2014. During 2015, they also entered into a Joint Venture with M/s Dubai Natural Gas Company Ltd. from its subsidiary concern IG Petrochemicals Ltd.

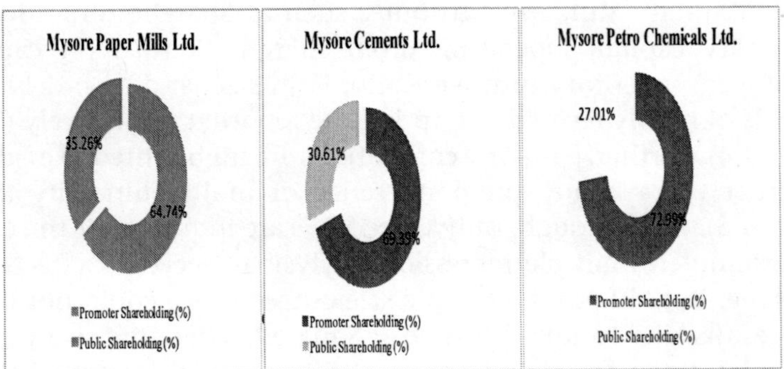

Figure 4.3: Shareholding Pattern of Active Mysore Industries.

IV. Research Methodology

The study uses secondary data obtained from the annual reports of selected SOEs; Money control; Economic times Bureau; Rediff money; and Bombay Stock Exchange (BSE). As Mysore Lamp Works Limited (MLWL) entailed financial distress since 1996 and thereafter the production being stopped, and hence financials do not apply here. The remaining three SOEs namely, Mysore Paper Mills Ltd.; Mysore Cements Ltd.; and Mysore Petro Chemicals Ltd. are the sample units for investigation. We intend to foresee the effects on non-government company (MPCL), state-government company (MPML) and subsidiary of foreign company (MCL) from 2002-2015. Each of these SOEs are listed in BSE. The remaining group of Mysore Industries are ignored due to the lacunas in obtaining sufficient financial data and have either failed to be listed in BSE/ NSE or have failed to be actively traded erstwhile. The secondary data on financials include Balance Sheet, Income Statement, Cash Flows, Ratios, Capital Structure and Management Discussions.

V. DATA ANALYSIS

Financial Highlights

The financial information of aforesaid SOEs such as Mysore Paper Mills Limited; Mysore Cements Limited; and Mysore Petro Chemicals Limited are collected from 2002-2015. In the first phase, we report descriptive statistics giving prime impetus to leverage. Leverage is measured by Total debt/ (Total debt + Equity Share Capital). Similarly, attributes such as Shareholding; Bonus in equity capital; Operating profit margin, Return on capital employed; Inventory turnover ratio; Firm size; and Non-debt tax shields of highly levered enterprises are reported respectively (See, Table 4.4). Further, pair-wise correlations are highlighted to evident whether there is any pre-ponderence of multicollinearity (See, Table 4.5). Even though, only three SOEs are inquired for the case, we attempted multiple regression analysis to see their effects on leverage. But, due to the sample size criterion, we could not infer the results due to low Adjusted R-Squared. Therefore, we report financial review based on leverage attributes which envisages their present financial position. The income statement and balance sheet indicators such as leverage, shareholding pattern, bonus in equity capital, OPM, ROCE, ITR, firm size and NDTS infer a group mean (stdev) of 0.52(0.19), 41.02(10.34), 11.49(0.21), 6.79(9.03), 1.39(20.92), 8.80(6.66), 5.49(0.36) and 0.07(0.04) respectively (See, Table 4.6). From the time aspect, leverage had an overall mean of 0.74 (See, Table 4.7) which exemplifies that, in some years these enterprises found it difficult to obtain financing [2008 (0.67), 2009(0.68), 2010 (0.71), 2011(0.71), 2012(0.73), 2013(0.70) and 2015(0.67)]. Therefore, we infer in comparison to cross-section, time period showed higher variation in leverage. In case of shareholding and bonus in equity capital, the overall mean stands at 39.19 and 14.06 which confines gradual divestment of stakes in these enterprises between 2008-2015. These insights evident they had to face intense competition and the need to modernise them was a daunting task. Operating profit margin witnessed mean of 5.25 in comparison to the years 2003-04 and from 2011-

2013 having a negative figure illustrates that these enterprises were under severe financial crunch. Return on capital employed presumes a mean of -1.19 rather has yielded (-33.67) in 2015 presumes the need to at least increase their net worth than the accumulated losses. The Inventory turnover ratio with an overall mean of 7.37 has shown positive signs wherein after 2013-2015. Interestingly, Firm size has a mean of 5.25 also has gradually begun to improve on a marginal basis. Non-debt tax shields rather shows astonishing figures due to the fact these enterprises are sick and rather expect state-government to rehabilitate their operations.

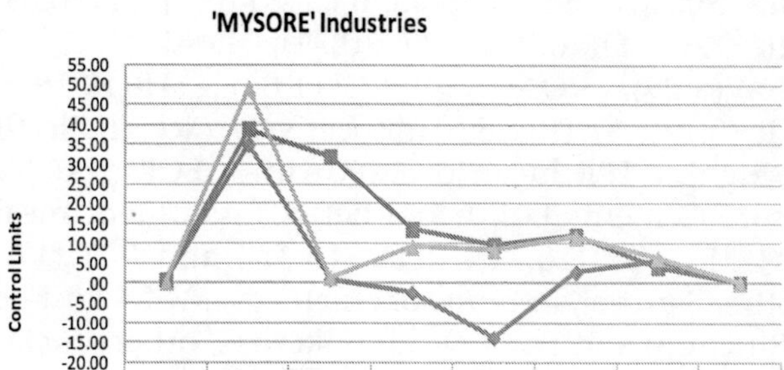

	Leverage	Share holding	Bonus	OPM	ROCE	ITR	Firm Size	NDTS
Mysore Paper Mills Ltd.	.66	35.07	1.00	-2.33	-13.80	2.87	5.89	0.06
Mysore Petro Chemicals Ltd.	.80	38.93	32.00	13.57	9.64	12.00	4.15	0.10
Mysore Cements Ltd.	.10	49.07	1.47	9.13	8.33	11.53	6.42	0.05

Fig 4.4: Financial Review: Graphical View.

Source: Author's Calculation.

In the second phase, we report the financial and operating performance of the selected SOEs to evident their vintage points. To measure the financial performance, both profitability and liquidity factors are examined (See, Table 4.8). In case of profitability, Mysore Paper Mills Ltd. asserts [OPM(-2.87); GPM (-6.58); CPM(-6.46); NPM(-9.76); PTPM(-10.14); RLTF(-1.81); ROE (-7.86)]; followed by Mysore Cements Ltd. [OPM(9.14); GPM(4.25); CPM(4.49); NPM(0.12); PTPM(0.37); RLTF(9.31); ROE(39.08)]; and Mysore Petrochemicals Ltd. [OPM(11.11); GPM(0.38); CPM(3.24); NPM(0.69); PTPM(1.32); RLTF(12.67); ROE (109.93)] respectively. The liquidity attributes adhere a group mean for Mysore Paper Mills Ltd. [CR (0.86), QR (0.63), and DER (4.92)]; Mysore Cements Ltd. [CR (1.27), QR (1.00), and DER (2.94)]; and Mysore Petrochemicals

Ltd. [CR (0.84), QR (0.77), and DER (0.79)] respectively. Though, there exists positive figures, Mysore Cements Ltd. had better liquidity as compared to other entities. For measuring the operating performance, factors such as sales, investment and efficiency are considered. Mysore Paper Mills Ltd. entails a group mean i.e. [MCR(0.43), ECR(0.22), TER(1.03), DR(0.03), PFR(0.28), MER(0.08), ROCE(-5.87), RONW(14.13), ROA(-0.79), ICR(-0.37), ITR(2.97), DTR(10.17), FATR(1.14), TATR(1.59)]; followed by Mysore Cements Ltd. [MCR(0.31), ECR(0.07), TER(0.91), DR(0.04), PFR(0.31), MER(0.11), ROCE(9.03), RONW(20.71), ROA(16.77), ICR(17.11), ITR(11.83), DTR(31.08), FATR(1.33), TATR(1.19)]; while for Mysore Petrochemicals Ltd. [MCR(0.31), ECR(0.07), TER(0.91), DR(0.04), PFR(0.31), MER(0.11), ROCE(10.00), RONW(5.09), ROA(1.79), ICR(1.87), ITR(12.19), DTR(18.93), FATR (0.77), TATR(1.62)] respectively (See, Table 9). MPML had the highest TER mean of 1.03 with a ECR of 0.22. In addition, Mysore Cements Ltd. had a better Investment mean with ROCE (9.03), RONW (20.71), ROA (16.77), and ICR (17.11) one after another. Further, in terms of efficiency, MCL had a better mean for DTR (31.08) and FATR (1.33). Likewise, other efficiency attributes like ITR (12.19) and TATR (1.62) are better effected in MPCL. The comparative financial ratios of Mysore Paper Mills Ltd. [PBT/NW (-0.37), PAT/NW(0.02), VA/EC(2.88), OP/NS(0.03), PBT/NS(-0.1), VA/NS(0.6), RES/NW(0.39), TD/NW(0.25)]; Mysore Cements Ltd. [PBT/ NW(0.21), PAT/NW(0.05), VA/EC(8.28), OP/NS(0.10), PBT/NS(0.01), VA/NS(0.60), RES/NW(1.07), TD/NW(-0.69)]; and Mysore Petrochemicals Ltd. [PBT/NW(0.12), PAT/NW(0.15), VA/EC(2.00), OP/NS(0.13), PBT/NS(0.06), VA/NS(0.29), RES/NW(0.08), TD/NW(-0.55)] are reported respectively (See, Table 10). In terms of VA/EC, Mysore Cements Ltd. a far better ratio of 8.28; with the RES/NW of 1.07.

After re-looking into both leverage dynamics and performance factors, it is quite evident firm size does matter because investment decisions are stranded decisively. In this case, disinvestment decisions in the aforesaid SOEs can elude nuances pertaining to capital expenditure, working capital requirements, dividend payments, and discharge of outstanding liabilities. Even though, SOEs enjoy luxury of being under the ambit of State Government, malaises adhere both allocation and disbursement of capital. As the tale goes, *higher the debt; higher the risk*. Hence, SOEs are revamped in meeting their promises to the creditors; stringent delivery terms from the suppliers; high level of order cancellations; inability to deliver products on time; increase in the borrowing cost of capital; and higher interest payments. Therefore, we connote these nuances lead to declining rate of capital formation; stagnant and falling market share; declining margins; rising cost of goods sold; and the inabilities that surpass scale economies.

VI. Discussions And Policy Implications

Thus, what remains bleak is the legacy of "MYSORE" for name sake which no longer portray flourishing empire of "MYSORE ESTATE" post-independent India. This could be due to excessive state interference in the affairs of these enterprises which have eventually led to business decisions being independent of political goals. The objectives were to oversee the milieu of SOEs against political interventions; stakeholders' stances; mal-administration; market competition; firm-specific determinants; and industry deterrence ambit their survival. This also tested few critical hypotheses for the benefit of policy-makers that include namely, stances held by different stakeholders to foresee performance and also the effects of internal and external constraints to highlight success of SOEs. The study was conducted to answer declining rate of capital formation; declining margins; rising cost of goods sold; stagnant and falling market share and the inability to achieve scale economies. Further, to be specific, investment in fixed assets; product development; brands; network of branches; skill improvement of employees; newer technology; role of unions towards business goals are the pre-dominant issues raised for discussion. We report Disinvestment decisions as an amicable solution to usher planned economic development in terms of grey earnings (value added); regional and national importance; employment opportunities; extensive use of local resources; exploit huge customer potential; and growth opportunities. To advocate, an effective disinvestment policy can curb nuances such as fiscal deficits, corporate governance, public-private partnerships; scarcity of resources, and operational constraints. The success of SEBI's public shareholding norms (minimum 10 per cent) in CPSEs to meet disinvestment targets through institutional private placements (IPPs), offer for sale, share buybacks, right issues, exchange traded funds (ETFs), closed auctions, and retail discounts can be implied to SOEs. We restrain our study to these selected SOEs, due to inequalities in obtaining financial history of various Mysore Industries. A comprehensive overview into them can reveal interesting rudiments.

VII. Conclusions

The anticipated case outcome evident that SOEs failed to modernise which eventually led to stiff competition by private entrants. Hence, we undermine adequate training, infrastructure, diversification, promotion, corporate social responsibilities, grey earnings, production capacity, recovery of bad loans, mal-administration, and state-government's interference as amicable target points. Due to these constraints, investment decisions also get politicised as there is no governing board to process investment proposals and neither are the cadres professionalised to effectively manage them. This has led them to be biased in introducing economic reforms as various political parties in power do not approve the nature and extent of reforms to be undertaken. Therefore, the economic well-being of a state can be examined carefully through SOEs to create employment opportunities, support large scale investments, control monopoly and improve standard of living. We infer from the anecdotes, political interference in regular affairs of the enterprise have a decisive influence on capital formation; higher minimum support prices of raw materials; rising cost of goods sold; skill development of employees; investment in fixed assets and inability to achieve scale economies. In this respect, the setbacks administered also include both banks and financial institutions who at times, express their inability to provide additional term loans and thus curtailing rehabilitation. Yet again, state government's stance triggers a weak link to forego the management, mal-administration; and self-centredness have kindled the renaissance of Mysore Industries. Therefore, we raise an alarming signal to protect our SOEs from the nightmares that can succumb and entail them to be known only in the history books and hence, raise the slogan "**RENAISSANCE OR BACKWATERS**" to stakeholders

Acknowledgement

The authors sincerely thank and acknowledge UGC (Selection and Awards Division, [Grant No. F.2-18/2011 (SA-I)], New Delhi, India for the external fellowship (SRF) assistance through the scheme *JRF in Sciences, Humanities, and Social Sciences.*

Bibliography

Altman, E. (1968). Financial ratios, discriminant analysis and the prediction of corporate bankruptcy. Journal of Finance, 23, 189-209.

Altman, E. (1993). Corporate financial distress and bankruptcy: A complete guide to predicting and avoiding distress and profiting from bankruptcy.

Anant, T., Gangopadhayay, and Goswami, O. (1992). Report of industrial sickness in India.

Andrade, G., and Kaplan, S. (1998). How costly is financial not economic distress? Evidence from highly leveraged transactions that became distressed. Journal of Finance, 53, 1433-1493.

Badrinath, R. (2004, Sept. 8). Mysore Lamps brand leased for pittance. Business Standard.

Bae, J. (2012). Predicting financial distress of the South Korean manufacturing industries. Expert Systems with Applications, 39(10), 9159-9165.

Balcaen, S., and Ooghe, H. (2004). 35 years of studies on business failure: An overview of the classic statistical methodologies and their related problems.

Beaver, W. (1966). Financial ratios as predictors of failure. Journal of Accounting Research, 4, 71-111.

Bellovary, J., Giacomino, D., and Akers, M. (2007). A review of bankruptcy prediction studies: 1930 to present. Journal of Financial Education, 33, 1-42.

Campbell, J., Hilscher, J., and Szilagyi, J. (2008). In search of distress risk. Journal of Finance, 63, 2899-2939.

Caplan, D., Dutta, S., and Marcinko, D. (2012). Lehman on the brink of bankruptcy: Case about aggressive application of accounting standards. Issues in Accounting Education, 27(2), 441-459.

Chan, K., and Chen, N. (1991). Structural and return characteristics of small and large firms. Journal of Finance, 46, 1467-1484.

Christidis, A., and Gregory, A. (2010). Some new models for financial distress prediction in the UK.

Dion global solutions limited. (2016). Mysore Petro Chemicals Limited. Moneycontrol.com.

Economic Times. (2016). Mysore Petro Chemicals Limited. Economictimesindiatimes.com.

Falk, R. (2005). Industrial sickness in Indian manufacturing.

Gopalan, R., and Xie, K. (2011). Conglomerates and industry distress. The Review of Financial Studies, 24(11), 3642-3687.

Goswami, O. (1996). Corporate bankruptcy in India: A comparative perspective. A monograph.

Guariglia, A., and Poncet, S. (2008). Could financial distortions be no impediment to economic growth after all? Evidence from China. Journal of Comparative Economics, 36(4), 633-657.

Guariglia, A., Liu, X., and Song, L. (2011). Internal finance and growth: Microeconometric evidence on Chinese firms. Journal of Development Economics, 96(1), 79-94.

Gutierrez, C., Olalla, M., and Olmo, B. (2009). The influence of bankruptcy law on equity value of financially distressed firms: A European comparative analysis. International Review of Law and Economics, 29, 229-243.

Kam, A., Citron, D., and Muradoglu, Y. (2005). The characteristics of corporate distress in an emerging market: The case of China.

Kaplan, S., and Stein, J. (1993). The evolution of buyout pricing and financial structure in the 1980s. Quarterly Journal of Economics, 108(2), 313-357.

Komera, S., and Lukose, J. (2014). Corporate Bankruptcy, Soft Budget Constraints, and Business Group Affiliation: Evidence from Indian Firms. Review of Pacific Basin Financial Markets and Policies, 17(3), 1-28.

Kornai, J., Maskin, E., and Roland, G. (2003). Understanding the soft budget constraint. Journal of Economic Literature, 41(4), 1095-1136.

Krishnaprasad. (2014, Jul. 28). High Court orders winding up of Mysore Lamp Works Ltd. The Hindu.

Kumar, S., and Bag, D. (2015). Disinvestment Dilemma:An Empirical Study. (I. K. (Eds.), Ed.) Research Issues in Applied Economics, 310-331.

Mishra, R., and Navin, B. (2002). Restructuring Public Enterprises in India: Privatisation and Disinvestment.

Nagaraj, R. (2005, Mar 26). Disinvestment and Privatization in India, Assessment and Options.

NDTV.Profit. (2016). Mysore Petro Chemicals Limited. ndtv. profit.com.

Ohlson, J. (1980). Financial ratios and the probabilistic prediction of bankruptcy. Journal of Accounting Research, 19, 109-131.

Pattanashetti, G. (2014, Dec 16). State to consider Mysore Lamps revival plan. The Hindu.

Pindado, J., Rodrigues, L., and Torre, D. (2008). Estimating financial distress likelihood. Journal of Business Research, 61, 995-1003.

Pursell, G. (1990). Industrial sickness, primary and secondary: The effects of exit constraints on industrial performance. The World Bank Economic Review, 4(1), 103-114.

Radono, G., Velarde, N., and Tarantino, E. (2016). Bankruptcy law and bank financing. Journal of Financial Economics, 1-20.

Shleifer, A., and Vishny, R. (1998). The grabbing hand: Government pathologies and their cures.

Shumway, T. (2001). Forecasting bankruptcy more accurately: A simple hazard model. Journal of Business, 74(1), 101-124.

Shyam Prasad, S. (2014, Aug. 30). Kannada film industry demands film studio at Mysore Lamps. The Times of India.

Som, L. (2013, June). Corporate Governance of Public Enterprises in India. ICRA Bulletin Money and Finance.

Veerendera, P. (2015, May 6). MPM: Contract workers seek immediate instatement. The Hindu.

Wohlschlegel, A. (2002). The economics of corporate bankruptcy law.

Wruck, K. (1990). Financial distress, reorganization, and organizational efficiency. Journal of Financial Economics, 27, 419-444.

Zmijewski, M. (1984). Methodological issues related to the estimation of financial distress prediction models. Journal of Accounting Research, 22, 59-82.

Table 4.1: *Mysore Industries: Identity Indicators*

State-owned Enterprises (SOEs)	*Year of Incorpn.*	*Reg No.*	*Age*	*Company Sub-category*	*Co. Status*	*Listed in BSE*	*Industry*
1	2	3	4	5	6	7	8
The Mysore Paints and Varnish Ltd.	11-11-1911	503	68	State- Government Company	Active	Listed	Trading
The Mysore Sugar Company Ltd.	30-01-1933	142	83	State- Government Company	Active	Listed	Manufacturing Food products and Beverages
The Mysore Spun Silk Mills Ltd.	08-05-1936	172	79	Non-Government Company	Dormant	Unlisted	Spinning, Weaving and Finishing of Textiles
The Mysore Paper Mills Ltd.	20-05-1936	173	79	State- Government Company	Active	Listed [BSE: 502405]	Paper and Paper Products
The Mysore Lamp Works Ltd.	26-08-1936	182	79	Non-Government Company	Liquidation	Unlisted	Electric Lamps
The Mysore Tobacco Company Ltd.	19-04-1937	199	78	State- Government Company	Active	Unlisted	Human Health Activities
The Mysore Coffee Curing Works Ltd.	15-09-1938	238	77	Non-Government Company	Active	Unlisted	Growing of Crops; Market Gardening; Horticulture
The Mysore Chrome and Tanning Company Ltd.	30-03-1940	261	75	State- Government Company	Active	Unlisted	Human Health Activities
The Mysore Match Company Ltd.	17-05-1940	264	75	Non-Government Company	Active	Unlisted	Human Health Activities
The Mysore Plantations Ltd.	20-11-1942	295	74	Non-Government Company	Active	Unlisted	Health and Social Work
The Mysore Electrical Industries Ltd.	13-02-1945	367	71	Non-Government Company	Active	Unlisted	Switchgear Equipments
The Mysore Alkali and Chemicals Ltd.	08-05-1947	472	68	Non-Government Company	Dissolved	Unlisted	Chemicals
The Mysore Trade Industries Ltd.	30-08-1947	499	68	Non-Government Company	Strike Off	Unlisted	Trading
The Mysore Cements Ltd. [Mycem]	13-05-1958	42301	57	Subsidiary of Foreign Company	Active	Listed [BSE: 500292]	Mfr. of Non-metallic Mineral products n.e.c
The Mysore Acetate and Chemicals Corpn. Ltd.	24-12-1963	1517	52	State- Government Company	Liquidation	Unlisted	Chemicals
The Mysore Sales International Ltd.	17-03-1966	1612	50	State- Government Company	Active	Unlisted	Human Health Activities
The Mysore Cosmetics Ltd.	25-03-1966	1615	49	State- Government Company	Liquidation	Unlisted	Cosmetics
The Mysore Minerals Ltd.	13-05-1966	1620	49	State- Government Company	Active	Unlisted	Human Health Activities
The Mysore Petrochemicals Ltd.	09-06-1969	1799	47	Non-Government Company	Active	Listed [BSE: 506734]	Commodity Chemicals
The Mysore Breweries Ltd. (SABMiller)	04-12-1970	1971	45	Non-Government Company	Amalgamated	Unlisted	Manufacture of Beverages
The Mysore Steels Ltd.	28-12-1973	2473	42	Non-Government Company	Active	Unlisted	Mfr. of Basic Iron and Steel
The Mysore Spinning and Mfr. Co. Ltd.	19-01-1974	2654	42	Non-Government Company	Dormant	Unlisted	Manufacturing (Textiles)

Authorised share capital	Paid up capital	Last AGM Date	Last Balance Sheet Date	Place	BIFR Case No.	BIFR Status	BIFR Date of last order
9	10	11	12	13	14	15	16
₹ 15,000,000	₹ 10,365,500	27-09-2014	31-03-2014	Mysore			
₹ 130,000,000	₹ 87,342,976	23-08-2014	31-03-2012	Mandya	601/2004	Declared sick/ DRS Awaited	23-05-2013
₹ 1,000,000	₹ 0	N/A	N/A	Channapatana			
₹ 1,500,000,000	₹ 1,188,934,270	30-12-2014	31-03-2014	Bhadravathi	601/2012	Pending determination of sickness	26-09-2013
₹ 150,000,000	₹ 118,102,328	12-09-2013	31-03-2013	Bengaluru	605/1996	Winding up recommended	18-07-2000
₹ 10,000,000	₹ 7,737,940	29-09-2015	31-03-2015	Bengaluru			
₹ 20,000,000	₹ 15,169,520	27-09-2014	31-03-2014	Chickmagalur			
₹ 10,000,000	₹ 7,574,452	18-09-2014	31-03-2014	Bengaluru			
₹ 1,000,000	₹ 499,658	28-09-2015	31-03-2015	Shimoga			
₹ 50,00,000	₹ 40,00,000	04-09-2014	31-03-2015	Chickmagalur			
₹ 100,000,000	₹ 99,860,000	29-09-2015	31-03-2015	Bengaluru			
₹ 1,000	₹ 0	N/A	N/A	Mangalore			
₹ 5,00,000	₹ 5,00,000	N/A	N/A	Bengaluru			
₹ 2,800,000,000	₹ 2,266, 131,200	07-08-2015	31-03-2015	Tumkur, Jhansi and Damoh			
₹ 140,000,000	₹ 0	N/A	N/A	Bengaluru			
₹ 750,000,000	₹ 201,766,000	28-09-2015	31-03-2015	Bengaluru			
₹ 1,500,000	₹ 0	N/A	N/A	Bengaluru			
₹ 70,000,000	₹ 60,000,000	21-11-2015	31-03-2015	Bengaluru			
₹ 150,000,000	₹ 65,834,880	24-08-2015	31-03-2015	Raichur and Tajola			
₹ 50,000,000	₹ 0	N/A	N/A	Bengaluru			
₹ 300,000,000	₹ 247,955,008	29-09-2015	31-03-2015	Mysore			
₹ 1,00,000	₹ 1,00,000	N/A	N/A	Mysore			

Table 4.2: Summary Table showing the different stances on M/s Mysore Lamp Works Ltd.

Stakeholder's Insights	*Background*	*Action*	*Scenario/ Effects*	*Impact*	*Remarks*
State Government's stance	Holds 91 per cent stakes. Loss suffered Rs 90 cRs (1993-2002).	References Global Investors Conference on 05/06.06.2000	Market share in the state was 20 per cent and 3 per cent nation-wide.	No plans to curb additional funds for revival.	Plan to execute a technology park project.
High Court of Karnataka's stance	On 18.7.00 Justice extends the time-span for revival.	On 23.1.14, recommends to float a global tender to mfr. LEDs.	On 28.7.14, defers the proceedings between BIFR and MLWL.	Recommends to merge with Mysore Minerals.	Due consideration raised for employees and the enterprise.
Employees and Union's stance	04.01.02, the state-govt. orders to wind-up the enterprise.	Workforce involves 1,556 workmen.	The state's Belaku project.	Request dishonoured	Blame the Management for the hindrances and constraints.
Bureaucrat's stance	Mr M.N.Vijay Kumar appointed as the new Managing Director.	Constraints in the MD salary, support staff and the official car.	Propose for the Bhagyajyothi and Kuteerajyothi projects.	AGM held on 12.9.13 connotes the material allegations	Management faced with corruption issues.
BIFR's stance	BIFR Case No. 605/96 registered in 1996	Winding-up of the company.	Financial distress (accumulated losses > net worth)	No concrete proposal for the change in management	Rehabilitate requires a whipping ₹ 19.91 crs
Enterprise's stance	Company Petition no. 231/2000	IDBI appointed as the Operating Agency (OA) u/s 17(3) of the Companies Act.	IDBI recommended to privatize the company.	Proposed ₹ 11.13 crs by the state-govt. or ₹ 14.22 crs from the sale of surplus land.	Banks and Financial Institutions undermine additional term loans.
Film Association's stance	To begin an official film studio in the MLWL premises.	Mrs Tara invokes the premises to the association.	More than 250 films have been shooted in the premises.	Put-forth the request to the state-government.	Seeking to utilise the premises for the welfare of the film association.

Source: Author's Compilation.

Table 4.3 Variable Definition: Financial and Operating Performance Indicators of "Mysore" Industries

I. Financial Performance Indicators

1. Profitability Attributes

Variables	Definition
Operating Profit Margin (per cent)	(Operating Profit / Net Sales)*100
Gross Profit Margin (per cent)	(Gross Profit/ Net Sales)*100
Cash Profit Margin (per cent)	(Cash Profit/ Net Sales)*100
Net Profit Margin (per cent)	(Net Profit After Tax/ Net Sales)*100
Pre-tax Profit Margin (per cent)	(Profit Before Tax/ Net Sales)*100
Return on Long Term Funds (per cent)	(Operating Profit/ Long-Term Funds)
Return on Equity	(Net Income/ Shareholder's Equity)

2. Liquidity Attributes

Variables	Definition
Current Ratio	(Current Assets/ Current Liabilities)
Quick Ratio	(Quick Assets/ Current Liabilities)
Debt-Equity Ratio	(Total Liabilities/ Shareholder's Equity)

II. Operating Performance Indicators

1. Sales Attributes

Variables	Definition
Material Cost Ratio	(Raw Materials Cost/ Net Sales)
Employee Cost Ratio	(Employee Cost/ Net Sales)
Excise Duty Ratio	(Excise Duty Cost/ Net Sales)
Manufacturing Expenses Ratio	(Manufacturing Expenses/ Net Sales)
Total Expenses Ratio	(Total Expenses/ Net Sales)
Depreciation Ratio	(Depreciation Cost/ Net Sales)
Power and Fuel Ratio	(Power and Fuel Cost/ Net Sales)
Selling and Distribution Ratio	(Selling and Distribution Expenses/ Net Sales)
Miscellaneous Expenses Ratio	(Miscellaneous Expenses/ Net Sales)

2. Investment Attributes

Variables	Definition
Return on Capital Employed	(Operating Profit/Total Capital)=ddEmployed)
Return on Net Worth	(Profit After Tax/ Net Worth)
Investment Turnover Ratio	(Net Sales/ Net Worth)
Return on Assets	(Operating Profit/ Total Assets)
Interest Coverage Ratio	(Operating Profit/ Interest Expenses)

3. Efficiency Attributes

Variables	Definition
Inventory Turnover Ratio	(Net Sales/ Inventories)
Debtors Turnover Ratio	(Total Sales/ Accounts Receivables)
Fixed Assets Turnover Ratio	(Total Sales/ Fixed Assets)
Total Assets Turnover Ratio	(Total Sales/ Total Assets)

III. Comparative Financial Analysis

Variables	Definition
(PBT/NW)	(Profit Before Tax/ Net Worth)
(PAT/ NW)	(Profit After Tax/ Net Worth)
(VA/EC)	(Valued Added/ Employee Cost)
(OP/NS)	(Operating Profit/ Net Sales)
(PBT/NS)	(Profit Before Tax/ Net Sales)
(VA/NS)	(Value Added/ Net Sales)
(RS/NW)	(Reserves/ Net Worth)
(TD/NW)	(Total Debt/ Net Worth)

Table 4.4: Descriptive Statistics

Variable	*Obs*	*Mean*	*Std. Dev.*	*Min*	*Max*
Leverage	44	0.66	0.26	0	0.94
Shareholding	44	41.16	13.95	27.01	76.48
Bonus in Equity Capital	44	10.91	14.70	0.62	32.18
Operating Profit Margin	44	6.69	11.29	-18.71	47.07
Return on Capital Employed	44	1.23	27.14	-149.76	38.41
Inventory Turnover Ratio	44	8.70	6.32	1.88	26.89
Firm Size	44	5.52	1.05	3.49	7.62
Non-Debt Tax Shields	44	0.07	0.05	0	0.32

Note: Highly levered enterprises.

Where, Leverage = [Total debt/ (Total debt + Equity share capital)]; Shareholding = Composition of promoter and public shareholding; Bonus in equity capital = Amount disbursed on Shareholder's equity; Operating profit margin = (Operating profit/ Net Sales); Return on Capital Employed = (Operating profit/ Total capital); Inventory turnover ratio = (Net sales/ Inventories); Firm size = ln (Net sales); Non-debt tax shields = (Depreciation/ Total assets)

Source: Author's Calculation.

Table 4.5: Pair-wise Correlation among the attributes.

Independent Regressors	SH	Bonus	OPM	ROCE	LIQ	ITR	FS	NDTS
Shareholding	1							
Bonus in Equity Capital	-0.09	1						
Operating Profit Margin	-0.02	0.43	1					
Return on Capital Employed	0.03	0.22	0.67	1				
Liquidity	-0.13	-0.25	0.40	0.40	1			
Inventory Turnover Ratio	-0.10	0.35	0.63	0.47	0.41	1		
Firm Size	-0.03	-0.90	-0.31	-0.11	0.31	-0.10	1	
Non-Debt Tax Shields	0.09	0.40	-0.09	-0.61	-0.35	0.04	-0.42	1

Table 4.6: Financial Review of Selected Mysore Industries [Cross Section]

SOEs	Leverage		Shareholding		Bonus		OPM		ROCE		ITR		Firm Size		NDTS	
	μ	σ	μ	σ	μ	σ	μ	Σ	μ	σ	μ	σ	μ	σ	μ	σ
MPML	.66	.03	35.07	0.26	1.00	0.00	-2.33	10.22	-13.80	40.77	2.87	.74	5.89	0.11	0.06	0.07
MPCL	.80	.14	38.93	12.21	32.00	0.00	13.57	11.09	9.64	11.06	12.00	4.06	4.15	0.37	0.10	0.03
MCL	.10	.39	49.07	18.57	1.47	0.64	9.13	5.77	8.33	10.94	11.53	15.17	6.42	0.61	0.05	0.03
All years	0.52	0.19	41.02	10.34	11.49	0.21	6.79	9.03	1.39	20.92	8.80	6.66	5.49	0.36	0.07	0.04

Table 4.7: Financial Review of Selected Mysore Industries [Time period]

Year	Var	LEV	SH	Bonus	OPM	ROCE	ITR	FS	NDTS
2002	µ	.81	42.33	12.00	8.33	2.33	5.67	5.14	.05
2002	σ	.15	6.43	17.35	7.57	4.62	2.52	1.15	.02
2003	µ	.80	50.67	11.67	2.67	-2.33	6.33	5.09	.06
2003	σ	.15	13.58	17.62	10.07	6.11	4.51	1.01	.01
2004	µ	.79	53.33	11.67	3.00	-1.67	6.67	5.16	.07
2004	σ	.15	16.50	17.62	6.00	0.58	3.51	1.21	.02
2005	µ	.80	51.67	11.67	7.00	4.67	7.33	5.25	.07
2005	σ	.15	16.04	17.62	6.24	5.03	6.11	.93	.03
2006	µ	.78	52.67	11.67	9.33	7.67	8.00	5.34	.07
2006	σ	.15	19.14	17.62	1.53	2.08	5.57	1.00	.03
2007	µ	.77	41.00	16.50	11.50	12.00	5.50	5.15	.07
2007	σ	.21	8.49	21.92	0.71	2.83	3.54	1.07	.05
2008	µ	.67	33.50	16.50	9.50	16.50	11.50	5.23	.10
2008	σ	.01	2.12	21.92	2.12	10.61	12.02	1.09	.10
2009	µ	.68	33.50	16.50	6.00	4.00	7.00	5.11	.07
2009	σ	.05	2.12	21.92	2.83	1.41	5.66	1.23	.05
2010	µ	.71	33.50	16.50	7.50	9.00	7.50	5.22	.06

(Continued)

2010	σ	.07	2.12	21.92	0.71	5.66	6.36	1.15	.05
2011	µ	.71	31.50	16.50	-4.50	-11.50	6.00	5.08	.07
2011	σ	.10	4.95	21.92	12.02	13.44	1.41	1.03	.04
2012	µ	.73	31.50	16.50	-7.00	-13.50	4.50	5.05	.08
2012	σ	.02	4.95	21.92	16.97	19.09	2.12	1.06	.05
2013	µ	.70	31.50	16.50	-3.50	-5.50	8.50	5.39	.07
2013	σ	.09	4.95	21.92	14.85	28.99	9.19	.71	.01
2014	µ	.75	31.00	11.33	7.00	-4.67	8.33	5.60	.07
2014	σ	.10	4.00	17.90	19.52	25.97	6.11	1.74	.02
2015	µ	.67	31.00	11.33	16.67	-33.67	10.33	5.69	.13
2015	σ	.16	4.00	17.90	30.01	101.65	7.64	2.08	.17
All years	µ	**0.74**	**39.19**	**14.06**	**5.25**	**-1.19**	**7.37**	**5.25**	**0.07**
All years	σ	**0.11**	**7.81**	**19.79**	**9.37**	**16.29**	**5.45**	**1.18**	**0.05**

Table 4.8: Financial Performance Indicators: Profitability and Liquidity

		Profitability		
Company Name	Year	OPM (per cent)	GPM (per cent)	CPM (per cent)
Mysore Paper Mills Ltd.	Mar '15	-13.23	-15.96	-17.83
Mysore Paper Mills Ltd.	Mar '14	-12.73	-15.34	-15.95
Mysore Paper Mills Ltd.	Mar '13	-13.94	-16.8	-17.48
Mysore Paper Mills Ltd.	Mar '12	-18.71	-21.87	-21.35
Mysore Paper Mills Ltd.	Mar '11	-12.7	-15.72	-16.57
Mysore Paper Mills Ltd.	Mar '10	7.39	5.02	6.97
Mysore Paper Mills Ltd.	Mar '09	3.68	1.18	0.08
Mysore Paper Mills Ltd.	Mar '08	8.1	2.11	2.58
Mysore Paper Mills Ltd.	Mar '07	11.96	6.1	3.35
Mysore Paper Mills Ltd.	Mar '06	8.95	3.17	0.48
Mysore Paper Mills Ltd.	Mar '05	5.06	-0.52	-0.01
Mysore Paper Mills Ltd.	Mar '04	-3.36	-3.18	-1.62
Mysore Paper Mills Ltd.	Mar '03	-7.79	-13.71	-6.63
Heidelberg Cement Ltd.	Mar '15	8.43	1.07	3.58
Heidelberg Cement Ltd.	Mar '14	6.99	4.14	5.59
Heidelberg Cement Ltd.	Mar '13	6.65	3.47	6.05
Heidelberg Cement Ltd.	Mar '12	11.93	8.61	9.77
Heidelberg Cement Ltd.	Mar '11	18.24	15.49	15.96
Heidelberg Cement Ltd.	Mar '10	12.85	10.06	18.79
Heidelberg Cement Ltd.	Mar '09	19.88	17.45	20.9
Heidelberg Cement Ltd.	Mar '08	11.73	8.97	0.56
Heidelberg Cement Ltd.	Mar '07	4.19	-3.77	-16.46
Heidelberg Cement Ltd.	Mar '06	7.88	-0.33	-1.12
Heidelberg Cement Ltd.	Mar '05	2.26	-3.76	-4.58
Heidelberg Cement Ltd.	Mar '04	3.43	-3.13	-0.99
Heidelberg Cement Ltd.	Mar '03	4.32	-3.07	0.4
Mysore Petro Chemicals Ltd.	Mar '15	25.92	17.09	17.25
Mysore Petro Chemicals Ltd.	Mar '14	6.93	4.53	3.93
Mysore Petro Chemicals Ltd.	Mar '13	4.78	-1.24	0.22
Mysore Petro Chemicals Ltd.	Mar '12	4.44	-1.64	1.17
Mysore Petro Chemicals Ltd.	Mar '11	8.39	2.72	6.25
Mysore Petro Chemicals Ltd.	Mar '10	8.44	1.72	5.97
Mysore Petro Chemicals Ltd.	Mar '09	11.47	6.47	10.65
Mysore Petro Chemicals Ltd.	Mar '08	10.75	3.88	16.5

				Liquidity		
NPM (per cent)	PTPM (per cent)	RLTF (per cent)	ROE (per cent)	CR	QR	DER
-20.36	-20.53	--	-42.72	0.51	0.38	--
-19.02	-19.09	--	-43.31	0.56	0.5	--
-21.24	-21.29	--	-42.43	0.6	0.51	--
-25.78	-25.08	-49.61	-51.77	0.77	0.91	--
-22.72	-23.00	-25.35	-35.74	0.98	0.55	21.91
3.71	5.17	17.3	26.10	0.96	0.83	2.65
1.27	-1.87	6.43	12.31	0.91	0.6	3.01
0.15	-0.89	12.18	27.36	0.9	0.81	3.62
0.69	2.89	17.04	36.84	1.06	0.61	3
-2.31	-0.05	11.64	26.25	1.03	0.66	3.34
-3.07	-3.49	4.39	13.56	0.97	0.67	2.94
-5.92	-7.45	-2.53	-9.97	0.93	0.65	2.22
-12.24	-17.21	-9.57	-18.68	1.06	0.48	1.64
-3.36	-6.67	0.95	45.02	1.27	1.07	1.65
2.79	4.14	3.09	34.07	0.91	0.69	1.24
2.95	4.29	2.93	29.02	1.34	1.14	0.97
7.29	10.55	12.38	45.72	1.05	0.85	--
14.24	17.32	24.2	75.73	1.98	1.72	0.02
15.59	13.88	21.8	62.61	2.22	1.92	0.05
16.11	16.64	34.31	75.10	2.47	1.96	0.04
-2.35	3.94	16.93	31.76	1.93	1.3	0.06
-20.97	-21.73	1.7	21.09	0.7	0.44	--
-6.17	-6.21	6.9	38.95	0.67	0.48	--
-10.84	-10.96	-0.56	11.98	0.65	0.44	--
-7	-10.34	-1.93	18.09	0.64	0.44	--
-6.7	-9.97	-1.62	18.92	0.72	0.65	19.47
8.44	11.09	38.5	157.21	1.38	1.26	0.22
1.53	2.31	18.01	139.61	1.39	1.23	0.6
-5.8	-3.98	17.99	53.26	0.85	0.93	0.97
-4.9	-4.90	-0.53	52.35	0.88	0.85	0.99
0.15	0.15	-2.39	104.70	1.21	1.08	0.96
0.64	-0.96	9.08	89.38	0.61	1.01	0.76
67.3	67.31	4.06	150.53	0.61	0.65	0.61
10.5	10.88	48.38	133.99	0.48	0.47	1.21

(Continued)

Mysore Petro Chemicals Ltd.	Mar '07	11	0.3	5.52
Mysore Petro Chemicals Ltd.	Mar '06	14.36	-0.56	-0.79
Mysore Petro Chemicals Ltd.	Mar '05	8.58	-14.24	4.58
Mysore Petro Chemicals Ltd.	Mar '04	12.09	-8.59	-9.13
Mysore Petro Chemicals Ltd.	Mar '03	17.3	-5.5	-19.94

Table 4.9 Operating Performance Indicators: Sales, Investment, and Efficiency

		Sales			
Company Name	Year	MCR	ECR	TER	DR
Mysore Paper Mills Ltd.	Mar '15	0.55	0.29	1.21	0.03
Mysore Paper Mills Ltd.	Mar '14	0.42	0.27	1.07	0.03
Mysore Paper Mills Ltd.	Mar '13	0.52	0.30	1.22	0.03
Mysore Paper Mills Ltd.	Mar '12	0.50	0.33	1.27	0.03
Mysore Paper Mills Ltd.	Mar '11	0.37	0.23	1.04	0.03
Mysore Paper Mills Ltd.	Mar '10	0.35	0.16	0.93	0.02
Mysore Paper Mills Ltd.	Mar '09	0.39	0.21	0.97	0.03
Mysore Paper Mills Ltd.	Mar '08	0.46	0.17	0.97	0.02
Mysore Paper Mills Ltd.	Mar '07	0.37	0.19	0.89	0.03
Mysore Paper Mills Ltd.	Mar '06	0.33	0.18	0.87	0.03
Mysore Paper Mills Ltd.	Mar '05	0.43	0.18	1.03	0.03
Mysore Paper Mills Ltd.	Mar '04	0.41	0.15	0.87	0.04
Mysore Paper Mills Ltd.	Mar '03	0.47	0.17	1.09	0.05
Heidelberg Cement Ltd.	Mar '15	0.27	0.08	0.94	0.07
Heidelberg Cement Ltd.	Mar '14	0.32	0.08	0.95	0.03
Heidelberg Cement Ltd.	Mar '13	0.31	0.08	0.93	0.03
Heidelberg Cement Ltd.	Mar '12	0.32	0.07	0.88	0.03
Heidelberg Cement Ltd.	Mar '11	0.31	0.07	0.82	0.03
Heidelberg Cement Ltd.	Mar '10	0.29	0.08	0.86	0.03
Heidelberg Cement Ltd.	Mar '09	0.25	0.09	0.81	0.02
Heidelberg Cement Ltd.	Mar '08	0.28	0.10	0.89	0.03
Heidelberg Cement Ltd.	Mar '07	0.34	0.06	0.95	0.05
Heidelberg Cement Ltd.	Mar '06	0.32	0.06	0.91	0.05
Heidelberg Cement Ltd.	Mar '05	0.34	0.07	0.98	0.06
Heidelberg Cement Ltd.	Mar '04	0.32	0.07	0.99	0.06
Heidelberg Cement Ltd.	Mar '03	0.33	0.08	0.95	0.07
Mysore Petro Chemicals Ltd.	Mar '15	0.05	0.30	0.51	0.08
Mysore Petro Chemicals Ltd.	Mar '14	0.09	0.31	0.63	0.09
Mysore Petro Chemicals Ltd.	Mar '13	0.70	0.11	0.94	0.02

-1.84	-1.77	11.83	109.86	0.67	0.48	--
-8.53	-7.14	7.4	157.97	0.66	0.45	--
-7.21	-6.60	10.27	60.09	0.6	0.43	--
-19.51	-19.04	-0.57	96.97	0.69	0.5	--
-31.73	-30.14	2.75	123.22	0.87	0.66	--

		Investment				Efficiency			
PFR	MER	ROCE (per cent)	RONW (per cent)	ROA	ICR	ITR	DTR	FATR	TATR
0.31	-0.06	-149.76	25.46	-25.82	-1.5	2.04	21.91	0.73	2.89
0.30	-0.08	-32.96	33.59	-19.25	-1.69	2.81	18.13	0.77	2.75
0.30	-0.13	-25.71	50.58	-12.78	-1.17	2.27	11.71	0.7	2.24
0.30	-0.23	-27.16	70.91	-6.32	-3.3	2.74	9.84	0.64	1.41
0.30	-0.04	-21.27	53.15	0.82	-2.77	5.01	7.94	0.66	1.51
0.33	-0.10	13.08	19.92	6.89	2.23	3.38	9.39	0.83	1.32
0.26	-0.07	4.9	7.17	5.94	0.64	3.3	6.59	0.79	1.4
0.24	-0.13	8.73	0.96	5.4	0.95	2.84	6.08	2.11	1.33
0.24	-0.07	14.39	3.89	5.46	1.51	3.2	7.57	1.83	1.4
0.25	-0.06	9.74	-12.81	5.24	1.05	3.21	7.47	1.71	1.28
0.29	-0.10	3.72	-13.59	5.93	0.48	2.49	7.03	1.47	1.14
0.22	-0.14	-2.17	-22.55	7.65	-0.32	3.42	8.9	1.5	1.19
0.33	0.07	-8.55	-28.02	10.47	-1.02	1.88	9.63	1.09	0.87
0.32	0.55	0.93	-4.96	36.19	0.19	7.17	46.31	0.48	0.56
0.28	0.50	3.01	3.7	36.73	5.34	7.74	48.13	1.06	0.59
0.26	0.48	2.93	3.64	35.3	12	8.93	40.7	1	0.63
0.22	0.02	12.38	8.2	33.8	33.09	22.76	37.39	0.91	1.14
0.19	0.02	24.2	18.53	31.03	65.76	26.89	44.75	1.03	1.31
0.25	0.03	19.29	24.86	31.96	48.3	22.57	47.35	0.9	1.29
0.29	0.04	34.31	30.1	20.53	55.04	18.01	41.52	0.87	1.77
0.30	0.02	16.93	-4.1	14.35	2.65	6.84	23.61	2.6	1.72
0.40	-0.01	1.29	91.27	-12.41	0.07	6.74	18.45	2.36	2.04
0.37	-0.03	5.61	93.45	-4.57	0.42	7.02	16.35	1.98	1.42
0.38	-0.03	-0.45	192.87	-6.33	-0.04	6.32	16.73	1.5	1.14
0.36	-0.05	-1.58	-140.63	-1.08	-0.19	6.9	13.69	1.43	1.09
0.38	-0.10	-1.37	-47.79	2.48	-0.19	5.9	9.14	1.14	0.84
0.03	0.21	38.41	24.65	44.46	10.13	17	6.55	0.29	0.92
0.03	0.45	18.01	14.14	36.22	2.8	14.56	4.15	0.29	1.04
0.05	0.65	14.65	9.44	32.84	1.96	14.82	13.25	0.96	3.11

(Continued)

Mysore Petro Chemicals Ltd.	Mar '12	0.59	0.19	0.93	0.06
Mysore Petro Chemicals Ltd.	Mar '11	0.66	0.17	0.96	0.06
Mysore Petro Chemicals Ltd.	Mar '10	0.66	0.13	0.91	0.06
Mysore Petro Chemicals Ltd.	Mar '09	0.71	0.13	0.97	0.07
Mysore Petro Chemicals Ltd.	Mar '08	0.66	0.10	0.88	0.05
Mysore Petro Chemicals Ltd.	Mar '07	0.69	0.09	0.90	0.06
Mysore Petro Chemicals Ltd.	Mar '06	0.66	0.10	0.89	0.08
Mysore Petro Chemicals Ltd.	Mar '05	0.64	0.10	0.84	0.08
Mysore Petro Chemicals Ltd.	Mar '04	0.62	0.14	0.90	0.12
Mysore Petro Chemicals Ltd.	Mar '03	0.63	0.11	0.89	0.10

Table 4.10: Comparative Financial Ratios

Company Name	Year	PBT/NW	PAT/NW	VA/EC
Mysore Paper Mills Ltd.	Mar '15	0.29	0.18	2.28
Mysore Paper Mills Ltd.	Mar '14	0.64	0.43	2.34
Mysore Paper Mills Ltd.	Mar '13	1.68	1.10	2.34
Mysore Paper Mills Ltd.	Mar '12	1.10	0.82	2.33
Mysore Paper Mills Ltd.	Mar '11	-7.93	-4.38	2.97
Mysore Paper Mills Ltd.	Mar '10	0.25	0.36	3.59
Mysore Paper Mills Ltd.	Mar '09	-0.10	0.21	2.78
Mysore Paper Mills Ltd.	Mar '08	-0.05	0.50	3.05
Mysore Paper Mills Ltd.	Mar '07	0.16	0.66	2.79
Mysore Paper Mills Ltd.	Mar '06	0.00	0.49	2.96
Mysore Paper Mills Ltd.	Mar '05	-0.15	0.22	3.31
Mysore Paper Mills Ltd.	Mar '04	-0.28	-0.13	3.12
Mysore Paper Mills Ltd.	Mar '03	-0.39	-0.18	3.62
Heidelberg Cement Ltd.	Mar '15	0.14	0.37	9.21
Heidelberg Cement Ltd.	Mar '14	-0.10	0.12	8.40
Heidelberg Cement Ltd.	Mar '13	0.05	0.09	7.57
Heidelberg Cement Ltd.	Mar '12	0.05	0.08	7.80
Heidelberg Cement Ltd.	Mar '11	0.12	0.14	7.49
Heidelberg Cement Ltd.	Mar '10	0.23	0.24	7.56
Heidelberg Cement Ltd.	Mar '09	0.18	0.17	7.58
Heidelberg Cement Ltd.	Mar '08	0.29	0.35	6.08
Heidelberg Cement Ltd.	Mar '07	0.07	0.21	6.11
Heidelberg Cement Ltd.	Mar '06	0.94	-0.19	10.21
Heidelberg Cement Ltd.	Mar '05	0.93	-1.24	9.78
Heidelberg Cement Ltd.	Mar '04	1.95	-0.44	9.64

0.07	0.51	-0.44	-21.76	29.74	-0.06	6.44	9.41	0.56	1.88
0.06	0.36	-2.17	-15.96	36.21	-0.36	6.91	10.67	0.59	1.66
0.05	0.03	5.3	0.45	41.99	1.35	11.96	14.49	0.58	1.69
0.05	0.03	2.64	1.63	41.8	0.71	10.63	12.05	0.49	1.58
0.04	0.19	23.99	19.93	17.18	5.98	20.21	14.82	0.61	3.46
0.05	-0.03	10.02	-28.01	-46.53	0.72	7.8	20.69	1.77	1.77
0.05	-0.03	7.37	3.16	-59.56	0.44	13.54	32.83	1.27	1.32
0.04	-0.07	10.05	14.96	-57.61	0.49	13.91	54.16	1.15	1.22
0.05	-0.03	-0.56	9.64	-49.05	-0.03	10.18	23.58	0.69	0.7
0.05	-0.04	2.75	34.01	-44.32	0.17	10.57	29.51	0.75	0.72

OP/NS	PBT/NS	VA/NS	RES/NW	TD/NW
-0.13	-0.21	0.66	1.54	-1.12
-0.13	-0.19	0.64	2.88	-2.22
-0.14	-0.21	0.70	5.90	-4.52
-0.19	-0.25	0.77	2.58	-4.10
-0.13	-0.23	0.67	-3.26	-6.91
0.07	0.05	0.58	-0.37	2.65
0.04	-0.02	0.58	-0.68	3.00
0.08	-0.01	0.51	-0.81	3.62
0.12	0.03	0.53	-0.81	2.93
0.09	0.00	0.54	-0.89	3.26
0.05	-0.03	0.60	-0.67	2.88
-0.03	-0.07	0.46	-0.30	2.19
-0.08	-0.17	0.62	0.04	1.64
0.16	0.06	0.60	0.74	1.08
0.08	-0.07	0.67	0.72	1.65
0.07	0.04	0.63	0.73	1.24
0.07	0.04	0.62	0.72	0.97
0.12	0.11	0.56	0.70	0.00
0.18	0.17	0.51	0.66	0.00
0.13	0.14	0.58	0.59	0.02
0.20	0.17	0.56	0.49	0.00
0.12	0.04	0.61	0.29	0.00
0.04	-0.22	0.62	2.05	-3.11
0.08	-0.06	0.59	4.63	-11.53
0.02	-0.11	0.64	6.00	-16.65

(Continued)

Heidelberg Cement Ltd.	Mar '03	-2.08	0.72	10.20
Mysore Petro Chemicals Ltd.	Mar '15	0.42	0.53	1.58
Mysore Petro Chemicals Ltd.	Mar '14	0.19	0.43	1.72
Mysore Petro Chemicals Ltd.	Mar '13	0.14	0.43	2.15
Mysore Petro Chemicals Ltd.	Mar '12	-0.15	0.18	1.84
Mysore Petro Chemicals Ltd.	Mar '11	-0.16	0.14	1.81
Mysore Petro Chemicals Ltd.	Mar '10	0.00	0.25	1.93
Mysore Petro Chemicals Ltd.	Mar '09	-0.02	0.21	1.97
Mysore Petro Chemicals Ltd.	Mar '08	0.65	0.88	2.16
Mysore Petro Chemicals Ltd.	Mar '07	-0.29	-0.29	2.28
Mysore Petro Chemicals Ltd.	Mar '06	0.03	-0.18	2.27
Mysore Petro Chemicals Ltd.	Mar '05	0.12	-0.27	2.00
Mysore Petro Chemicals Ltd.	Mar '04	0.09	-0.12	2.02
Mysore Petro Chemicals Ltd.	Mar '03	0.33	-0.22	2.28

0.04	-0.10	0.67	-4.38	17.34
0.47	0.38	0.47	0.77	0.22
0.26	0.11	0.54	0.72	0.60
0.07	0.02	0.24	0.70	0.97
0.05	-0.04	0.35	0.66	0.99
0.04	-0.05	0.31	0.72	0.96
0.08	0.00	0.25	0.76	0.76
0.08	-0.01	0.26	0.76	0.61
0.11	0.67	0.22	0.42	1.21
0.11	0.11	0.21	1.22	-2.49
0.11	-0.02	0.23	1.17	-2.27
0.16	-0.07	0.20	1.17	-2.41
0.09	-0.07	0.28	1.20	-2.92
0.13	-0.19	0.25	1.23	-3.42

5

Innovative Business Solutions Using Big Data Analytics—An Empirical Analysis on Retail Customer Behaviour

Dr.Vinay M R and Mr.Prakash K

I. INTRODUCTION

The last few years have witnessed significant changes in the way the business sector views business management. With the modern internet facility, e-commerce and e-marketing are occupying a very important place in the retail business. A number of small and big online retail units are emerging today in the current market as a result of digitalization and globalization. This results in a severe competition among these various retail businesses making it very complicated for a long term successful survival. The business leaders will have to make key decisions to address many challenges and fierce competition in the market to make their business frontrunner. These decisions need to be taken based on appropriate and accurate information, insights and reliable facts to address the challenges and to make effective decisions especially in the light of changing market structure.

The business follows various tactics and ideas to retain their existing customers and attract new customers to expand their market, sales and revenue. But, this is a big challenge in the current retail world as there are many new retailers emerging with attractive deals and discounts. Hence, the major challenge is to retain the customers and understand their behaviour, requirements and churn reasons. This can be achieved to an extent by effective campaigning of the products to the appropriate target customer group, introducing various Cross-/Up-/down sell opportunities and providing optimized discounts etc.

This paper discusses the importance of **Big Data Analytics** approach* to provide innovative and effective strategic business solutions based on empirical analysis that we have performed for one of our **Retail clients** recently. The paper focuses on all aspects of Customer Behaviour Analytics – Purchase pattern, trend, profiling, segmentation, attrition and loyalty etc., also various Cross-/Up-/Down sell opportunities not only within the business line, but also across different business lines of the company. This provides a broader way for Data Monetization. Finally, we found that there is a high potential value in the data to achieve all the business objectives.

I.I IMPORTANCE OF THE TOPIC

The Big Data analytics provides more useful insights and strategies that help the business to address many business challenges and to become a successful player in the market through innovative business solutions. These strategies would be developed using different approaches based on statistical analysis, predictive modelling, forecasting and extensive market research etc.

Big Data Analytics helps the business to determine optimal prices, recalculate entire risk portfolios to mitigate future risks, analyse customer behaviour to derive new strategies for customer acquisition, retention, campaign optimization and high redemption rate. The retail companies across the globe are nowadays showing immense interest in using Big Data Analytics to convert their raw data into optimum business insights. This paper will educate business leaders to focus on meaningful and effective utilization of the available information and convert them to strategy making insights through innovative approaches.

II. About our Client

Our client is one of the leading multinational and multi-business media company based in Switzerland. It operates in more than 14 countries across the globe with the worldwide staff accounting to approximately 8,000 employees. The major businesses are e-commerce, publishing newspapers and magazines, digital newspapers, web property, online ticketing solutions, mobile platforms and apps, TV and radio stations etc.

The paper focuses on one of its major businesses – online Retail platform. The business sells various 'Products' and 'Coupons' to its customers via, web portal and mobile app. The client is facing many challenges in the current scenario like customer attrition, customer dissatisfaction, change in customer behaviour and revenue loss etc. as a result of the great revolution in digital space like internet, social media, online sales and digitalization. Hence, the client wanted to find strategic solutions and derive insights from the data that they had shared with us to address these challenges and meet their objectives. The client shows immense interests towards retaining their customers, profit maximization, market expansion and sales improvement etc.

II.I. Current Business Scenario and Focus Area

The current business scenario of our client has been changing rapidly due to immense competition, new market entrants, the digitalization of the services and changing customer behavior. Their major sales include 'Fashion', 'Sport', 'Food and Beverages', 'Travel coupons', 'Home and Living' and 'Wine' etc. The company also provides attractive discounts for both 'Products' and 'Coupons' to grab the attention of the buyers to purchase more 'Products' and 'Coupons'.

In the current business scenario of our client, there could be customers who purchase only 'Products', only 'Coupons' or both from their online shopping platform. The business is looking for optimizing conversion of both new and existing buyers into 'Hybrid customers' ('Products' and 'Coupons'), market expansion, personalization of offers, improve campaign efficiency, improve customer base, and maximize sales and profit. There is also a high necessity to determine the optimum discount rates that can be given to its customers to improve the sales, profit and revenue.

The focus is specifically on Customer Behaviour Analytics space with the following key objectives:

- Provide strategic business insights and recommendations for overall customer relationship improvement, sales & revenue maximization
- Explore opportunities for Cross-/Up-/Down sell within and across different business lines
- Identify opportunities to improve campaign efficiency
- Explore opportunities for data monetization within & across business lines
- Support the business in their Digital Transformation journey and in maximizing value from data through Big Data Analytics.

II.II. Business Objectives and Proposed Solution

The paper focuses on providing analytical solutions and strategic recommendations to the client to meet their business objectives like growth, acquire and retention. The overall objective of this engagement is to explore and identify the **analytical opportunities, perform extensivecustomer analytics and modelling, derive insights, recommend the strategic business solutions** to improve customer engagement and relationship. The objectives and proposed solutions isillustrated below:

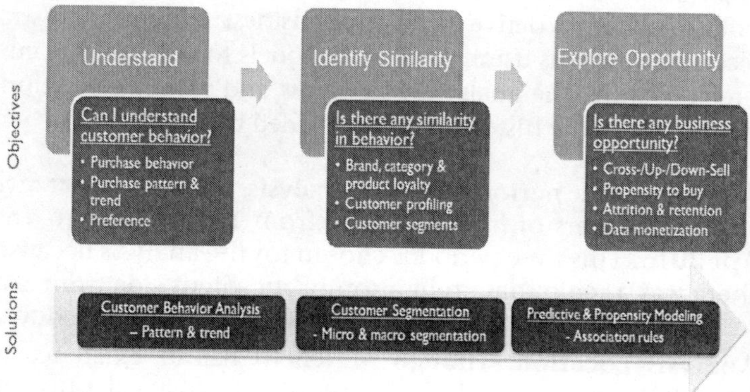

Figure5.1: Business Objectives and Proposed Solution

- **Customer behavior analysis:** Understand customer purchase behavior, pattern, preference and trend to identify the opportunity to expand market
- **Customer Profiling:** Study the customer behavior and characterize them based to their previous purchase patterns considering various factors such as frequency, recency and monetary etc.
- **Customer Segmentation:** Investigate the opportunity to create various segments of the customers in order to identify the targetable customers which would increase profitability and enhances the scope for data monetization
- **Propensity/Probability modeling:** Develop propensity/ probability models which can be used to understand propensity and behaviors of the customers, their attrition and purchase associations.

The client also wanted to use the customer information of one business to improve the sales and market base of the other business lines through targeted campaigning. Hence, there is a major objective to explore the opportunities for data monetization within and across different business lines. All these business strategies provides scope for market expansion, introduction of Cross-/Up-/Down sell opportunities, efficient campaigning, revenue optimization and sales growth.

III. Methodology

III.I. Scope of Business

The major scope of the business is to perform extensive Customer Behaviour Analytics to derive innovative business solutions and strategic recommendations using predictive models to enhance the customer relationship. The analytical solutions and recommendations are extracted using the historical data provided by the client:

- **Analysis time period:** For the analysis, we had about two and a half years of historical data from **1st Jan 2013 to 15th Apr 2015.** This time period is chosen for the analysis because, there was a major data migration in the client side from SAP to Hadoop in 2012 and several new services were introduced
- **Analysis Location:** Though the client has its existence in 14 countries, our analysis is completely focused only on **Switzerland** location since 80% of the customer base is from Switzerland
- **Data Monetization:** To explore opportunities of data monetization across other business lines, we selected two other main businesses of the client—**Publishing Newspaper and Magazines, Digital newspapers and apps.**

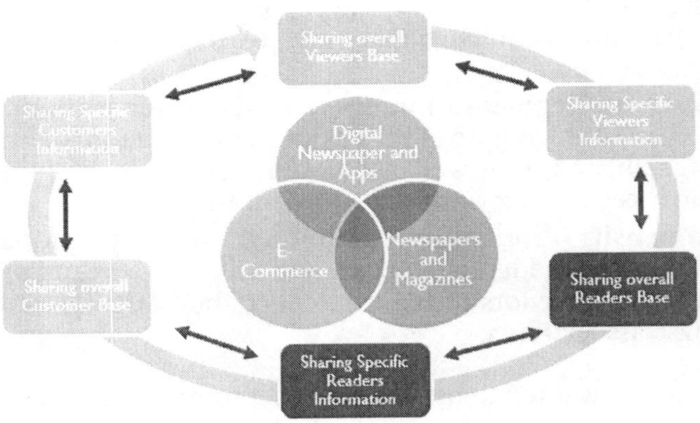

Figure 5.2 Business Discovery Phase

Note: *Across business analysis is done with the assumption that there could be an overlap in their customer base across different business lines.*

We performed our analysis in two phases:

- **Phase I:** Perform the Customer Behaviour Analysis such as purchase pattern, preference, trend, profiling, segmentation, developing attrition models and propensity models etc. within the business line
- **Phase II:** Explore various marketing opportunities across different business lines – Publishing newspapers and Magazines, Digital Newspapers and Mobile Apps (Data Monetization).

III. II. Hypothesis Setting

The hypothesis is formulated considering the current business scenario, business objectives and inputs, available data and analytical techniques. The analysis is performed based on the data extracted from the client's big data platform related to demographic and geographic information of the customers, their transactions and the product specific details. The main focus of this project is to analyze, measure and predict the customer behavior using the available information and data. The hypotheses set for this project are listed below:

- Historical data is the appropriate reflection of the customer behaviour in the near future
- Customer behaviour can be predicted using many related factors like purchase pattern, preference, trend and loyalty etc.
- The data has a high potential value to provide strategic business insights and recommendations.

> The above Hypothesis is proved with the analysis of available data and major finding is that we can develop appropriate business recommendations for Revenue growth

III.III. Key Assumptions

Below are the initial and major assumptions based on the interaction with the business regarding the project:

- Client is having all the required data for analysis
- There is no significant change in the business during the analysis period
- Analysis is limited to structured data available within each business
- The implementation of the algorithms in the target systems is not in scope of the project
- The data meets the required quality.

III. IV. Tools and Techniques

We have used different tools and statistical techniques based on the requirements and business inputs to explore various marketing opportunities that can be recommended for market and sales expansion, increased profitability and customer retention:

- The data is extracted from the client's big data platform—Hadoop using Hive
- Various analytical and statistical techniques are performed with the help of R
- Developed several models like RFM, Association rules, Segmentation, Profiling and Optimization etc.

Figure 5.3: Tools and Techniques

III.V. Major Analytical Steps

The customer analytics life cycle passed through 6 major standard and robust procedural phases which are dependent and associated with each other and be resolved until each phase meets specific criteria. The operation starts from understanding customer business environment and ends in deriving results, developing recommendations, implementation and incorporation of findings in the system. Finally, continuous improvement of accuracy and efficiency of model performance is being maintained through regular calibration. They have been illustrated below in the diagram:

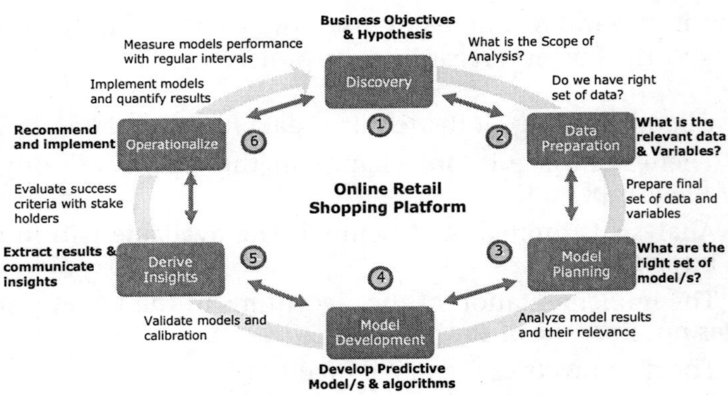

Figure 5.4: Major steps followed in Customer Analytics

We have attempted to explain all the major steps below in a consolidated way as they are very vital and informative in nature:

- **Business objectives and hypothesis:** We initiated our assignment from discovery phase where we understood the business scenario, objectives and available data in the Big Data platform
- **Data extraction, preparation and sampling:** In the second stage, we finalized the list of variables and time period for our analysis. The analysis time period is from 1st Jan 2013 to 15th Apr 2015
- **Model planning and development of predictive models/algorithms:** We designed many models and finalized very accurate and efficient models based on the results. We developed separate models for individual objects starting viz., segmentation models, association rules and propensity models
- **Derive results, develop strategic solutions, recommendations and operationalization:** We derived insights from model results and converted them into strategic solutions and business recommendations. Finally, we developed action items which business can implement based on its priority and preference.

The data is extracted from Hadoop data base using Hive. The entire data was stored in the client's Big Data platform.

IV. Solution Development Process—Within Business

We have developed various statistical and analytical models using the data extracted with respect to the customer transactions, purchase pattern, trend, demographic and geographic information and loyalty etc. With the availability of data, business requirements, key objectives and analytical solution framework we developed 14 solutions that can address all the objectives of our client. The 14 point solutions are illustrated below:

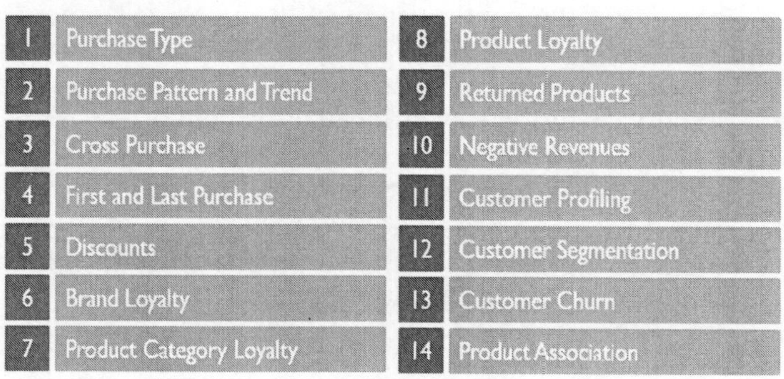

Figure 5.5: 14 Point Solutions and Opportunities

- **Understanding Customer Behaviour**
  - The analysis initially started with understanding customer behaviour in terms of purchase category, pattern, trend, product loyalty and then profiling of customers
  - In the next step, our analysis extended to address the impact caused by the discounts provided by the client. We have developed statistical analysis and insights for the better optimization of discount percentage
  - We have identified the products responsible for negative revenues and provided appropriate business recommendations to avoid continuous revenue leakages
- **Customer Profiling and Segmentation**
  - We created segments considering the customer's interest, profession and purchase patterns based on their profiles
- **Customer Churn Analysis**
  - We developed several attrition models for customer churn analysis focusing on how recently they have made a transaction and how many times they have transacted in the entire analytics scope
- **Association Rules**
  - Finally, we developed association rules to identify the next likely purchase and alternate purchase with the current purchase pattern

All these analysis are done with the available data to prove that the data has a high potential value which is one of the business objectives of our client.

IV.I. Purchase Category

The client sells both 'Products' and 'Coupons' to its customers via, online web portal and mobile applications. On understanding the purchase category of the customers, we have classified them into three categories – 'Product customers', 'Coupon customers' and 'Hybrid customers':

- **Product Customers:** Customers who have purchased only 'Products' during the entire analysis period
- **Coupon Customers:** Customers who have purchased only 'Coupons' during the entire analysis period
- **Hybrid Customers:** As the name suggests, this category includes customers who have purchased both 'Products' and 'Coupons' during the entire analysis period.

The customer groups and their behaviour in terms of purchase category are illustrated below:

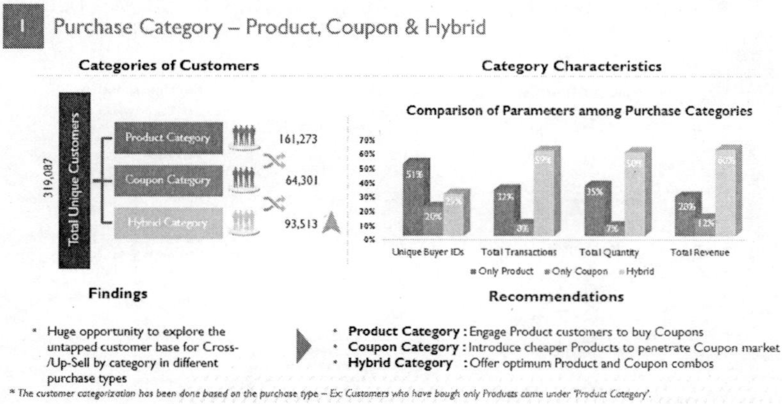

Figure 5.6: Opportunity Area 1—Purchase Category

Hence forth, we have performed our analysis separately for all the three categories. We have identified that they have a customer base of around 300,000 unique customers from the data provided by the client. As shown in the above figure, the 'Product customers' are more in number when compared to the other categories. As shown in the chart above, it is evident that though the count of 'Hybrid customers' is very less when compared to the other categories of customers they are contributing more in terms of transactions, quantity sold and revenue earned. The major recommendation here is to sell more 'Coupons' to 'Product customers' and products to 'Coupon customers' with the aim of converting almost all the 'Product' and 'Coupon' customers into 'Hybrid' which is one of the business objectives. Hence, converting 'Product' and 'Coupon' customers into 'Hybrid' can increase the number of transactions, quantity sold and in turn the revenue of the company. **Introducing Cross sell opportunities to 'Product' and 'Coupon' customers and up sell opportunities to 'Hybrid customers' will eventually increase their sales and revenue.**

IV.II. Purchase Pattern and Trend

The patterns in which the customers purchase their required products are analyzed from the given dataset to understand their preference, trend and affinity towards different 'Products' and 'Coupons'. We have created several transaction classes based on the number of transactions done by each customer during the entire analysis period and mapped them accordingly to each transaction class. The different classes and the corresponding findings are shown below:

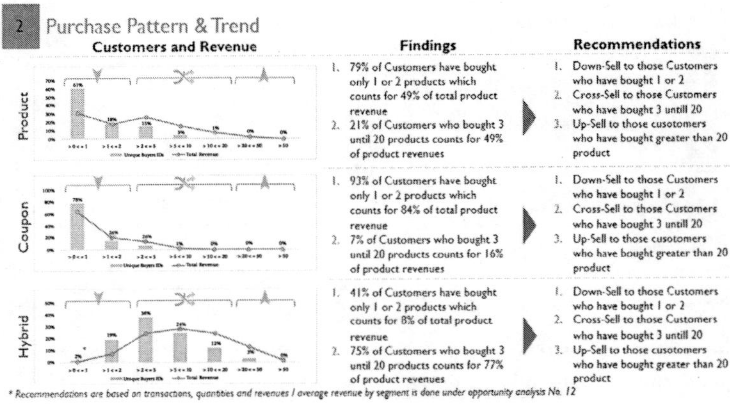

Figure 5.7: Opportunity Area 2—Purchase Pattern and Trend

The transaction classes indicate the number of transactions made by the customers in the entire analytics scope. In the graph above, x-axis indicates the different transaction classes [>0<=1, >1<=2, >2<=5, >5<=10, >10<=20, >20<=50, >50] and y-axis indicates the percentage of customers that fall under each class. The red line across the green bars in the graph indicates the revenue generated by the customers in each transaction class. It can be seen that, around 80%-90% of the 'Product' and 'Coupon' customers have purchased only once or twice in the entire period considered for analysis.

After analysing the pattern of purchase, trend and the transactions we have come up with appropriate marketing opportunities for each transaction class in all the three categories of people:

- Provide Down sell opportunities for those customers who have made only one or two transactions in the entire scope
- Provide Up sell opportunities for those customers who have made more than 20 transactions in the entire scope
- Provide Cross sell opportunities for those customers who have made 2 to 20 transactions in the entire scope.

IV.III. Cross Purchase Analysis

The customers' interests and preference change from time to time depending upon the industrial revolution, technology development, income and lifestyle. So analyzing the interests of the customers over a period of time is a very important factor in Customer Behaviour Analytics to retain customers in a business. We have done Cross-purchase analysis to know how the interests of the customers changes from buying 'Products' to 'Coupons' and vice-versa as shown in the below figure:

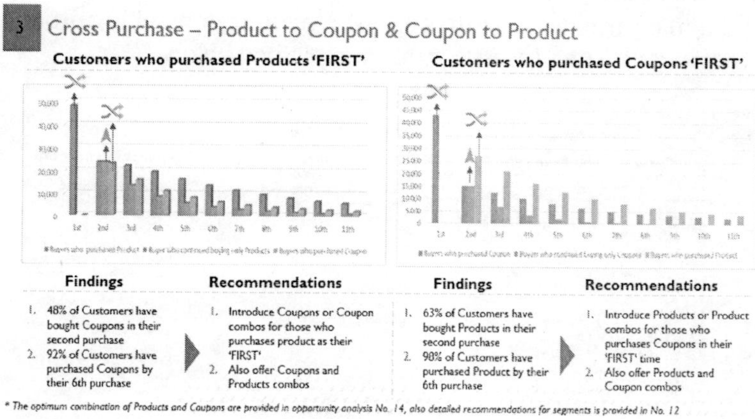

Figure 5.8: Opportunity Area 3 – Cross Purchase Analysis

For this analysis, we started with two sets of data:

- Customers who purchased only 'Products' in their first transaction
- Customers who purchased only 'Coupons' in their first transaction.

We have observed how the customers have changed their interests from buying 'Products' to 'Coupons' and 'Coupons' to 'Products' in their successive transactions. It is clear from the above graph that about 50%-60% of the customers who purchased 'Products' have shifted to buy 'Coupons' and those who purchased 'Coupons' have shifted to buy 'Products' in their very next transaction. Also, around 92%-98% of the customers who bought 'Products' have changed their interests to buy 'Coupons' and vice-versa by the end of 6th transaction. We have derived useful insights from this analysis and provided appropriate business recommendations for increasing the sales and revenue.

The major recommendation here is to **introduce Cross sell opportunities** (introduce 'Coupons' to people buying 'Products' and 'Products' to people buying 'Coupons') **to the customers immediately after their first purchase** so that there is a high possibility to increase the 'Hybrid' customer base.

IV.IV. First and Last Purchase Analysis

In a retail business, there are certain products or brands that are the most purchased items by the customers. Identifying the products which are first bought by the customers has significance in improving the sales and popularity of those products. The business can take measures to introduce those 'Products'/'Coupons' to all the customers and make intense measures to push medium/low selling products in the market. The process is further explained below:

Figure 5.9: Opportunity Area 4 – First and Last Purchase Analysis

In the above graph, x-axis denotes the top selling products and x-axis denotes the count of customers purchasing the corresponding products. The blue bar represents the number of customers purchasing the corresponding 'Products'/'Coupons' in their first transaction and orange bars represents the number of customers purchasing the corresponding 'Products'/'Coupons' in their last transaction.

From the analysis, we have identified the top 'Products'/'Coupons' being purchased as a first item and also the items which are purchased in the last transaction by the customers. We can recommend the business to introduce:

- **Up sell opportunities** for the 'Products'/'Coupons' that are the top first purchased by the customers
- **Down sell opportunities** or related cheaper items for the 'Products'/'Coupons' that are mostly purchased last by the customers
- **Cross sell opportunities** for all the 'Products'/'Coupons' to intensify sales and growth.

IV.V. Analysis of Discount Codes

Nowadays, it has become a trend for all the retail sectors to provide attractive discounts to its customers with the aim of customer retention, increasing sales and revenue. Hence, discount codes provided by these retail companies should be in such a way that they don't compromise their profit and expected revenue. If a business fails to introduce proper optimization of these discount codes, it may lead to revenue loss and continuous revenue leakage. Our client also provides various discount codes to the customers with the idea of increasing the sales and revenue. We have done extensive analysis here to optimize the discount codes so that the client does not face negative margin and revenue loss. The classification of the discount coupons is explained as:

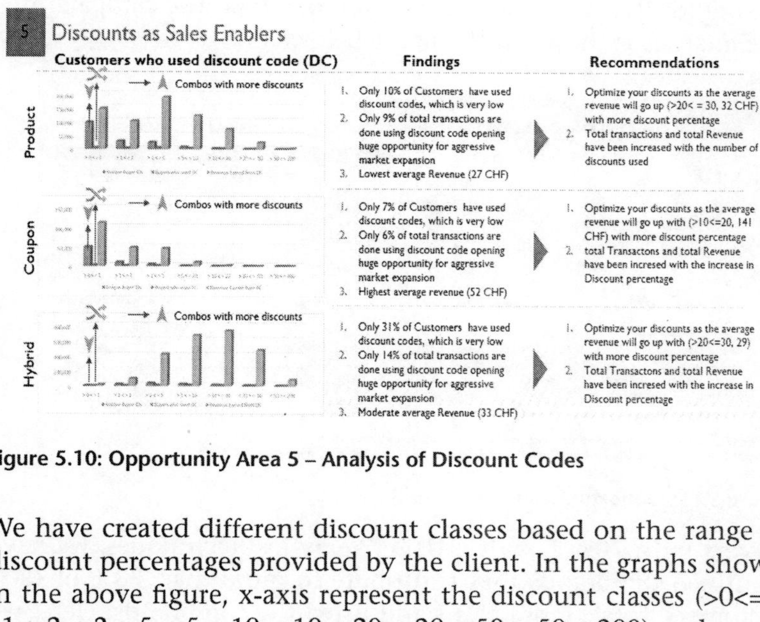

Figure 5.10: Opportunity Area 5 – Analysis of Discount Codes

We have created different discount classes based on the range of discount percentages provided by the client. In the graphs shown in the above figure, x-axis represent the discount classes (>0<=1, >1<=2, >2<=5, >5<=10, >10<=20, >20<=50, >50<=200) and y-axis represents the number of customers who fall under each class. The orange bar indicates the number of customers who used discount codes in their transactions under each class.

It is evident from the graph that the customers using these discount codes are very few in number (around 10%) in all three categories of customers ('Product', 'Coupon' and 'Hybrid'). From the analysis, **we came up with the optimized discount percentage for all the three categories of customers, say 20%-30% for 'Product**

customers', 10%-20% for 'Coupon customers' and 20%-30% for 'Hybrid customers' that can be recommended to the business for implementing in the current scenario. The optimized discount percentages are identified by analyzing the historical transactions and the revenue generated by the discount codes in the past.

IV.VI. Brand Loyalty

Brand Loyalty refers to the situation in which the customers persistently stick to only one or two brands without any compromise in terms of price, quality and features. Identifying those brands and selling appropriate products to the customers help the business in increasing the sales and revenue. Instead of campaigning all the products to all the customers, they can concentrate only on the brands that the customer is loyal to and do the campaigning. The analysis is shown in the figure below:

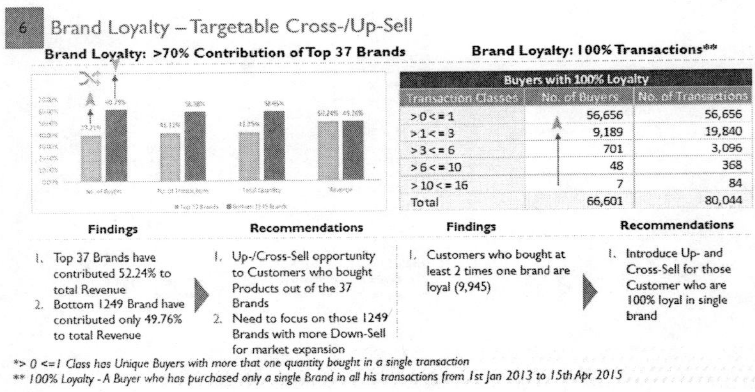

Figure 5.11: Opportunity Area 6 – Brand Loyalty

Buyers with 70% Loyalty: Using analytical techniques, we have identified the brands that contribute to more than 70% of each customers' total transactions and listed the top brands. Here, we have selected a threshold of 70% loyalty. From all these analysis, the major finding is that the top 37 brands contribute to more than 50% of the total revenue earned by the client and the remaining 1249 brands contribute to the rest of the total revenue.

We have given the following recommendations to the client to increase their sales and revenue:

- Recommended the client to provide Up sell opportunities with more valuable and expensive products to the customers purchasing the top 37 loyal brands

- Recommended to sell the remaining 1249 brands with Cross sell or Down sell opportunities for market expansion.

Buyers with 100% Loyalty: We have also identified the brands that contribute to 100% of each customer's total transactions in the entire time period considered for analysis. There are 9,945 customers who have purchased only a single brand in the entire scope. As these customers are loyal to only one brand, the business can sell only those brands with more valuable products, i.e., Up sell opportunity to the appropriate customers.

IV.VII. Top Product Categories and Products

There are a few 'Products'/'Product categories' and 'Coupons'/' Coupon categories' that are contributing more in terms of revenue. We have identified those top selling items from the historical data and derived business insights out of it.

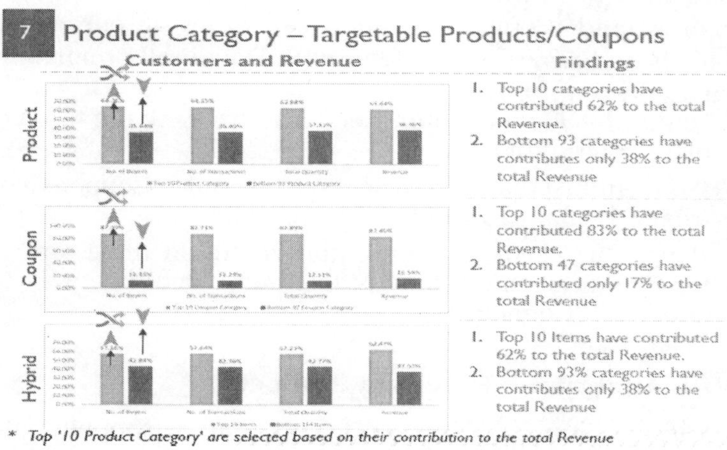

Figure 5.12 Opportunity Area 7 – Product Category

- Found the 'Product' and 'Coupon' categories that are contributing more in terms of revenue
- It is identified that the top 10 'Product' and 'Coupon' categories accounts to more than 60% and 80% of the total revenue respectively
- Hence, the client can concentrate more on these top selling 'Product' and 'Coupon' categories instead of focusing on all the categories.

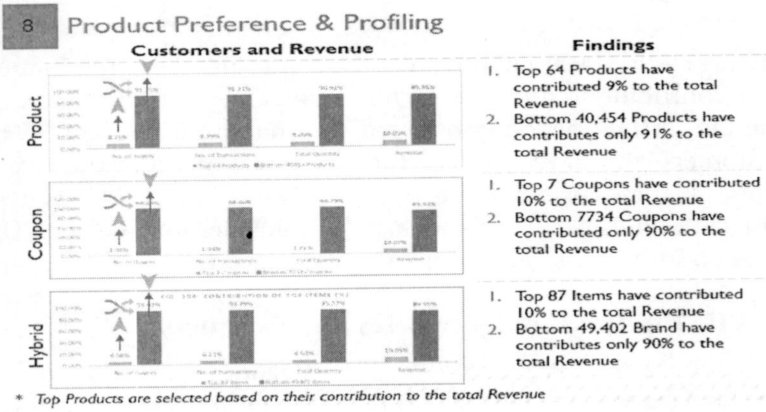

Figure 5.13 Opportunity Area 8 – Top Product

The major recommendation here is to **introduce Up sell and Cross sell opportunities to push those top 'Products'/'Product categories' and 'Coupon'/'Coupon categories' in the market and focus on the rest of the items with Down sell opportunity for market expansion.**

- Found the 'Products' and 'Coupons' that rank the top most place in terms of revenue
- It is identified that the top 64'Products' and 7 'Coupons' contribute to about 10% of the total revenue
- Hence, the client can concentrate more on these top selling 'Products' and 'Coupons' instead of focusing on all the 'Products'/'Coupons'.

IV.VIII. Analysis on Returned Products

The customers purchase products from an online shopping platform based on their interests, demand and necessity. After receiving the product, there are chances of returning those products back to the retail sector due to several reasons like product failed to meet their expectations in terms of quality, color and design etc. The returning of those purchased products leads to loss of revenue due to the shipping costs, packaging costs and other related costs involved in shipping the product to the receiver. There can be a set of few such products that are continuously being returned by the customers. Refraining from selling those products to the customers helps the business in evading the unnecessary costs involved. The method of identification of those products and development of strategic insights are explained as:

9 Returned Products and Gross Revenue Loss

Contribution of Top 44 Products

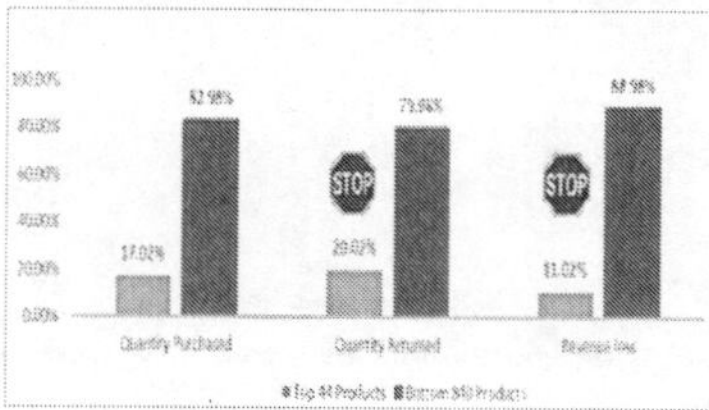

Products with Highest Return Rate

Product	Quantity Purchased	Quantity Returned	Revenue loss
Tischventilator Â«coo	214	19	118
Kissen 65x100cm Â«H	38	16	285
Gutschein im Wert vo	686	14	140
3er-Set Socken schwa	368	13	91
30er-Set Entgiftungsp	3,333	12	281
SÃ¼sses Dreierlei im	24	12	85
Antischnarch-Schiene	1,530	8	109
1h Tennisplatzmiete i	124	8	80
Smartstick in Schwarz	2,298	8	49
Drehregal Â«TobiÂ» v	401	6	141

Opportunities

1. 44 Products contribute to 20% of total Returns in terms of quantity and 11% of total returns in terms of Revenue.
2. Total 884 Products have been returned after purchase (1,234 quantity)
3. Total 884 Products have been identified for being returned because of various reasons
4. These Products can be stopped immediately as they are causing for revenue leakages

Recommendations

1. Regular review of returned Products in regards of quantity returned and verify quality issues for those with high quantity and revenue loss –
2. Mitigate possible reputation issues and do not Cross-/Up-Sell

Figure 5.14: Opportunity Area 9 – Analysis on Returned Products

From the various analysis that are performed, we have identified those products which are continuously being returned by the customers and listed the top returned products from the past data. During the analysis period, 884 products are being returned after purchase and amongst those products the top 44 returned products accounts for about 20% of the total returned products in terms of quantity and 11% in terms of revenue loss.

STOP **Stop-Selling**	Avoid selling Products and/or Coupons as they are causing Revenue leakages

The concept of stop selling recommends the business to **immediately stop the selling of those continuously returned products in order to avoid revenue leakages.** The business has to regularly review those products to identify the reasons behind their failure in the market to avoid revenue loss.

IV.IX. Analysis on Negative Revenue

Negative revenue results when the business sells products below the margin price or when they provide huge discounts that compromise their profit. These products will be of serious threat to the sales and revenue earned by the companies. Identifying such products and analyzing the reasons behind selling them at negative margins is very important and efficient in avoiding revenue loss. The process is further explained below:

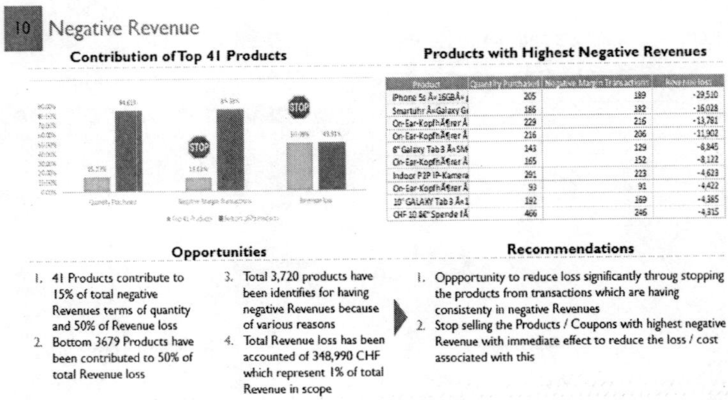

Figure 5.15: Opportunity Area 10 – Analysis on Negative Revenue

With the given data, we have found the products that are consistently sold at negative margins during the scope of analysis (1st Jan 2013 to 15th Apr 2015). The business sells more than 3600 products in its shopping platform. Among those products, we have identified around 41 products that are significant in causing negative revenues. These 41 products contribute to about 50% of the total revenue loss and 15% of total negative revenues in terms of quantity. The graph show in the above figure represents how the top 41 negative revenue generating products and the rest 3629 products accounts for the revenue loss in terms of quantity, number of transactions and revenue. Business, rather than concentrating on all the 3600 products, it is feasible and effective for the business to focus only on those top 41 products that accounts for 50% of the revenue loss.

STOP **Stop-Selling**	Avoid selling Products and/or Coupons as they are causing Revenue leakages

The business has to take immediate actions to reduce these loses by stop selling such products with highest negative revenue. Hence, there **is high possibility to avoid negative revenues if the client refrains from selling only those 41 products.**

IV.X. Customer Profiling

Business wanted to identify similarity and difference among their customers using different parameters. The objective is to create various segments of the customers based on the similarity of their behaviours in terms of number of transactions, recency of transaction, average money spent, average time between transactions and number of categories bought etc. Before segmenting the customers into different segments, it is essential to profile them according to their behaviour using the above parameters. The below figure explains the process of profiling the customers under various parameters:

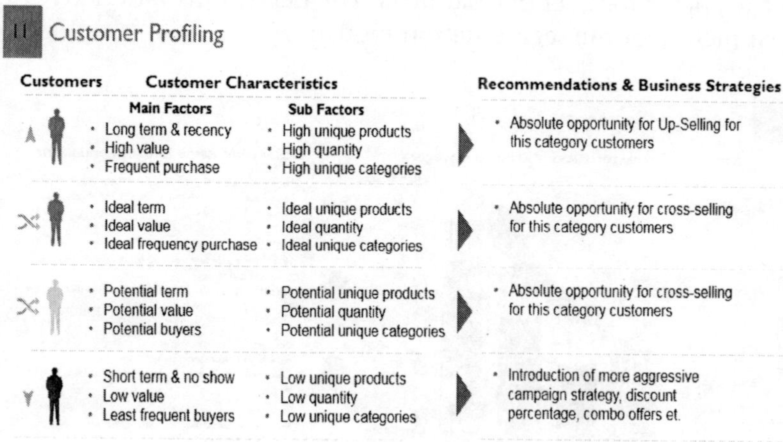

Figure 5.16: Opportunity Area 11 – Customer Profiling

We analyzed the customer behaviours in terms of different parameters available in the data:

- **Main Factors:** The major factors considered for profiling the customer includes their frequency, recency and monetary value
- **Sub-Factors:** We have also used the other potential variables suitable for the analysis such as quantity purchased, number of unique products purchased and number of unique categories purchased.

Based on the customers' profiles, we have provided strategic business recommendations to the client to implement appropriate marketing opportunities. But, the business cannot concentrate on each and every customer (approx. 300,000 customer base) and make the decision at individual level. Hence, it is essential to segment these customers into several segments according to their profiles using various propensity/probability modelling methods.

IV.XI. Customer Segmentation – RFM Model

We have created several segmentation models using the variables available in the data. After running several models, we came up with the extended RFM model which best suited our objectives and hypothesis. This is a very important part of Customer Behaviour Analytics as this helps the business to understand their customers' preference and to identify the customers who are valuable and loyal to them over a period of time. Using this information, they can do effective campaigning of their products and services to the appropriate set of customers. The below illustration gives a clear picture of the segmentation model:

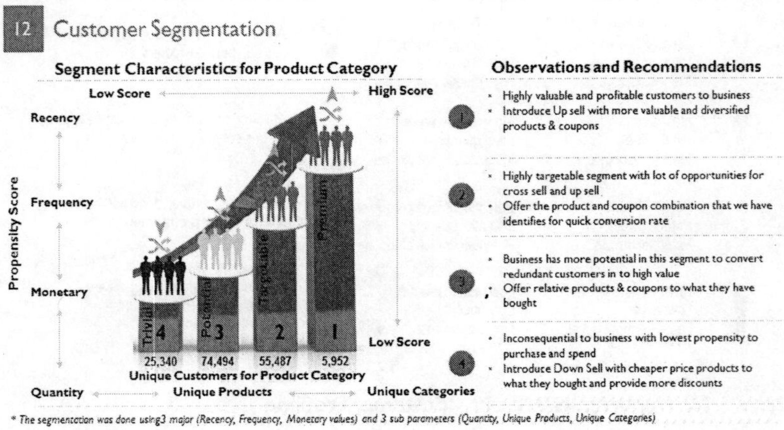

Figure 5.17: Opportunity Area 12 – Customer Segmentation

We have created four segments of customers – 'Premium', 'Targetable', 'Potential' and 'Trivial' using the extended RFM model:

- **Variable selection:** The required variables are selected based on the business inputs, SME's decision and data availability. We had selected 6 major transaction related variables
- **Factors/Parameters:** Recency, Frequency and Monetary as the major factors. Quantity, Unique products and Unique Categories as the sub-factors
- **Weightage:** Weightage is given based on the business importance and clients' requirement. The weightage is given only for major factors. Recency is given 3, Frequency 5 and Monetary 2
- **RFM-V Classes:** The classes are created based on the range and distribution of the respective factors. The classes are also given weightage based on their significance
- **Scoring & Ranking:** The scoring is done based on the RFM-V equation which we derived from the above exercise and all the customers are ranked accordingly

- **Discrepancy measures:** Model discrepancies are measured using variance tests.

IV.XII. Customer Attrition Analysis

Customer churn is one of the major threats for any business as this leads to significant leakage of revenue and profit. A customer is considered to be churned when his latest/last transaction is beyond a certain time period. The various customer segments and their average churn period are shown below:

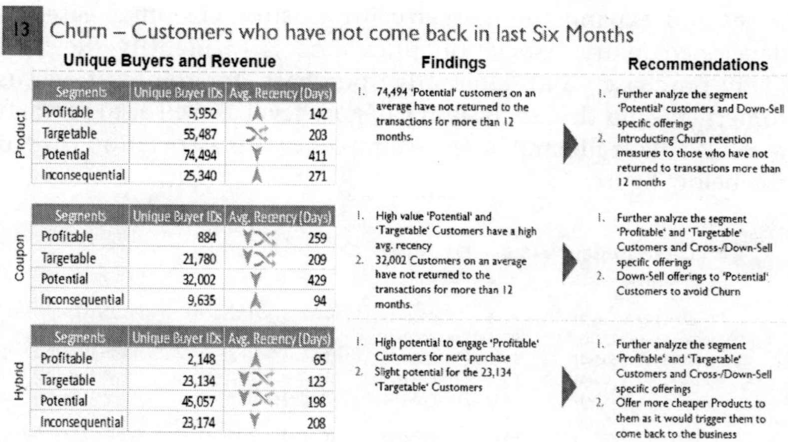

Figure 5.18: Opportunity Area 13 – Customer Attrition Analysis

Several attrition models are run to obtain the finest results for our data. The attrition analysis is done separately at both customer category level and customer segment level. The major reasons for the customer leaving the client are analyzed from the data by identifying their last transaction details like 'Products'/'Coupons' purchased, date of purchase etc.

As shown in the above illustration, the 'Premium' group of customers has recently made their transaction and hence, there is a large possibility to introduce Up sell opportunities to them by selling more valuable, expensive products related to their previous purchases. There is a large possibility to introduce Cross-/Up sell opportunities to 'Targetable' customers to convert them to 'Premium' customers. 'Potential' customers have not performed many transactions for about a year. These customers need to be treated with more consciousness as they are in the verge of being churned in the near future. They should be provided related products with Cross sell opportunities to retain them as loyal customers. The next set of customers is the 'Inconsequential/Trivial' customers who have not done any transaction for more than a year. The business can suggest them to purchase products with Down sell opportunities by providing cheaper alternatives as it would trigger them to come back to the business.

IV.XIII. Product Association

Business wanted to identify the scope for Cross-/Up sell opportunities and expand the market using existing customer base. We developed many association rules models to identify the 'next likely purchase', and 'alternative purchase' for the existing customers. We did this analysis at category level as well as at segment level. We have illustrated few examples of our association rules in the below figure:

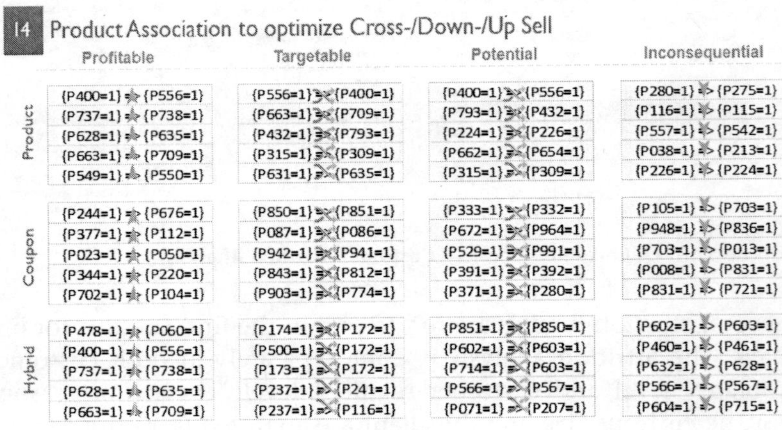

Figure 5.19: Opportunity Area 14 – Product Association

Product association/affinity for customers is done using Apriori technique. Below are the steps which are followed for developing association rules:

- **Variable selection:** The required variables are selected based on the business inputs, SME's decision and data availability. We had selected top 1000 products based on highest revenue contribution
- **Transactions:** The affinity is measured at each transaction level. All the transactions which are pertaining to the top 1000 products are considered for developing association rules

- **Rule Development:** The rules are developed using Apriori technique after several attempts based on the confidence, support and lift with various combinations
- **Rule Classification:** The classification of rules are done based on the business requirements and at each category and segment level
- **Performance Measures:** Confidence, support and lift are used as performance measures for the final rule development.

V. Solution Development Process – Across Business Lines

As mentioned in the objectives earlier in this paper, the business also needs to recognize if there is a possibility to give space for Data Monetization. Hence, we have extended our analysis across the different business lines of our client. The below figure shows the different business lines of the company:

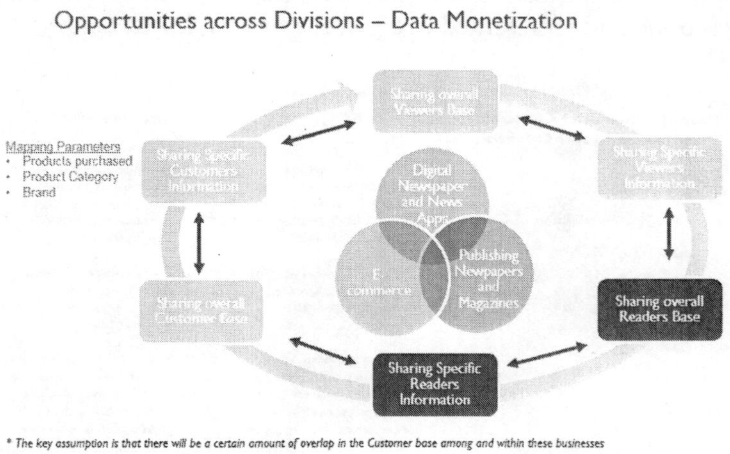

Figure 5.20: Opportunities across Business Lines – Data Monetization

The client wanted to use the customer base of one business to improve the sales and market base of the other business lines with the assumption that there could be an overlap in their customer base. Hence, there is a major objective to explore the opportunities for data monetization within and across different business lines. All these business strategies provides scope for market expansion, introduction of Cross-/Up-/Down sell opportunities, efficient campaigning, revenue optimization and sales growth.

For across business analysis, we have considered two other major businesses of our clients:

- Publishing Newspapers and Magazines
- Digital Newspapers and News Apps.

Based on the interests of the customers towards different 'Products'/'Coupons' purchased online, we have mapped them to the other business lines and explored various marketing opportunities that can be recommended to expand the market and customer base of the other business lines using the available customer base of 300,000 customers and their transaction details.

V.I. Across Business Lines: E-Commerce to Digital Newspaper and News Apps

E-Commerce to Digital Newspaper

Initially, we started our across business analysis with mapping the customers of e-commerce to Digital Newspaper channels. This mapping is done and represented in a graph which is shown below:

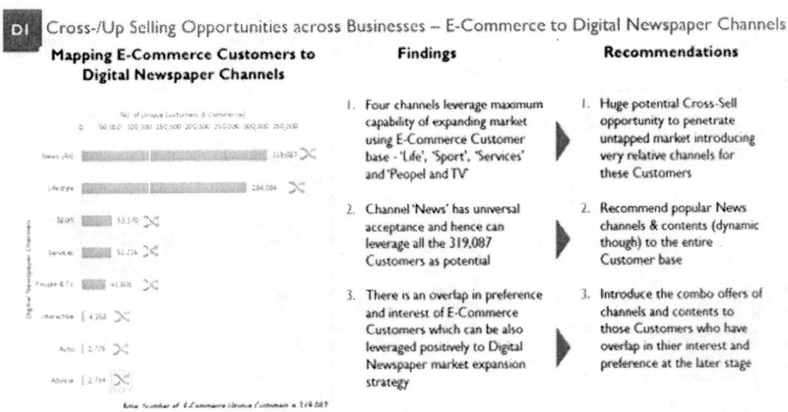

Figure 5.21: E-Commerce to Digital Newspaper Channels

The mapping of the customers of e-Commerce is done by analyzing the various parameters and characteristics like purchase history, brand purchased, category purchased and quantity purchased etc. This mapping is done with the assumption that there is a probability of certain overlap of the customers of these different business lines. This overlap will be excluded when business starts the actual campaigning.

From the digital newspaper website, we collected the different channels like 'News', 'Lifestyle', 'People & TV' and 'Sport' etc.

Since 'News' becomes common to all type of customers, we mapped all the 300,000 customers of e-Commerce to the 'News' Channel. From the purchase pattern, category and purchase type of customers of e-Commerce, we identified that about four channels of Digital Newspaper Company leverage the maximum capability of expanding market using e-Commerce customers. These top four channels are 'Life', 'Sport', 'Services' and 'People & TV'. Hence, there is a huge potential to introduce Cross sell opportunities to penetrate untapped market introducing much related channels to the e-Commerce customers. Also, there are circumstances in which the customer may be mapped to two or more channels of Digital Newspaper. The business can provide related combo offers to those customers who appear in one or more channels, e.g.: if an e-Commerce customer has purchased more 'Sports' and 'Food' related products, then he can be mapped to both the 'Sport' and 'Lifestyle' channel of Digital Newspaper. In that case, the business can do campaigning of a related combo offer ('Sport' and 'Lifestyle' Magazines) to the customer.

E-Commerce to Digital Newspapers' Online Retail Product Categories

Our Digital Newspaper and Mobile Apps client also has an online shopping platform that provides e-Commerce services to its customers. So, there is a high significance to map the customers of our e-Commerce business to the Digital Newspaper business. We received the product categories that are sold from the shopping platform of Digital Newspaper business and mapped the customers of e-Commerce business for market expansion as shown below:

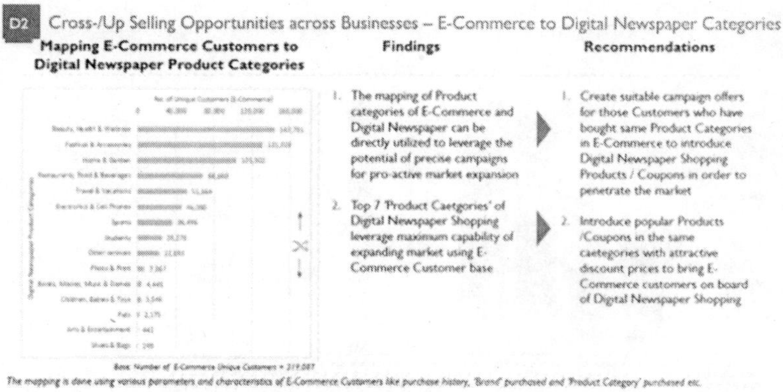

Figure 5.22: E-Commerce to Digital Newspaper Product Categories

E-Commerce to News Apps

We also mapped the e-Commerce customers to the Mobile Apps which is shown below:

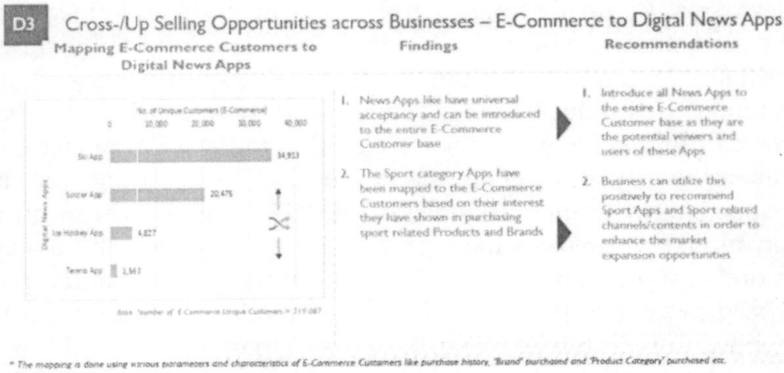

Figure 5.23: E-Commerce to Digital News Apps

V.II. Across Business Lines: E-Commerce to Print Newspapers and Magazines

As explained in the previous topic, we have also performed the across business Cross-/Up sell analysis between e-Commerce business and the daily Newspaper and Magazine publishing business.

E-Commerce to Print Newspapers and Magazines

We began the analysis with mapping the customers of e-Commerce to the Newspapers using the purchase history, purchase category, brands purchased, products purchased and quantity etc. Below is the illustration of the mapping of the customers of e-Commerce to Newspapers:

Figure 5.24: E-Commerce to Newspaper and Magazine Publishers

Since 'News' becomes common to all type of customers, we have mapped all the 300,000 customers of e-Commerce to the Newspaper and Magazine publishing business. The business can do effective campaigning of the Newspaper to all the e-Commerce customers by leveraging the customer base of one business to another.

The business can take the following steps to increase their market and customer base:

- Introduce Cross-/Up sell with more valuable and diversified offers to the 'Premium' customers of e-Commerce
- There is a large opportunity to offer Cross sell opportunity to the 'Targetable' customers by providing ideal combinations that are very popular and most preferred by business
- Business can offer relatively cheaper combinations to the 'Potential' set of customers as it can leverage them to valuable customers
- Introduce Down sell opportunity with cheap offers and provide more discounts to the 'Inconsequential/Trivial' customers of e-Commerce.

E-Commerce to Print Newspapers and Magazines' Major Categories

Using the customer details, we mapped the customers of e-Commerce to the major categories of Newspapers and Magazines publishing business as shown below:

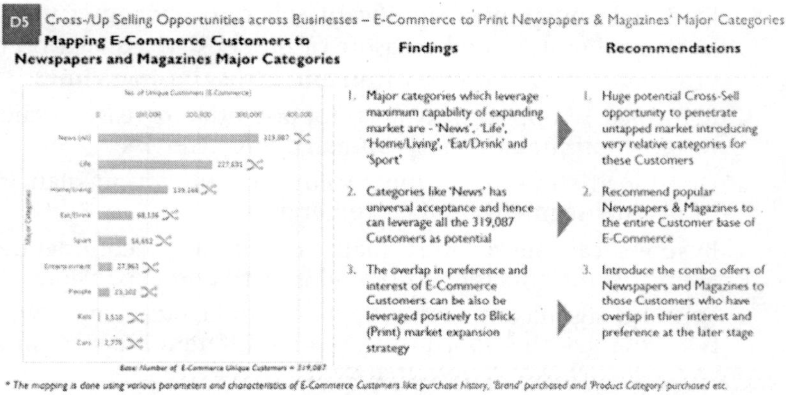

Figure 5.25: E-Commerce to Newspaper and Magazine Publishers' Major Categories

E-Commerce to Print Newspapers and Magazines' Sub-Categories

In a microscopic level, mapping of customer is also done at sub-category level and identified the various marketing opportunities as illustrated below:

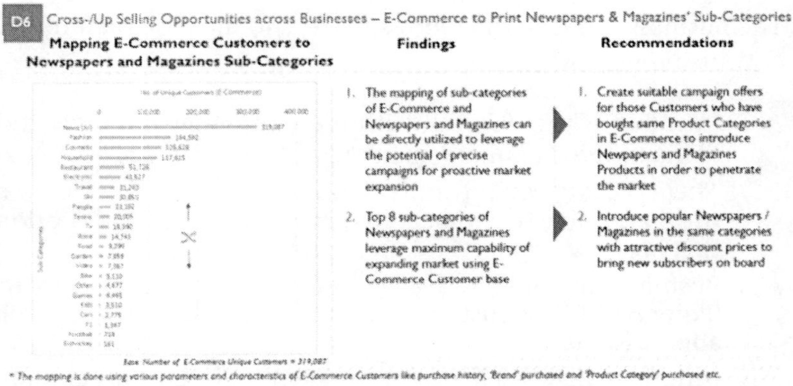

Figure 5.26: E-Commerce to Newspaper and Magazine Publishers' Sub-Categories

VI. Major Findings and Conclusion

VI.I. Summary and conclusion

We did work on all the pre-defined objectives and tested hypothesis accordingly using the available data. We also added few additional objectives based on the updated information:

- Explored and proved significant scope for customer profiling, segmentation and measure of propensity, association of products, Cross-/Up sell within and across business lines
- Identified 14 opportunity areas for potential increase in sales, revenue, profitability and campaign effectiveness
- Developed strategic business solutions and action plan for individual segments and customer groups
- Business can successfully plan, incorporate recommended actions & insights for substantial growth and expansion
- Found a significant scope for data monetization by identifying marketing opportunities across different business lines using available and potential data.

VI.II. Customer Profiling and Segmentation

Identified and created various customer segments based on their similarity in the customer behaviour and business expectations using the extended RFM-V model:

- Identified 4 ideal customer segments – 'Premium', 'Targetable', 'Potential' and 'Inconsequential' - using individual parameters like frequency, recency, monetary and other related factors
- There is a high possibility to get more profit from 'Premium' set of customers
- The 'Targetable' and 'Potential' customers need to be treated with more exciting opportunities to convert them into 'Premium' ones
- There is a high risk of customer churn in the 'Inconsequential' segment.

VI.III. Cross-/Up sell and Association Rules

Developed various business strategies and recommendations based on the association rules developed using Aprori technique:

- These rules can be used to offer appropriate Cross-/Up sell opportunities or combo offers to the right set of customers at the right time
- This will help to improve campaign efficiency through targeted and customized offers
- The developed association rules also contribute to overall market expansion.

VI.IV. Data Monetization

Performed various analysis across the different business lines to explore the scope for data monetization with the available data:

- We have found that the customer base of one business can be used to increase the market and customer base of other two businesses by studying their purchase preference, history, preferred brands and products etc. and mapped them accordingly
- There is a lot of scope for the utilization and monetization of the customer data of our clients to expand their other businesses.

VII. Strategic Business Recommendations and Next Steps

VII.I. Strategic Business Recommendations

We have developed customer engagement and profitability improvement strategies based on the results, insights derived from our analytics and model results. The various business insights, recommendations and the corresponding business impacts that can be observed after deployment are illustrated below:

Our Business Strategy Recommmendations (Short Term)

ID	Business Strategy	Business Impact	Opportunity Areas
A	Increase Hybrid Customer Base	• Increase total Revenue and average Revenue by transaction • Strengthen Customer Loyality	1 2 3
B	Optimize your Discounts	• Increase total Revenue and average Revenue by transaction • Increase of total transactions	2 5
C	Improve Brand/Product Loyality	• Strengthen Customer/Brand/Product Loyality • Strengthen the Brands	6 7 8
D	Effective Campaigning based on Segments	• Strengthen Customer Loyality • Improve response and convertion rate	4 11 12
E	Optimize Offers based on affinitiy	• Increase propensitz of accepting offers • Reduce campaining costs	13 14
F	Avoid Revenue Leakages and Customer Churn	• Reduce Revenue Leakage ratio • Increase Customer retention	9 10 13

Figure 5.27: Business Strategies, Impacts and Recommendations

All the identified opportunity areas and the corresponding business strategies are mentioned in the above figure which can be implemented to obtain the potential business impacts for the respective strategies.

Next Steps

All these analysis are done for a Pilot project and because of the work done in a very short time period, we have won a long time engagement with the same client as an achievement. In this extended project, we will be working on the deployment of our recommendations to see the results in the near future. Also, we will be working on Advanced Customer Behaviour Analytics to derive more significant and potential insights for the business to increase their sales, revenue, market and customer base.

VIII. Appendix

List of Variables

Below are variables and their description used for our analysis at different stage. We have also created many derived variables based on the actual variables required for modeling:

Variable Name	Variable Type	Description
BuyerID	Numeric	MD5 hash of Latin_Email field
CreationDate	Date	When the e-mail is recorded
FirstPurchaseDate	Date	Date of first purchase
LastPurchaseDate	Date	Date of last purchase
NumberOfDiscountCodesUsed	Numeric	Number of Discount Codes used for each transaction
RevenueGenerated	Numeric	Indicator of revenue generated by this user
Margin I	Numeric	MarginI on variant Level
OrderID	Numeric	Moosehead Order Number ID
Price	Numeric	Price of variant
Quantity	Numeric	Purchased Quantity of this variant
RevenueAfterRefunds	Numeric	Net revenue after refunds
TransactionDate	Date	Date of purchase
VariantID	Numeric	MooseheadVariantID
Brand	Character	Brand of the product
CategoryID	Numeric	Category of the Product
DiscountPercent	Numeric	Discount given for a product in percentage
ProductGroupID	Numeric	Product group of the variant
ProductID	Numeric	Moosehead ProductID
ProductTitle	Character	Name of the product
Supplier	Character	Supplier name
ProductRecordType	Character	Whether a product or a coupon

Figure 5.28: Table containing list of variables and their description

Model Development Process

We have defined the process of development of all the models and illustrated below:

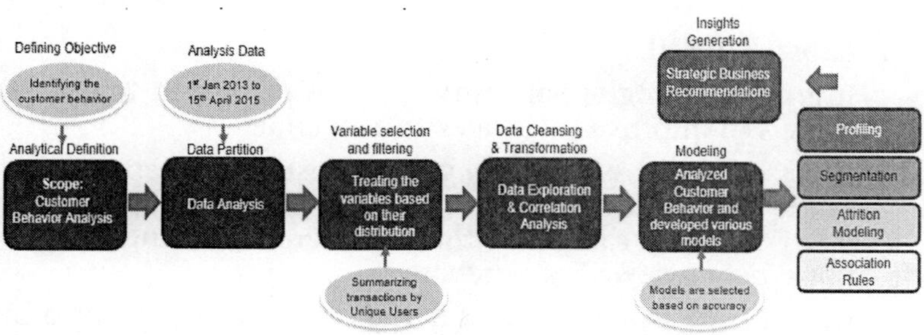

Figure 5.29: Model Development Process

XI. Acronyms

We have defined below the key words that we have used throughout the paper for more understanding:

- **Product Customers**

  The set of customers who have purchased only 'Products' during the analysis period from 1st Jan 2013 to 15th Apr 2015

- **Coupon Customers**

  The set of customers who have purchased only 'Coupons' during the analysis period from 1st Jan 2013 to 15th Apr 2015

- **Hybrid Customers**

  The set of customers who have purchased both 'Products' and 'Coupons' during the analysis period from 1st Jan 2013 to 15th Apr 2015

- **Brand Loyalty**

  If a customer sticks to only one or two brands in the entire scope, i.e., most of his/her transactions are pertaining to one or two brands

- **Negative Revenue**

  Negative revenue results when the business sells products below the margin price or when they provide huge discounts that compromise their profit

- **Returned Products**

  Returned products are a set of few products that are continuously being returned by the customers due to various reasons like quality issues and expired etc.

- **Cross-/Up sell**

  It is a marketing opportunity that can be offered to the customers to improve their sales and revenue:

  Cross sell:A Cross sell is to get the customer to spend more money to buy adding more 'Products' and/or 'Coupons' from other (related) categories than the 'Products' and/or 'Coupons' being viewed or purchased

  Up sell: An Up sell is to get the customer to spend more money – buy a more expensive model of the same type of 'Products' and/or 'Coupons', or add features/warranties that relate to the 'Products' and/or 'Coupons' in question

- **RFM (V) Segmentation**

  Segmenting customers based on their Recency, Frequency and Monetary as major factors and few related sub-factors together giving weightage to these parameters based on the business inputs. The output of this model is the propensity score for the respective segments based on the individual customer scoring.

Reference:

NA

6

Financial Liberalisation and Industrial Growth in India

Dr Niranjan R

I. Introduction

The nexus between international financial integration [IFI] and economic growth continues to be one of the most debated issues among macroeconomists and these debates very often heave several issues both from theoretical and policy perspectives. International financial integration is likened to the opening of domestic financial systems, such as financial markets, and institutions to the rest of the world and the internationalisation of financial assets and liabilities managed by resident entities. Over the last two and half decades, there has been an increase in the degree of international financial integration; countries are relaxing the restrictions on cross-border capital movements, deregulating domestic financial markets and offering competitive investment environments to encourage foreign investment. As a result, issues such as IFI and its impact on macro economy in general, real and financial sector in particular, have been a topical area of research and the volume of contributions to the issue is growing both regionally and globally.

Debating on the measurement issues of financial integration, many researchers provide a wide array of indicators as a proxy to gauge the level of international financial integration. Firstly, the de jure indicators are the proxy for the prerequisites of international financial integration and de facto indicators are the consequences of international financial integration. Other quantity based measures are savings and investment correlations pioneered by Feldstein and Horioka (1980) and lastly the price/arbitrage based measure gauges through the Law of One Price (LOOP)[1]. The LOOP seeks to equate rates of return of comparable assets across different

[1] Pioneered by Cournot (1927) and Marshall (1930), it mainly says that in the absence of administrative and informational barriers, the risk adjusted returns on identical assets should be comparable across markets.

markets/economies; the financial markets are integrated when the law of one price holds.

Majority of developed economies have open accounts coupled with liberalised financial sectors. Following the trend, developing and emerging countries have opened up their economies mostly between the mid-1980s and in early 1990s. Since then the financial systems and institutions have changed drastically and changes in information technology increased the degree of financial integration. However, the empirical support on IFI is ambiguous with economists putting both positive [creating growth opportunity] and negative [creating financial instability and crises] impacts of IFI. Financial Integration has a casual effect on its long run economic performance, permitting financial development with better resource allocation, enhancing competition, portfolio and risk diversification, liquidity boost and access of domestic firms to foreign funds, allowing higher profitability and growth. At the same time deregulation may trigger financial instability - banking crises, financial crises and currency crises which have been experienced by both developed and developing economies in the 80s and 90s and recently the global financial crises. These macroeconomic instabilities question the feasibility of IFI through sudden liberalisation of the financial sector.

In Indian perspective, from early 1950s to until the mid-1980s the evolution of the real, financial and external sector is guided by protected policies. These sectors policy framework liberalised from the mid-80s and this process accelerated with the initiation of new economic policy in the backdrop of balance of payment crises in 1991. The reforms in the real sector included deregulation and delicensing of industries, according a greater role to the private sector and gradual shift from direct physical controls to indirect controls (Chandrasekhar, 1988; Ahluwalia, 1991). The financial sector reforms shared the centre stage of the economic liberalisation; the Narasimhan Committee [GoI, 1991] recommended a gradual deregulation of the financial sector, including phasing out of directed credit, interest rate de-regulation and lowering of SLR and CRR to release resources for private sector. The policy of deregulation resulted in the abolition of the office of controller of capital issues, giving way to free pricing of capital issues and making equity finance an attractive source of funds for the corporate sector and empowered SEBI for regulation of capital markets. Meanwhile, foreign institutional investors have been allowed to invest in both equity and debt markets. Access to foreign funds has also been increased through liberalised external commercial borrowings (ECBs) and allowing recourse to

GDRs, ADRs and foreign currency convertible bonds (FCCBs). This enabled industries to take advantage of interest rate differentials between markets and raise cheaper funds. The reforms initiated in these areas constituted a major step towards reducing micro economic rigidities and lead to efficient allocation of resources primarily guided by market forces.

The broad approach to external sector reform was laid out in the report of the High-level Committee on Balance of Payments, headed by C. Rangarajan, in 1993. The devaluation of the rupee in July 1991 and the subsequent transition to the market-based exchange rate regime constituted an important aspect of the open trade policy regime. The reform also led to the elimination of quantitative restrictions on imports (barring a few sensitive items) and a drastic reduction in customs duties. With a distinct change in the overall policy stance, the reform marked a shift in emphasis from import substitution to export promotion, moving away from direct subsidies to indirect promotional measures. Regarding, the currency market, reforms included a market-based exchange rate system, introduction of convertibility of the rupee for external transactions on current account, and a compositional shift in cross-border capital inflows from debt-creating to non-debt-creating flows. With this macroeconomic integrational backdrop the paper examines the interaction between financial integration and dynamics of industrial growth in India by employing panel data regression models.

This section outlines the salient features of manufacturing sector across the industries by gross value added and external financial dependence. Since the nature of these industries varies according to their production process one can expect substantial variation in the composition of the variables. The change in gross value added of industries is shown in fig. 1. The top five manufacturing industries are MBM[2], MCCP, MONMP, MFB and MMVT add up to about 72.89per cent, rest of ten industries contribute of about 24.60per cent of gross value added in 1990. The top five industries of 1990 maintained their position in 2007, but the share increased marginally to 74.12per cent. MONMP and MMVT increased their share from less than 8 per cent to 11per cent and MCCP witnessed biggest decline in its share from 24.24per cent in 1990 to 15.68per cent in 2007. The share of remaining ten industries declined from 24 per cent to 21per cent from 1990 to 2007.

[2] See Appendix for industry abbreviations.

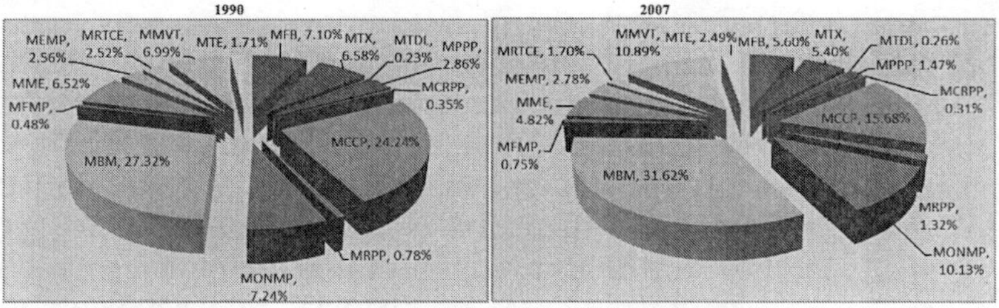

Fig 6.1: Change in the C omposition of Gross Value Added of Manufacturing Corporate Sector

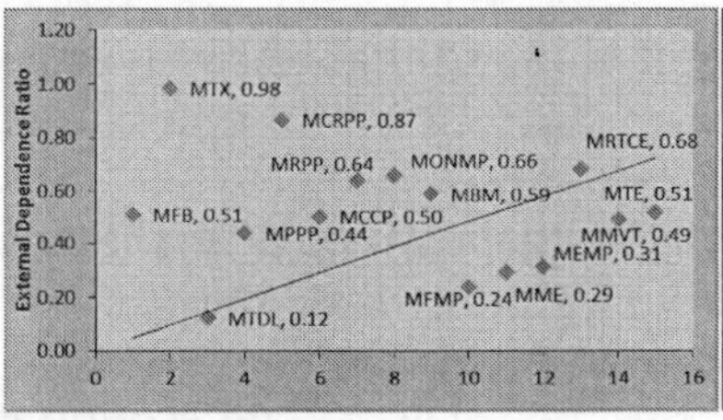

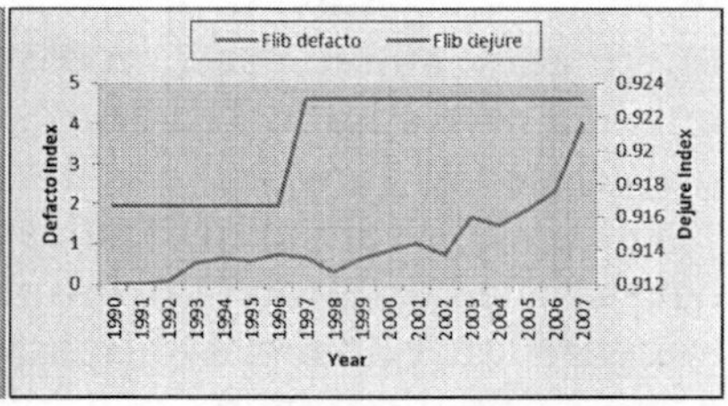

Fig 6.2: Average External Financial Dependence of Indian Industries (1990-2007)

Source: CMIE Prowess and author's computations. For industries abbreviations refer appendix.

Fig 6.3: Indices of Financial Integration for India

Defacto Index is author's computation (see Data Methodology Section) and Dejure Index is Jacques Minane Index

The pattern of external financial dependence[1] of industries is shown Figure 6.2. It is found that MTX, with value of 0.983 is the highest external financial dependent industry followed by MCRPP (0.866) and MRTCE (0.684). Meanwhile, industries such as MONMP, MRPP, MBM, MTE, MFB, MCCP, MMVT and MPPP are also highly dependent on external finance. The MEMP, MME, MFMP and MTDL are least dependent on external finance.

The Figure 6.3. depicts the trends in the indicators of financial integration proxied by Jacques Miniane dejure index[2],

[1] The external financial dependence of an industry is whose share of investment that cannot be financed through internal cash flows or retained earnings. It is computed as capital expenditure minus cash flow from operations divided by capital expenditure of an industry.

[2] Jacques Miniane's dejure index is binary indicator take value of "1" if there is an existence of capital controls and "0" otherwise. The considered controls are Controls on capital market and money market instruments, control on collective investment securities, derivatives and other instruments, control on credit operations: Commercial and financial credits, controls on direct investment, liquidation of direct investment, control on real estate, controls on provisions specific to commercial banks and other credit institutions and controls on institutional investors: Limits (max.) on securities by non-residents and portfolio invested abroad and dual exchange rate.

and the defacto index.[3] The defacto measure of restrictions on international capital flows shows a strong trend towards liberalisation, indicating an increased growth in cross-border capital inflows. In respect to dejure measure, compared to 80s, it changed in the early 90s and remained stable till 1996 and started to increase till 1998 and thereafter maintained stability. As, we observed that literature tends to support the claim of deregulation is beneficial, with liberalisation of financial markets helps in reducing the cost of capital, mobilize household savings, allocate resources efficiently, diversify risks, induce liquidity and reduce information and transaction costs. It is found that on an average, financial liberalisation leads to a one per cent increase in annual real economic growth over a five-years period.[4]

Many have argued that industrial deregulation and liberalisation have opened up greater opportunities for growth. Levine, R (2001) evidenced that financial liberalisation improves the functioning of domestic financial markets, banks and hence accelerate economic growth. By liberalising restrictions on international portfolio flows tends to enhance stock market liquidity, thus, boosting productivity growth, which in turn promotes economic development by encouraging improvements in financial system. Financial Integration affects the functioning of the domestic markets, the cost of capital, the diversification ability of local participants, the level of prices and foreign capital flows. Bekaert, Harvey and Lundblad (2005), shows that stock market liberalisation promote economic growth particularly in countries with more developed financial markets and higher quality institutions. They find that industries that face better growth opportunities experience significantly higher value added growth following liberalisation. Gupta,N and Kathy Yaun (2005); Barry Eichengreen, Rachita Gullapalli and Ugo Panizza (2009), found similar results, where liberalisation is followed by an increase in the industry value added, growth in investment and average market globalization. This is consistent with the view that financing constraints are reduced when the financial markets are liberalised. However, Levchenko A. Andrei,

---

[3] Measured as the ratio of the stock of inward FDI to GDP, the ratio of the stock of inward FDI and portfolio investment to GDP, the net flow counterparts of these two ratios, and the average current account deficit over the period (Prasad, Rajan, R and Zingales (2007).

[4] Bekaert, G, Harvey and C Lundblad (2005).

Ranciere and Thoeing (2009), analyses the effects of financial liberalisation on growth and volatility at the industry level for a large sample of countries. They estimate the impact of liberalisation on production, employment, firm entry, capital accumulation, and productivity. Financial liberalisation is found to have a positive effect on both growth and volatility of production across industries. The positive growth effect comes from increased entry of firms, higher capital accumulation, and an expansion in total employment. By contrast, they do not detect any effect of financial liberalisation on measured productivity. Finally, they opine that growth effects of liberalisation appear to be temporary rather than permanent. Vanassche, Ellen (2004), studied the impact of financial integration on growth at the industry level and evidenced that financial openness has a positive effect on growth of industrial sectors, regardless of their characteristics. Moreover, industries that rely relatively more on external finance grow disproportionately faster in countries with more integrated financial systems. However, relating to the industry-specific effect of financial openness, it decreases when the development of the domestic financial system is controlled. And finally he tested the hypothesis that financial integration improved growth also by enhancing the functioning of the domestic financial system. He found strong evidence of this indirect transmission channel of financial openness on growth. In contrast to these results, Vlachos, J and Daniel Waldenstorm (2002), using Rajan and Zingales (1998) methodology, found that industries which are highly dependent on external financing do not experience a higher growth in value added among countries with liberalised equity markets. They find a significant and positive effect of liberalisation on the creation of firms and growth opportunities in production, other than value added with the countries have relatively well developed financial markets. They attribute the decline in value added to vertical industrial disintegration and corporate outsourcing. Since outsourcing means breaking up of value added chains, it could result in a pattern of increased firm creation, increased production and zero growth in value added. At the micro level Laeven, L (2003), in a relative perspective between small and large firms investigated the impact of financial market reforms on financing constraints of firms in developing countries. He found that liberalisation affects small and large firms differently. Small firms are financially constrained before liberalisation but become less constrained after liberalisation. However, large firms are less constrained before liberalisation but become higher as financial liberalisation proceeds. He hypothesised that financial liberalisation has adverse effect on the financing constraints of large firms, because these firms had better access to preferential directed credit, before liberalisation. On the other hand, few research works focused on the impact of liberalisation on export performance of firms. Manova (2008) and Beck (2003), shows that equity market liberalisation that enhance the access of foreign investors lead to a larger increase in exports for firms. They evidenced that financially dependent sectors export more and have stronger trade balances in countries with better developed financial markets. In case of India, using firm level data Oura, H (2008) examined the development of different segments of a financial system, corporate financing patterns and firm growth in India. Consistent with earlier research findings, he found that in more recent years firms are increasingly relying on external funds to finance their investment. Moreover he finds that financial system in India is not channelling funds into industries with higher external finance dependence, where the debt financing does not allocate funds according to the firms external finance dependence, while equity financing system does. Similarly, he found that firms that are more dependent on external finance grow more slowly.

II. Data and Methodology

In order to examine the interaction between financial integration and dynamics of industrial growth in India the study makes use of two digit industries classified on the basis of the Annual Survey of Industries, National Industry Classification (NIC) code 2004, which is regarded as benchmark for industry classification, prepared according to their economic activity. According to National Industry Classification (NIC), the manufacturing sector commences from NIC 15 and ends at NIC 36, in whole the manufacturing sector contains 22 two digit industries, and out of it the study selected 18 major industries for panel analysis starting from 1990 to 2007. The data for eighteen industries of the Indian manufacturing sector for the post liberalisation period (1990-2007) is drawn from Centre for Monitoring Indian Economy's (CMIE) computerised database PROWESS. In order to estimate empirically the impact of financial integration and financial development on industry growth the study employs the following regression models of Vanassche, (2004).

Model 1

$$GVA_{ij} = \text{constant} + \beta_1 \text{ Fraction of value Added}_{ij} + \beta_2 \text{ FI} + u_{ij}$$

Model 2

$$GVA_{ij} = \text{constant} + \beta_1 \text{ Fraction of value Added}_{ij} + \beta_2 EX_{ij} \cdot \text{FI} + u_{ij}$$

Model 3

$$GVA_{ij} = \text{constant} + \beta_1 \text{ Fraction of value Added}_{ij} + \beta_2 EX_{ij} \cdot \text{FI} + \beta_3 Ex_{ij} \cdot \text{FD} + u_{ij}$$

$GRVA_t$ is the growth rate of real value added of industry_t where, Gross Value Added is the sum of wages and salaries, interest payments, rent paid, profit after tax and depreciation, GVA for each industry is deflated by Whole Sale Price Index (WPI). Share is the share of Industry in real gross value added where we expect industries with larger share to grow more slowly and therefore a negative sign for β_2. External is the measure of dependence on external finance for industry. In order to measure the external dependence we use the Rajan and Zingales (1998) methodology[5], an industry's dependence on external finance is defined as capital expenditures minus cash flow from operations divided by capital expenditure. The study also take into consider the influence of interaction between the external financial dependence of an industry with the measures of overall financial development (FD).[6] The variable FD, the financial development indicator is an average of finance size, finance activity and finance efficiency of the financial sector. Finance size is a measure of the overall size of the financial sector and is defined as the log of the sum of private credit and stock market capitalisation. Similarly, finance activity is a measure of the overall activity of financial intermediaries and markets. It is defined as the log of product of private credit (the value of credits by financial intermediaries to the private sector divided/ GDP) and value trades (the value of total shares traded on the

[5] An industry's dependence on external finance is defined as capital expenditures minus cash flow from operations divided by capital expenditure.

[6] Finance Development = Average of finance-activity, finance-size, and finance-efficiency Finance-activity = log (total value traded as share of GDP x claims on private sector by financial institutions as share of GDP) Finance-size = log (market capitalisation and claims on private sector by financial institutions as share of GDP) Finance-efficiency = log (total value traded as share of GDP divided by banks overhead costs as share of total assets)

stock market divided by GDP). Recent empirical works (Levine, Loayza and Beck, 2000) have evidenced the importance of private credit which exerts a large positive and robust influence on economic growth. On the other hand, we measure the efficiency of financial intermediaries and markets, and are defined as the log of ratio of value traded and overhead costs, which equals the overhead costs of the banking system relative to the banking system assets. Empirically, a large overhead cost reflects inefficiencies in the banking system and therefore, as a proxy for negative indicator of banking sector inefficiency. Finally in order to capture the financial openness defacto measure is used. In finance literature, to examine the effect of financial liberalisation, two separate measures are employed, firstly, the dejure measure of financial integration where its measures are quality based which concentrate on events such as changing regulations and the response of the monetary authorities to financial flows. On the other hand, the second category refers to de facto measure, measuring the actual observed outcome of the enforcement of existing regulations on financial markets. However, many empirical works (Prasad, Rogoff, Wei and Kose, 2003; Aizenman and Noy, 2003; D. Ozdemir and C. Erbil 2008) have tested the reliability of these two measures and advocated for defacto measure as an appropriate and more realistic tool to assess and to capture the effects of financial openness. Hence, in order to capture the effects of financial liberalisation on industry growth we followed Prasad, Raghuraman and Zingales (2007), defacto measures of openness. The measure is a ratio of the stock of inward FDI to GDP, the ratio of the stock of inward FDI and portfolio investment to GDP, the new counterparts of these ratios and the average current account deficit over the period.

III. Estimation Methodology

Since, we have Panel data the study make use of the panel estimation models; the fixed effects model and the random effects model are applied to explore the interaction between financial integration and industrial growth. The fixed effects model takes into account the industry specific effects whereas the random effects model considers the time effect.

The fixed effects model is expressed as:

$$GVA_{it} = \alpha_i + \beta X_{it} + u_{it}, \quad i = 1 \ldots N; \; t = 1 \ldots T$$

where, GVA_t is Gross value added of ith industry in t[th] period, X_{it} is vector of k explanatory variables of ith industry in t[th] period, β is parameters to be estimated and u_{it} is error term and assumed $\sim N(0, \sigma^2)$. α_i, 1,...N are constant coefficients, specific to each industry. Fixed effect model assumes that differences across the considered industries appear by means of differences in the intercept term. These individual coefficients are estimated together with vector of parameters β.

The random effects model is defined as:

$$GVA_{it} = \alpha_i + \beta X_{it} + u_{it}, \quad i = 1 \ldots.., N; \; t = 1, \ldots., T$$

In the random effects model, the α_i are treated as random variables rather than fixed constants. The α_i are assumed to be independent of the errors u_{it}, i.e., $\alpha_i \sim N(0, \sigma^2_\alpha)$ and $u_{it} \sim N(0, \sigma^2_u)$. The GVA_{it}, β, X_{it} are defined as prior. Since α_i are random, the errors now are $w_{it} = \alpha_i + uit$[7]. The presence of α_i produces a correlation among the errors of the same cross-section unit, though the errors from the different cross-section units are independent. In random-effects (error component) models when the variances of the individual-specific effect and error term are unknown, generalised least squares method (GLS) is the standard way for estimation of parameters (Baltagi, 2005). Finally, to select an appropriate model from fixed effects and random effects model, the study employed Hausman test. The null hypothesis indicates that the individual effects are uncorrelated with the regressors. This shows that the estimations of the fixed effects panel model are not statistically different from the estimate of the panel model with random effects. The null hypothesis is not rejected, so it is sensible to conclude that the individual effects are not correlated with exploratory variables in the model.

IV. Empirical Results and Discussion

Since, we make use of panel time series data; the unit root test has applied to ascertain the stationarity of the data series. A variety of procedures for the analysis of unit roots in a panel context have

[7] The composite error term w_{it} consists of two components, α_i, which is the cross-section, or individual-specific, error component, and u_{it}, which is the combined time series and cross-section error component. The term error components model derives its name because of the composite error term w_{it} which consists of two (or more) error components.

been developed.[8] Here we make use of IPS test developed by Im, Pesaran and Shin (2003). IPS, using the likelihood framework, suggested a new more flexible and computationally simple unit root testing procedure for panels (which is referred as t-bar statistic), that allows for simultaneous stationary and non-stationary series (Barbieri, Laura, 2006). The IPS is based on averaging individual Dickey-Fuller unit root tests computed for each cross-section unit in the panel when the error term u_{it} of the model is serially correlated, possibly with different serial correlation patterns across cross-sectional units when T and N are sufficiently large. The IPS test results presented in Table 6.2 in appendix show that except GVA and share all other variables are non-stationary, and they are stationary at first difference, except financial integration (FI) hence we have taken respective difference of all the variables for estimation.

After stationary tests, the parameters are estimated by using panel data models, to distinguish between the two models the Hausman statistic is used to test the null hypothesis that the regressors and individual effects are not correlated. Failure to reject the null hypothesis implies that the random effects model will be preferred. If the null hypothesis is rejected, the fixed effects model is held appropriate. The Hausman test statistic is significant in all the three models and hence the null hypothesis is rejected, which indicates that industry specific effects are correlated with the regressors. This suggests that the fixed effects model is appropriate, and consistent. Since the fixed effects model is the appropriate one, interpretation of the results will be focused on fixed effects model only. Table 6.2 presents the results of all the three models where in column (a) shows the first order effects of financial integration on industries growth, irrespective of their characteristics. In the model the dependent variable is the growth rate of real value added (GVA), and the model majorly focuses on

---

[8] There are different types of panel unit root tests. One of the first unit root tests to be developed for panel data is that of Levin, Lin and Chu (2002) and the second is that of Hadri (2000). Both test assume that the autoregressive parameters are common across cross-section units, while Levin, Lin and Chu (2002) uses a null hypothesis of a unit root, while that of Hadri (2000) uses a null of no unit root. Unlike Levin, Lin and Chu test Hadri test is applicable to small–T, large–N panels. A third test is referred to as the IPS test developed by Im, Pesaran and Shin (2003). In this test the null hypothesis is that of a unit root, where this test is applicable to sufficiently large T and N.

the coefficient of the financial integration variable (FI) and its sign and significance. The variable share is positive and significant at one per cent level in all three

Table 6.1: Estimation Results of Panel Models [Random Effects Model]
Dependent Variable: *Growth of Value Added (GVA)*

Regressors/Model	*Model 1*	*Model 2*	*Model 3*
	A	*B*	*C*
C	19.00231 (2.60558) (0.0000)	20.88714 (2.404586) (0.0000)	20.58046 (2.319882) (0.0000)
SHARE	0.043781 (0.267214) (0.8700)	-0.027844 (0.248898) (0.9110)	-0.023044 (0.240027) (0.9236)
FI	3.482567 (3.367425) (0.3021)	--	---
EXFI	--	-8.992357 (2.185647) (0.0001*)	5.701371 (3.912584) (0.1463)
EXFD	--	--	9.093315 (2.039957) (0.0000*)
Hausman Test	10.150824 (0.0062*)	11.465283 (0.0032*)	11.380513 (0.0098*)
R^2	0.004	0.062	0.131
DW	2.25	2.14	2.20
No. of Observations	240	255	255

Table 6.2: Estimation Results of Panel Models [Fixed Effects Model]
Dependent Variable: *Growth of Value Added (GVA)*

Regressors/Model	*Model 1*	*Model 2*	*Model 3*
	A	*B*	*C*
C	0.598046 (5.355298) (0.9112)	3.824016 (4.966596) (0.4421)	2.018917 (4.536371) (0.6567)
SHARE	2.992676 (0.810794) (0.0003*)	2.658519 (0.754290) (0.0005*)	2.910173 (0.684948) (0.0000*)
FI	0.452479 (2.388921) (0.8499)	--	---
EXFI		-9.496935 (2.179883) (0.0000*)	2.371301 (3.378153) (0.4834)

EXFD		--	8.434318 (1.804768) (0.0000*)
Hausman Test	10.150824 (0.0062*)	11.465283 (0.0032*)	11.380513 (0.0098*)
R^2	0.076	0.152	0.225
DW	2.12	2.05	2.16
No. of Observations	240	255	255

* Significant at 1 per cent, **Significant at 5 per cent and *** Significant at 10 per cent.

Models. The coefficient of the indicator of financial integration (FI) is positive, though not statistically significant. The result suggests that, controlling for other variables, the integration of financial systems promotes growth of all industries. To provide an indication of the economic significance of financial integrational effect, the values of the financial integration (defacto) measure, in first phase (1990-95) has increased from 0.008617 to 0.590746, while in second phase (1996-2000), it has increased from 0.727897 to 0.839414, and final phase (2001-07), the financial integration measure increased at rapid pace from 0.994976 to 4.006385. The economy wide effect of financial integration on growth is thus significantly [though not statistically] positive. To assess the sector specific effects of financial integration the model (1) is augmented by including the interaction term between the industry's external financial dependence and financial integration. If financial openness facilitates credit access, this effect will be specifically noticeable in respective industrial sectors, which are highly dependent on external finance. The presence of industry specific effect is justified with a positive and significant coefficient of the interaction term. The coefficient of the interaction term is negative and significant, suggesting that besides a positive effect on growth of all industries, financial integration has negative or marginal influence on sectors which are dependent on external finance. However, when the financial development interaction term is added to the regression model, the coefficient of the interaction term (external financial dependence and financial integration) turns positive. One of the interpretations of this result is that the integration of financial systems may have improved growth also by increasing the level of domestic financial development.

Further to test the influence of financial integration and domestic financial development the model (2) is augmented by adding an interaction term, the industry's dependence on external finance and a measure of domestic financial development, to evidence any direct transmission channel emanating from financial integration to growth of domestic financial sector. The results presented in column (3) of Table 6.3, shows that the financial integration and financial development variable coefficient is positive and statistically significant. The results highlight that more financial integration coupled with financial development seem to have direct effect on industry growth in real value added the finding consistent with the results of similar empirical works Vanassche, Ellen (2004), Edison *et al* (2002).

VI. Conclusion

The association between international financial integration [IFI] and economic growth continues to be most debated issue. The current study deals with this debate by focusing on the dynamics of industrial growth and financial integration in India. The study assesses this link for a panel of selected major fifteen manufacturing industries (classified under NIC 2004) for the period from 1990 to 2007. Examining the economy wide effects, industry's external financial dependence, domestic financial development and there interaction with financial integration impacting on industrial growth, is the major contribution of the study to previous literature in respect to India. The result suggests that, controlling for other variables, the integration of financial systems promotes growth of all industries regardless of their characteristics. Specifically focusing industry's external financial dependence and interaction with financial integration, the study finds that besides a positive effect on growth of all industries, financial integration has negative or marginal influence on sectors which are dependent on external finance. However, when the financial development interaction term is added to the regression model, the coefficient of the interaction term turns positive. Finally, the results of the third model indicates that the financial integration and financial development [interaction] variable coefficient is positive and statistically significant. The results highlights that more financial integration coupled with financial development seem to have direct effect on industrial growth.

Appendix

Table 6.A: List of Manufacturing Industries based on NIC selected for the study

NIC Code	*Industry*	*Study Code*
NIC 15	Manufacture of Food Products and Beverages	MFB
NIC 17	Manufacture of Textiles	MTX
NIC 19	Manufacture of Tanning and Dressing of Leather	MTDL
NIC 21	Manufacture of Paper and Paper Products	MPPP
NIC 23	Manufacture of Coke, Refined Petroleum Products	MCRPP
NIC 24	Manufacture of Chemicals and Chemical Products	MCCP
NIC 25	Manufacture of Rubber and Plastic Products	MRPP
NIC 26	Manufacture of Other Non-metallic Mineral Products	MONMP
NIC 27	Manufacture of Basic Metals	MBM
NIC 2	Manufacture of Fabricated Metal Products	MFMP
NIC 29	Manufacture of Machinery and Equipment	MME
NIC 31	Manufacture of Electrical Machinery and Apparatus	MEMP
NIC 32	Manufacture of Radio, Television and Communication Equipments	MRTCE
NIC 34	Manufacture of Motor Vehicles Trailers and Semi-trailers	MMVT
NIC 35	Manufacture of Transport Equipment	MTE

Table 6.B: Results of Panel Unit Root Test (Im, Pesaran and Shin)

	Individual Intercept		*Individual Intercept*		*Individual Intercept and Trend*		*Individual Intercept and Trend*	
Variable	*Level*		*Difference*		*Level*		*Difference*	
	Statistic	*Probability*	*Statistic*	*Probability*	*Statistic*	*Probability*	*Statistic*	*Probability*
GVA	-7.26552	0.0000*			-5.34971	0.0000*		
Share	-1.53699	0.0621			-1.36336	0.0864		
FI†	15.0930	1.0000	-4.99446	0.0000*	13.2935	1.0000	-4.12673	0.0000*
ExFI	2.68320	0.9964	-4.37732	0.0000*	2.37529	0.9912	-2.38646	0.0085
ExFD	-0.29873	0.3826	-4.06131	0.0000*	2.71886	0.9967	-2.11103	0.0174*

† Second difference, * Significant at 1 per cent, **Significant at 5 per cent and *** Significant at 10 per cent.

Table 6.C: Descriptive Statistics of the Variables

Variable	*Obs*	*Mean*	*Std.Dev*	*Min*	*Max*
GGVA	270	21.44593	30.0417	-53.82011	178.5832
SHARE	270	6.365051	7.325837	0.1966196	32.98037
EXFI	270	0. 4545803	0.9808274	-6.249511	3.316173
EXFD	270	1.121589	1.890165	-13.32037	5.711501
FDEFACTO	270	0.9976067	0.9546134	.0086169	4.006385

References:

Abiad and Mody (2005), *Financial Reform: What Shakes It? What Shapes It?*, The American Economic Review, 95 (1), 66-88.

Ahluwalia, I. Judge (1985), *Industrial Growth in India- Stagnation since Mid-Sixties,* Oxford University Press, Delhi.

Ahluwalia, I. Judge (1991), *Productivity and Growth in Indian Manufacturing,* Oxford University Press, Delhi.

Baltagi (2005), *Econometric Analysis of Panel Data,* 3rd Edition, John Wiley & Sons, England.

Barryeichen Green, Rachita and Ugo Panizza (2009),*Capital Account Liberalisation, Financial Development and Industrial Growth: A Synthetic View.*

Barbieri, Laura (2006), *Panel Unit Root Tests: A Review.*

Beck (2003), *Financial Dependence and International Trade, Review of International Economics,* 11, 296-315.

Bekaert, Harvey and Lundblad (2005), *Does Financial Liberalisation Spur Growth?,* Journal of Financial Economics, 77, 3-56.

Buch, C. M., J. Dopke and C. Pierdzioch, (2002), *Financial Openness and Business Cycle Volatility,* Working Paper, KielInstitute for World Economics.

Caprio G.A. and Summers (1993), *Finance and its Reform, Beyond Laissez-Faire,* Working Paper No. 1171, World Bank.

Chandrasekhar, C. P. (1988), *Aspects of Growth and Structural Change in Indian Industry,* Economic and Political Weekly, 23.

Chinn and Ito (2002), *Capital account liberalisation, institutions and financial development: Cross country evidence,* Working Paper 8967, National Bureau of Economic Research.

Cournot (1927), *Researches into the Mathematical Principles of the Theory of Wealth,* trans. by Nathaniel T. Bacon, New York: Macmillan.

Edison, H., Levine, R., Ricci, L. and Slok, T. (2002), *International Financial Integration and Economic Growth,* Journal of International Money and Finance, 21, 749-776.

Edison and Warnock (2001), *A Simple Measure of the Intensity of Capital Controls,* International Finance Discussion Papers, Number 708, Board of Governors of the Federal Reserve System.

Feldstein and Horioka (1980), *Domestic Savings and International Capital flows,* Working Paper 310, National Bureau of Economic Research.

Grilli and Milesi-Ferretti (1995), *Economic Effects and Structural Determinants of Capital Controls,* IMF Staff Papers - International Monetary Fund, Vol. 42, No. 3, pp. 517-551.

Gupta, N and Kathy Yaun (2005),*On the Growth Effects of Liberalisation,* unpublished manuscript, Indiana University.

Im, Pesaran and Shin (2003), *On the Panel Unit Root Testing Using Non-linear Instrumental Variables,* Working paper, https//www.econ.cam.ac.uk/faculty/pesaran/

Laeven,L (2003), *Does Financial Liberalisation reduce financing constraint?,* Financial Management, 32 (1), 5-34.

Lane and Milesi-Ferretti (2003), *International Financial Integration,* IIIS Discussion Paper No. 03.

Lane and Milesi-Ferretti (2006), *The External Wealth of Nations Mark II: Revised and Extended Estimates of Foreign Assets and Liabilities,* 1970–2004, IMF Working Paper, World Bank.

Levchenko, A, Romain Rancièreand Mathias Thoenig (2009), *Growth and Risk at the Industry level: The Real Effects of Financial Liberalisation,* Journal of Development Economics, 89, 210-222.

Levine, R (2001), *International Financial Liberalisation and Economic Growth*, Review of International Economics, 9(4), 688-702.

Manova K (2008), *Credit Constraints, Equity Market Liberalisation and International Trade,* Journal of International Economics, 76, 33-47.

Marshall, Alfred (1930), *Principles of Economics: An Introductory Volume,* 8th ed. London: Macmillan.

Miniane, J (2004), *A New Set of Measures on Capital Account Restrictions,*IMF Staff Papers, International Monetary Fund, 51 (2), 276-308.

Mody and Murshid (2002), *Growing Up With Capital Flows,* IMF Working Paper, World Bank.

Narasimhan Committee (1991), *Report of the Committee on the Financial System.*

Oura, H (2008), *Financial Development and Growth in India: A Growing Tiger in a Cage,* IMF Working Paper WP/08/79.

Ozdemir, D and C, Erbil (2008), *Does Financial Liberalisation Trigger long run Economic growth? Evidence from Turkey and other Recent EU members.*

Prasad, E, K. Rogoff, S-J Wei and M. A. Kose (2003), *The Effect of Financial Globalization on Developing Countries: Some Empirical Evidence, IMF* Occasional Paper, Washington D.C. International Monetary Fund.

Prasad, Raghuramand Zingales (2007), *Foreign Capital and Economic Growth,* NBER, Working Paper No. 13619.

Quinn (1997), *The Correlates of change in International Financial Regulation,* American Political Science Review, 91 (3), 531-551.

Rajan and Zingales (1998), *Financial Dependence and Growth,* American Economic Review, 88, 559-586.

Schmukler,S and Vesperoni (2001), *Firms financing choices in Bank-Based and Market Based Economies,* ed Financial Structure and Economic Growth: A Cross Country Comparison of Banks, Markets and Development. The MIT Press, London.

Sinha, Chandan and Pradhan C Narayan, (2008), *India's financial openness and integration with Southeast Asian countries: an analytical perspective,* BIS Papers No. 42.

Tarapore, S.S. (1997), An Assessment of Indian Economic Reforms, Prajnam, 25.

Vanassche, E (2004), *The Impact of International Financial Integration on Industry Growth,* Katholieke Universiteit Leuven, Belgium.

Vlachos, J and Daniel Waldenstorm (2002), *International Financial Liberalisation and Industry Growth,* Working Paper No. 586, IUI, The Research Institute of Industrial Economics, Sweden.

7

Voluntary Retirement Scheme in Public Sector Banks: Critical Issues

Professor D.S. Leelavathi

Introduction

Globalisation which aims at integrating Indian economy with the rest of the world has called for greater efficiency, competitiveness and flexibility in various economic activities. As a consequence of this, a series of changes in the form of reforms have been introduced in various sectors of the economy, including the banking sector. Apart from introducing reforms in the banking sector as suggested by Narasimham committee, though of late, it has also embarked upon the employee restructuring mechanisms of which Voluntary Retirement Scheme (VRS) is the most widely debated as well as practiced unlike in other sectors. VRS is the most human technique to provide overall reduction in the existing strength of employees. It is a common method for trimming the excess employees. It is a generous tax-free severance payment to persuade the employees to voluntarily retire from the company.

The main objective of VRS is to 'right size' or 'smart size' and 'down size' the work force so as to reduce labour cost (wage constitutes to nearly 12 per cent to 13 per cent of total expenses of bank) and increase competitiveness. Downsizing in a narrow sense can be defined as 'planned elimination of positions or jobs. Economists perceive VRS as a measure to shed the excess work force whose marginal productivity is '0' or 'negative'. Technical modernisation demands replacement of redundant labour with capital. VRS is not an alien to the banking sector because such schemes have been introduced in the industry sector, particularly the public sector industries since 90's under exit policy. The intensions have been maintaining cost effectiveness in a competitive world on the one hand and on the other, creating labour market flexibility.

Employers refer to VRS as golden handshake while employees brand this as 'Voluntary Retirement Scheme with iron handshake'. In India, Government employs more than 70 per cent of the organised work force and now it is using all its channels to reduce work force without antagonising the trade unions. It is envisaged in the New Economic Policy that VRS can provide minimum sustenance and security to the retired individual and his family. In the public sector all those who have attained 50 years of age and 20 years of service, and in private sector, 40 years of age and 10 years of service are eligible for opting VRS.

The first budget of the new millennium has boldly stated that the government is very serious about downsizing its own size and hence several posts and cadres in bureaucracy have been abolished. The Prime Minister has stated that each government department would downsize by 10 per cent by 2004 and would adopt VRS which is similar to the ones being offered by the public sector units. The banking sector is the most dominant segment of the financial sector accounting for about two-third of the assets of the organised financial sector.

The banking sector reforms along with Basel norms 1, 2 and 3 meant for streamlining the global financial system have brought in revolutionary changes in the banking industry. Coupled with IT resolution and e-banking, the diversification of banking sector services and products have initiated massive labour restructuring, focusing on VRS and retraining. Wage bill in PSBs constitutes the second largest expense for the bank apart from interest paid on borrowings. Competition between public and private sector banks, foreign and domestic banks have resulted in a significant reduction in transaction cost, higher profitability and increased business per employee. In 2011, the public sector banks in India opted for VRS to downsize their work force on account of following general reasons:

- To face business recession.
- Due to intense competition.
- Joint ventures and foreign collaborations.
- Takeovers and mergers.
- Obsolescence of product / Technology.
- Changes in technology, production process, innovation, new product line and
- Realignment of business due to market conditions.

Twenty seven public sector banks (PSBs) and nineteen Nationalised banks have taken the decision to rationalise/ restructure their work force through VRS. The decision is based on the recommendations of the committee compromising representatives of Indian Bank Association (IBA), PSBs and the Ministry of Finance. The committee recommended a series of measures to improve the efficiency of banks including VRS and three years sabbatical and VRS. This will help them improve their cost-income ratio, re-profile their aging work force and give a fillip to computerisation. Accordingly, those who have completed 40 years of age and 15 years of service can opt for VRS. The government has approved these measures. Since then several PSBs have introduced VRS. The total staff of the 27 PSB is nearly 8.83 Lakh and is expected that there will be reduction of about 15 per cent in staff strength through VRS. Both Punjab National Bank and Syndicate Bank would be extending VRS to about 6,000 workers in each bank. Similarly, close to 14 per cent of Bank of India staff has opted for an early exit. If job security is what once drove people towards nationalised banks, it is now the lure of fat settlement amount and future risks that are making them to accept VRS. However, non-eligibility criteria includes specialist officers/ employees under service bonds/ special arrangements, employees under pending disciplinary action and any other as may be specified by the bank.

Steps taken before introducing VRS

- An undertaking from the employee availing VRS not to seek reemployment in the organisation or any other institution where the bank has a major shareholding.
- Banning re-employment in all Public sector banks.
- Freezing vacancies created by employees availing VRS.
- Sanctioned VRS and any new recruitment should only be in accordance with manpower plan.
- Before introducing VRS, banks were required to complete their manpower planning and identify the number of officers/staff who could be considered redundant.

How foreign banks do it?

Retreat, Downsizing and right sizing are old hat for India's legion of foreign banks. Most of them have been doing it for years for one of several reasons – Mergers, downsizing or restructuring economy measures to stay fit and competitive. CITI bank has introduced VRS in the past when it found that its older managers stagnating in the corner and younger ones had no ways to rise up in the hierarchy. Offering VRS to older lot is a good way to clean people blocking the top slots while also lowering the cost structure. These kinds of exit typically offer payback in two years or less from the savings.

Following the footsteps of national trend, even in Karnataka, nearly 10,000 bank employees, officers and clerical staff are going home with attractive 'Golden handshake' package. For example, Vijaya Bank, one of the five major banks of the state, accounted for a major share in VRS with 2,782 personnel putting in their papers out of which only 100 papers were rejected. The bank has decided to reduce its work force by 17 per cent. Similarly, 15 per cent of the work force of the Karnataka Bank with its 2,400 branches has opted for voluntary retirement. Dena Bank topped the national list with its 27 per cent of its work force opting out whereas in Syndicate Bank it was 21 per cent and in Andhra Bank 20 per cent of officers and nine per cent of clerical staff opted for VRS.

Apart from the general reasons, most specific reasons for introducing VRS are as follows:

- Poor performance and low level of competitive efficiency in PSBs.
- Fear of reducing the retirement age to 58.
- Surplus and redundant labour in PSBs.
- Computerisation of banks.
- Rationalisation of branches.
- Abolition of Central Banking Recruitment Board.
- Attractive opportunities for talented workers.
- To settle the immediate financial commitment of the workers.
- In the hierarchical structure of banking work force, an employee at the lowest level have to go through at least 10 promotions to reach the top. This complex procedure may be one of the causes for VRS.
- Also, while promoting the employees, usually seniority counts and not the performance.

Bank of India chairman, K.V. Krishnamurthy says there was one urgent need to cut costs in the PSBs. In India, the percent of the total cost of staff in the PSBs accounts for 60 to 70 per cent against the global standard of 30 per cent. The productivity is low and there is not enough work for everybody. In fact, three years sabbatical without pay was also advocated. The State Bank has appointed the Nationalised institution of Bank management to work out the best staffing patterns.

All the above reasons could have formed a strong rationale for bank employees for opting VRS. Further, VRS in the banking sector would lead to certain immediate changes which are more positive in nature, for example:

1. Increase in productivity and efficiency.
2. The average age profile of employees will reduce.
3. Young and enthusiastic work force dominates the employee structure.
4. Gives an opportunity to introduce new technology/ computerisation.
5. The staff - cost will come down.
6. Promotional opportunities will go up.
7. VRS will give banks an opportunity to revise their HRD policies.
8. The tier structure could be rationalised.

However, VRS needs to be very carefully designed in such a way that it would not create a more disastrous results rather than benefits. It is in this background that the paper intends to explore certain critical issues in VRS and those issues need to be taken care of while planning / designing VRS in PSBs.

VRS package included two months' salary for each completed year of service or the salary for the remaining number of months of service left, whichever is lesser. Pension includes commuted value of pension, banks contribution towards provident fund as the case maybe. Similarly, gratuity as per gratuity act/ service act, Provident fund is settled as per bank rules and leave encashment as per accumulated leaves.

II. Critical Issues of VRS in PSBs

1. Financing of VRS in PSBs

In the industry sector, the National Renewal Fund (1992) was the main source of financial assistance for settling VRS amount due to workers. However, in case of PSBs, there is a lot of confusion. The ministry of finance has rejected banks proposals to fund VRS through external commercial borrowing (ECBs). The main reason being, the government doesn't want to externalise its liabilities where it is unnecessary. Profit making banks have been permitted to fund VRS through any means, including internal accruals, public issues, private issues, private placements and market borrowings. However, when it comes to ECBs as means of funding downsizing plans, the finance minister has taken the position that banks should consider other rupee alternatives.

The weak financial position of some banks will not enable them to settle VRS amount completely. Under such circumstance, they provide 50 per cent cash and the remaining in the form of worker bonds which carries an interest rate of 10 per cent. Similar practice is also found in the public sector industries.

2. Capital adequacy ratio

The banks offering VRS are sensitive to the fact that it would affect their Capital Adequacy Ratio (CAR). In fact, the Indian Bank Association has requested that VRS should be excluded while calculating **CAR**. The VRS package approved by the finance minister gives banks an option either to show the expenses incurred on accounts of VRS over the next five years or debit in one shot. In both the cases, the net worth will fall, thereby affecting CAR of the bank. CAR compromises of tier 1 and tier 2 capitals and net worth is part of banks tier 1 capital.

However, the experts feel that any exception made on calculating CAR would mean reverting from the RBI decision to move towards international account practice. According to a recent study of the IBA, the average CAR of all PSBs stand at 10.96 per cent in the year 1999 – 2000, marginally above the nine per cent mandatory requirement under RBI norms.

3. Employees opting for VRS to lose out on pension.

The bank employees have learnt that pension will be lesser under the special VRS – VRS – 2000 designed by the government as against the Pension Act that they would be entitled to under standard VRS that has been in force in all PSBs. In terms of notification issued by IBA, pension will be calculated on the basis of actual years of service only, unlike old pension scheme which provided for adding five years of notional service to the years of actual service rendered. This notification will affect all those employees between 20 – 30 years of age. Affected employees feel somewhat cornered since under the scheme, they cannot withdraw their VRS application once they submit the forms. They complain that the terms were changed after submission of application whole bank officials assert that the notification is the nature of a clarification since this is a new scheme.

4. Re-engineering of branch rationalisation

In case of downsizing of labour in PSBs, invariably bank branching needs utmost importance. In fact, this has been a major reason for surplus work force in PSBs. However, the logic behind branch expansion is quite obvious. But, gradually, the cost of operation became heavier than the benefit and proved uneconomical and the work competition was totally marginalised. In the present context of labour restructuring in the PSBs, branch rationalisation could be re-approached from two perspectives, namely structural and macro. At the structural level, they need to analyse which branch in which region need to exist, which one to consolidate and where to grow? At the Micro level, they need to analyse where and how many outlets should be located in certain city or area and thus need to build distribution density.

5. Controversy regarding treating the VRS expenditure as capital or revenue expenditure

Till recently VRS expenditure was tested as revenue expenditure and charged against Profit and loss account of assesses. Consequently, the taxable net profit would come down sharply and thus assesses had to pay lower tax on profit arrived after VRS payments. However, in a circular dated January 23, 2001 by Central Board of Direct Taxes, VRS expenditure is now treated as capital expenditure for taxation purpose. This means such expenditure will be disallowed for the purpose of computing taxable income. The reasoning of the income tax authorities is that, since expenditure is expected to yield benefits in the long run, there is no need for allowing a deduction. This move is most likely to hit PSBs and some pharma companies which have resorted to VRS.

However, in case of personal income tax, according to the latest condition, an amount of up to ₹ 5 lakh will be exempted from tax calculations if received under VRS or Voluntary separation scheme. Nowadays, asset management companies like Sundaram finance, K.P. Mutual Fund, Prudential ICICI and a few others have started a wing to assist those who have opted VRS.

6. The post-VRS adjustments in banks

The real trouble for the banks begins after VRS programme is over. The balance between generalists and specialists will be disturbed and human resource management becomes a nightmare. International banks world over, regardless of their size are shrinking in numbers through mergers and acquisitions. Millions of staff across the ranks was laid off under cost cutting compulsions. Merger scenario is one of compatibility and integration among the resultant staff, which demands a good lot of homework.

In India, top management personnel in banks usually opt for VRS. This would upset the chain of command and qualifying service criteria for promotion that needs to be worked out. The second fall out would be, the unpredictability of who is going and who is staying back and at what level. In our banking system 90 per cent of work force constitutes generalists and 10 per cent specialists in credit, foreign exchange personnel and IT or accounting experts. VRS has to strike balance between these two. Of those seeking VRS in PSBs, nearly 30 to 35 per cent of them the banks want to retain. Thus, rationing of VRS becomes a very difficult exercise. However, in India, such issues have scarcely been thought of and much less debated. Some banks are actually facing the acute shortage of staff. There would be around 90,000 bank employees out of payrolls in the first shot aggressive VRS push. As it has been rightly pointed out at bank Economists conference in that VRS has boomeranged on the PSBs on account of not being planned properly.

7. Implications for women workers

A significant promotion of women work force in the organised sector is found concentrated either in teaching or in banking sector. However, VRS in the PSBs has far reaching implications especially for women employees. Among those who are accepting VRS, women workers constitute a significant proportion. The survey report of the NSS reveals that with the standard of living rising during the post-reforms period, some Indians (especially women) seem to be finding affordable to stay out of labour market.

In the PSBs women workers opting for VRS feel that it provides an excellent opportunity to pursue their hobbies and interests, care for their familiar without worrying about income repercussions. This also has contributed to some extent for declining female work participation rate in the organised sector and once again when they enter the invisible household service, the national income accounting becomes still more partial and incomplete. Also, the exit of women workers from the organised labour market adversely affects their empowerment and decision-making capabilities.

However, when some of the women employees were interviewed by the Times of India group, their response was wide and varied. Some of them stated that they can start the service industries, where as some expressed their willingness to support their husbands and children in their pursuit, some wished to join medical transcription, information technology, start small industries etc. But all these adventures are also associated with a series of risks and uncertainties where in ex-women workers may have to face harsh realities. At the same time, all of them agreed that employment prospects in PSBs are very weak and unpromising and as such VRS is really a golden opportunity. All said and done, unless one is extremely well equipped and prepared, it is not advisable to venture into areas which need major investment in infrastructure.

8. Counselling of post-VRS investment by the workers

When workers get huge amount of money varying from 5 to 15 lakhs after VRS, naturally the problem of managing the money, at individual level do arise. Productive and careful investment and management of money is rather difficult at least for some of them. Although bank people have a better knowledge of how to make their money grow, some of them are bound to lose their balance either knowingly or unknowingly and therefore a proper guidance and counselling regarding the effective management of VRS amount is very much appreciated. Already some banks and mutual funds are on their way offering such survives to their clients.

Similarly, if we look at the macro perspective, when more and more workers accept VRS, the understanding is more liquidity is created which in turn has its own effects not only on money circulation but also on the stock market. When people have more disposable income in their hand, how do they invest and where do they invest etc.., receives utmost importance. The stock market analysts believe that PSB staff opting for VRS is expected to invest in mutual funds and stock markets. The stock brokers have to invest around 15 to 25 per cent of the VRS amount to enter the stock market. At present IDBI is preparing schemes for such category of investors and some mutual funds too are following it.

9. Resolving Door syndrome

Another problem in VRS in PSBs is rehiring or resolving syndrome where the employee awaiting VRS is rehired by the same organisation within the same sector. If proper HR assessment and skill gaps are not undertaken before designing VRS, the risk of re-hiring continues. The risk of rehiring is higher in an organisation that is being restructured as opposed to being closed. Therefore, it is essential to undertake detailed Human Resource audit before designing the VRS schemes and careful considerations need to be given to minimise rehiring risks in an organisation that is being restructured. Some of the measures taken in India include banning of reemployment in the same sector/agencies, undertaking from employees not to seek reemployment, freezing vacancies created by staff seeking VRS.

10. Erosion of intellectual capital

VRS is PSB has led to almost intellectual bankruptcy since most of the experienced managers have opted for VRS and who were also confident of getting a still better job with their rich experience. Once overstaffed PSBs are now facing a severe shortage of latent with experience states AK Khondelwal report in 2012. The RBI has already termed 2010-20 as the decade of retirement for PSBs as estimated 3.4 lakh employees in all categories will retire by 2020. McKinney report (2013) on the Indian banking structure say 87 per cent of general managers will be superannuated in three years from now (2016 - 2017) leaving a huge gap of those responsibly for implementing the Policy. On top of that, between 60 to 90 per cent DGMs at PSBs are set to retire by the end of the same fiscal. The bank bench marking survey says, by 2020 this number could be somewhere between 93 to 100 per cent. Nachiket Mor committee (2014) recommends universal banking and financial inclusion by 2020, however, the coverage is not even 50 per cent. Can this be achieved in the shortage of DGMs expertise in the field?

III. Changing For Better

Despite significant challenges created on account of the above discussed issues, the PSBs have been able to face these challenges on account of several reforms introduced based on the recommendations of the expert committees. Although in the beginning VRS was a bad term, now the time has come where the workers claim that VRS is their birth right and management has no right to take away the same. In fact, there are strikes against the non-implementation of VRS. Since VRS implementation several PSBs have improved their competitive efficiency and this healthy environment has even created quite a good number of job opportunities. This goes in tune with the argument that in the long run more jobs would be created, provided restructuring takes place in the banking sector.

At present, the PSBs employ more than Seven lakh people. Of these, large number of people will be retiring in next five to six years. To fill this gap and to take up the growing business, the banks are on a recruitment spree as can be seen in media and vacancy announcements. Only this year about 40,000 vacancies- both clerical and officers- have been created in PSBs due to retirements, resignations and VRS. Tremendous expansion of business has contributed to the expansion of employment opportunities. They have started recruiting from the campuses, taking MBAs from different discipline, agriculture graduates, chartered accountants etc. There are well defined progression path in each PSB. The expansion mode in which PSBs in India are has been creating number of opportunities for young people to choose banking as their career. In brief, labour downsizing, which has become a major component of the restructuring package of the PSBs has started yielding better results.

IV. CONCLUSION

It is true that VRS is one of the best options of corporate India to get rid of excess labour force. It is also in tune with what is going on in India and rest of the world. However, brutal retrenchment can ruin the organisations reputation and destroy the chances of retaining talent, besides demotivating and demoralising the work force. The exit policy should be based on consistency compassion and cooperation. For this purpose the schemes need to be strategically designed in such a way that it strikes a balance between both the interest of those who opt for it as well as the requirement of the bank. A few studies have shown that many organisations/ companies that have trimmed work force not only have failed to see a rebound in earnings but also found their ability to compete has eroded further. This is the obvious reason why usually highly skilled personnel with lot of market demand prefer to opt for VRS. Thus, those workers whom the bank really wants to get rid of remain undisturbed. Hence, if the VRS is not carefully designed, the problem becomes much worse. Careful VRS plan requires both short-term as well as long-term vision and effective measures to implement the same.

References

- www.banknetindia.com/banking/vrs.htm
- RBI- Annual Report https://org.in/scripts/notificationuser
- www.business-standard.com/why the bank VRS worked/or did it
- https://www.scribd.com/doc/VRS in PSBs
- www.thehindu.com/2011-02 - VRS in banks-how many imponderables?
- Times of India.indiatimes.com>business-now VRS is a must for bank employers. March 29, 2002.
- Indiatoday.intoday.in>Archives>Economy Feb 25 2001 -VRS for PSU bank staff gets good response.
- How to manage employee exit? Business Standard.22/03/2004.
- Mckinsey Report (2013) on 'The Indian Banking Sector'.
- Nachiket Mor Committee Report' – 2014 on universal banking and financial inclusion.
- World Bank Report: Review of VRS in South Asian Banks.
- Raj Kapil and Uma Kapil (ed): Decade of Economic Reforms in India: past, present and future, Academic Foundation, 2002, New Delhi.

8

Financial Analysis of Public, Private and Foreign Banks in India

Seyed Mehdi Pourkiaei and
Prof. S. Mahendra Kumar

I. Introduction

Banks play a stellar role in the development of the nation with its high social content and commitment. These act as a development agency and are the sources of hopes and aspirations of the masses. The structure of the banking system is determined by two basic factors – Economic and Legal. Banks are key financial intermediaries or institutions that serve as "middle men" in the transfer of fund from servers to those who invest in real assets as house, equipment and factories. In performing this function financial intermediaries improve the well-being of both saver and investor. By improving economic efficiency they raise living standard of the society. The banking sector is considered to be an important source of financing for most businesses. They play a very important role in the effort to attain stable prices, high level of employment and sound economic growth. They make funds available to meet the needs of individuals, businesses and the government. In doing this, they facilitate the flow of goods and services and the activities of governments. The commercial Banking system provides a large portion of the medium of exchange of a given country, and is the primary instrument through which Monitory Policy is conducted, through their deposit mobilisation and lending operations. Commercial banks make the productive utilisation of ideal funds, thus assists the society to produce wealth. Commercial Banks are the institutions specifically designed to further the capital formation process through the attraction of deposits and extension of credit.

II. History of Banking in india Prior to 1969

The Indian banking system has undergone major changes in the past fifty years. Structural, financial and geographical changes have taken place in Indian banking system. The banking activity has now reached the common people. Looking back the history of Indian banking system, it is observed that Indigenous Bank was an old form of Indian banking system.

Money lending operation in India was found in the Vedic period i.e. 2000 to 1400 B.C. In the Buddhist period, ample evidence of the existence of *sresthis* or bankers has been obtained. They were mainly engaged in lending money to traders, to merchant adventures for going to foreign countries, to explorers to extract valuable materials from forests and to kings for meeting financial difficulties due to war or other reasons against the pledge of movable or immovable property or personal surety.

From the writings of few Muslim historians, European travellers, State records and the Ain-i-Akbari it is reported that under the early Muslim and Mughal rulers in India indigenous bankers played a major part in lending money, financing internal and foreign trade and giving financial assistance to rulers during periods of stress. The indigenous bankers were usually known as kothiwals, sarafs, shroffs, seths, chettis or mahajans. They varied in their size from petty money-lenders to substantial shroffs who carried on large and specialised business. They used to grant loans against all kinds of securities such as gold, jewellery, land, promissory notes, hundies etc. they also lent against personal credit of the borrowers. The East India Company established banks on Western lines in India. As a result, banks and government treasuries were established. Indigenous bankers with reduced resources with a smaller scale of business could not compete with the commercial banks. In spite of the progress of the join-stock banks, indigenous bankers still carried on a large amount of banking business throughout India because, area of work of join-stock banks was restricted to metropolitan areas and important commercial centres. But work of indigenous bankers was still concentrated in rural areas.

The first join-stock bank under European management in Kolkata known as the 'Bank of Hindustan' was established in 1770 by Alexander and Co., one of the leading Agency Houses. This was the first bank to issue notes. This bank went into liquidation in 1832 with the fall of the Agency House of Alexander & Co. Thereafter, East India Company established three Presidency Banks in India. 'The Bank of Bengal', the first of the Presidency Banks was established in 1806 as 'The Bank of Calcutta' and received its charter as 'The Bank of Bengal' in 1809. Other two Presidency Banks 'The Bank of Bombay' and 'The Bank of Madras' were established in 1840 and 1843, with a share capital of 50 lakh and 30 lakh respectively. East India Company contributed 3 lakh in each case and obtained the right to appoint some of their directors.

The Imperial Bank of India Act, 1920 was implemented by amalgamating three Presidency Banks into the 'Imperial Bank of India' in 1921. It had right to hold government funds and manage the public debt and not to issue currency. The branches of this bank were performing their functions as clearing houses. It was anticipated that the Imperial Bank should gradually be developed into a full-fledged Central Bank. In fact, it performed certain central banking functions such as banker to government. But after the establishment of Reserve Bank it ceased to function as a central bank. It functioned purely as a commercial bank.

On the basis of the recommendation of the Hilton Young Commission of 1926, the Reserve Bank of India Act was passed in 1934 to establish a Central Bank in the country as a share-holders' bank. Reserve Bank of India commenced its operation on 1st April 1935. It was originally constituted as a private shareholders' bank with a fully paid-up share capital of five crore. In order to bring integration between its policies and those of government it was nationalised on 1.1.1949. Revolutionary changes were found in the Indian banking structure after Second World War. Many banks began to open branches in different places. The banks started investing funds on government securities. But till the time of independence, Indian banking system was not sound even if there were hundreds of small banks under unscrupulous management. In 1949, Banking Regulation Act was passed with a view to restructure commercial banks in India. For the first time, the Act introduced the licensing system for banking business. This Act gave extensive controlling powers to the Reserve Bank of India and the government over the commercial banks. It had laid down rules and regulations for the opening of banks, their branches and minimum capital required for opening a bank etc.

In 1955, the State Bank of India Act was passed. Rural Credit Survey Committee recommended that the government should establish a strong state-owned commercial bank which would undertake rapid expansion of banking facilities in rural areas. The State Bank of India (Subsidiary Banks) Act was passed in September 1959, enabling the State Bank of India to take over eight state-owned or state-associated banks as its subsidiaries. The eight subsidiaries of State Bank of India were as follows: (i) The State Bank of Bikaner, (ii) The State Bank of Jaipur, (iii) The State Bank of Indore, (iv) The State Bank of Mysore, (v) The State Bank of Patiala, (vi) The State Bank of Hyderabad, (vii) The State Bank of Saurashtra and (viii) The State Bank of Travancore.

III. Reforms in Banking Sector in India

Banking Sector reforms were initiated to upgrade the operating standard health and financial soundness of the banks. The Government of India setup the Narasimham Committee in 1991, to examine all aspects relating to structure, organisation and functioning of the Indian banking system the recommendations of the committee aimed at creating at competitive and efficient banking system. Another committee (Khan Committee), was instituted by RBI in December, 1997 to examine the harmonisation of the role and operations of development financial institutions and banks. It submitted its report in 1998. The major recommendations were a gradual move towards universal banking, exploring the possibility of gain full merger as between banks, banks and financial institutions. Then the Verma Committee was established (1998) this committee recommended the need for greater use of IT even in the weak public sector banks, restructuring of weak banks but not merging them with strong banks, VRS for at least 25 per cent of the staff. The Banking Sector reforms aimed at improving the policy frame work, financial health and institutional infrastructure, there two phase of the banking reforms. Narasimham Committee provided the blueprint for the initial reforms in banking sector following the balance of payment crisis in 1991.

IV. REVIEW OF LITERATURE

Bodla B S and Verma Richa (2008-09) have attempted to view the Earning Quality of Indian banks as per CAMEL Model. This paper highlighted the earning quality in terms of operating profit and net profit, fund based and fee based income of the banks. Earning Quality determined the profitability of the banks.

The study covered 88 scheduled commercial banks for the time period 1991-92 to 2005-06. The study period was further divided into three sub-periods 1992-95, 1996-00 and 2001-06. T-test was applied to examine the significance of difference in various parameters between various sub-periods and across various sectors. It was concluded that on the whole the banks operating in India have shown appreciable improvement in their fee-based income. It was found that banks of foreign origin were ranked on the top on the basis of their earning quality. Profitability of Scheduled Commercial Banks was growing continuously due to increasing fee-based income and curtailment of operating expense.

Kalluru Siva Reddy and Sham Bhat K (2009) have investigated the effects of foreign banks entry on the operations of public sector banks in India for the period 1996-2007. Variables employed to mark the intensity of foreign bank's presence that ratio of number of foreign banks to the total number of banks in the country. Net interest margin to total assets, Non-interest income to total assets, profits before tax to total assets, overhead expenses to total assets, non-performing loans to total loans were the variables which measure the income, profitability and costs of public sector banks. The empirical results revealed that foreign bank entry usually increases competition in the banking industry as was evidenced by increasing profitability of banks. It was concluded that foreign bank entry in the Indian banking system adversely affects the operations of PSBs.

Singh Ram Pratap and Chatterjee Biswajit (2009-10) have compared the performance of 40 Indian commercial banks regarding deposit mobilisation in the reform period. The paper made use of a non-parametric approach that is Data Envelopment Analysis (DEA). It uses the Window Analysis developed by Klopp. Time span used for the present study is five years that is 2001-02 to 2005-06. One important objective of the study has been to see whether bank ownership mattered in respect of deposit mobilisation. The result suggests that the public sector banks have fallen behind the in-sample private sector commercial banks in terms of deposit mobilisation.

Kodian Narander, Kumar Shalinder and Kodan Anand Singh (2010) have conducted a study on implementation of Basel Norms in Indian banking sector. The main objective of this study was to observe whether Indian banks, particularly the public sector banks are ready to implement Basel Norms within the outer limit of year 2006. This study concluded that banks in India particularly public sector banks are ready to migrate to Basel Accord II only at a conceptual and academic level. They have to travel a long distance when it comes to organisational and technological readiness to go ahead, only then they can compete with international competition smoothly.

Kajal Chaudhary and Monika Sharma (2011) have made a comparative analysis of services of Public Sector Banks and Private Sector banks. They believed that it is right time to take suitable and stringent measures to get rid of non-performing asset (NPA) problem. Further they have suggested that an efficient management information system should be developed and the bank staff involved in sanctioning the advances should be trained about the proper documentation and charge of securities and motivated to take measures in preventing advances turning into NPA. They have also recommended that Public banks must pay attention on their functioning to compete with private banks and all the banks should be well versed in proper selection of borrower/project and in analysing the financial statement.

Neha Rani and Dinesh Gaba (2014) have concluded that private sector banks are performing better than other banks because it's substandard, doubtful, losses advances are increasing but their share in total gross advances are decreasing and they have also found that foreign banks performance is better than scheduled commercial banks and public sector banks. It was also established from the study that public sector banks are not performing well because their percentage share of standard advances are consistently decreasing and percentage share of substandard and doubtful advances in total gross advances are consistently increasing. Further, it was revealed that gross non-performing asset (NPA) of public sector banks are also increasing. The authors have suggested that public sector banks should decrease their NPA by adopting different measures.

V. Objective of The Study

The main objective of present study is to compare the performance of public, private and foreign banks in India by applying CAMEL method. The paper attempt to test the hypothesis that the "performance of foreign banks is better as compared to performance of private and public sector banks".

Study Sample

Twelve banks comprising of four public, four private and four foreign banks on the basis of stratified random sampling has been selected to reach out the findings. The selected banks are as follows:

The Selected Banks for the Study

PUBLIC SECTOR BANKS	PRIVATE SECTOR BANKS	FOREIGN BANKS
Canara Bank	HDFC Bank	CITI Bank
Punjab National Bank	Karnataka Bank	Bank of America
Andhra Bank	South Indian Bank	Barclays Bank
Bank of India	Laxmi Vilas Bank	Abu Dhbi Bank

Performance Analysing Public, Private and Foreign Banks

For the purpose of the study, several methods have been taken into consideration for analysis. The performance of a bank can be measured by a number of indicators. Profitability is the most important indicator because it gives an insight into the broad indication of the capability of a bank to increase its earnings. For measuring the performance of selected banks the present study has employed the CAMEL methods.

VI. Emphirical Analysis

Table 8.1 analysis Credit Deposit Ratio through Regression analysis is undertaken for the period 2003-04 to 2013-14.

Table 8.1: Credit Deposit Ratio for the period 2003-04 to 2013-2014

Bank Category	R^2	*F-value*	*p-value*	*Year*		*Constant*	
				Coefficient	*p-value*	*Coefficient*	*p-value*
Private Banks	0.340	5.162	0.046	0.950	0.046	72.430	0.000
Public Banks	0.920	114.25	0.000	3.234	0.000	40.591	0.000
Foreign Banks	0.827	47.798	0.000	4.604	0.000	37.165	0.000

Source: Computed from Secondary Data.

Table 8.1 indicates the regression analysis result of Credit Deposit Ratio as dependent variable and time as independent variable. As a result of analysis within **Private Bank** category Credit Deposit Ratio has been significantly explained by years with R^2

value is 0.340, significant F-value is 5.162 as P-value is 0.046 (P value should be ≤ 0.05) and significant coefficient of year value is 0.950 (even here P-value is 0.046 which is ≤0.05).

As a result of analysis within **Public Bank** category Credit Deposit Ratio has been significantly explained by years with R^2 value is 0.920, significant F-value is 114.251 as P-value is 0.000 (P value should be ≤ 0.05) and significant coefficient of year value is 3.234 (even here P value is 0.000 which is ≤0.05).

As a result of analysis within **Foreign Bank** category Credit Deposit Ratio has been significantly explained by years with R^2 value is 0.827, significant F-value is 47.798 as P-value is 0.000 (P value should be ≤ 0.05) and significant coefficient of year value is 4.604 (even here P-value is 0.000 which is ≤0.05).

Table 8.2: Interest Income as Percentage to Total Income for the period 2003-04 to 2013-14

Bank Category	R^2	*F-value*	*p-value*	*Year Coefficient*	*Year p-value*	*Constant Coefficient*	*Constant p-value*
Private Banks	0.542	11.847	0.006	0.427	0.006	78.093	0.000
Public Banks	0.735	27.688	0.000	0.784	0.000	82.208	0.000
Foreign Banks	0.673	20.557	0.001	2.759	0.001	46.919	0.000

Source: Computed from Secondary Data.

Table 8.2 indicates the regression analysis result of Interest Income as Percentage to Total Income as dependent variable and year as independent variable.

As a result of analysis within **Private Bank** category Interest Income as Percentage to Total Income has been significantly explained by years with R^2 value is 0.542, significant F-value is 11.847 as P-value is 0.006 (P value should be ≤ 0.05) and significant coefficient of year value is 0.427 (even here P-value is 0.006 which is ≤0.05).

As a result of analysis within **Public Bank** category Interest Income as Percentage to Total Income has been significantly explained by years with R^2 value is 0.735, significant F-value is 27.688 as P-value is 0.000 (P value should be ≤ 0.05) and significant coefficient of year value is 0.784 (even here P-value is 0.000 which is ≤0.05).

As a result of analysis within **Foreign Bank** category Interest Income as Percentage to Total Income has been significantly explained by years with R^2 value is 0.673, significant F-value is

20.557 as P-value is 0.001 (P-value should be ≤ 0.05) and significant coefficient of year value is 2.759 (even here P-value is 0.001 which is ≤0.05).

Table 8.3 depicts the analysis of Non-Interest Income to total Income for the period 2003-04 to 20013-14.

Table 8.3: Non-Interest Income as Percentage to Total Income for the period 2003-04 to 2013-2014 using Regression Analysis

Bank Category	*R^2*	*F-value*	*p-value*	*Year*		*Constant*	
				Coefficient	*p-value*	*Coefficient*	*p-value*
Private Banks	0.542	11.846	0.006	-0.427	0.006	21.907	0.000
Public Banks	0.735	27.688	0.000	-0.784	0.000	17.792	0.000
Foreign Banks	0.673	20.560	0.001	-2.759	0.001	53.081	0.000

Source: Computed from Secondary Data.

Table 8.3 indicates the regression analysis result of Non-Interest Income as Percentage to Total Income as dependent variable and year as independent variable.

As a result of analysis within **Private Bank** category Non-Interest Income as Percentage to Total Income has been significantly explained by years with R^2 value is 0.542, significant F-value is 11.846 as P-value is 0.006 (P value should be ≤ 0.05) and significant coefficient of year value is -0.427 (even here P-value is 0.006 which is ≤ 0.05).

As a result of analysis within **Public Bank** category Non-Interest Income as Percentage to Total Income has been significantly explained by years with R^2 value is 0.735, significant F-value is 27.688 as P-value is 0.000 (P value should be ≤ 0.05) and significant coefficient of year value is -0.784 (even here P-value is 0.000 which is ≤ 0.05).

As a result of analysis within **Foreign Bank** category Non-Interest Income as Percentage to Total Income has been significantly explained by years with R^2 value is 0.673, significant F-value is 20.560 as P-value is 0.001 (P value should be ≤ 0.05) and significant coefficient of year value is -2.759 (even here P-value is 0.001 which is ≤ 0.05).

Table 8.4: Interest Expense as Percentage to Total Expenses for the period 2003-04 to 2013-2014 using Regression Analysis

Bank Category	*R^2*	*F-value*	*p-value*	*Year*		*Constant*	
				Coefficient	*p-value*	*Coefficient*	*p-value*
Private Banks	0.009	0.090	0.771	-0.084	0.771	60.142	0.000

Public Banks	0.438	7.802	0.019	1.57	0.019	55.365	0.000
Foreign Banks	0.070	0.756	0.405	0.382	0.405	31.804	0.000

Source: Computed from Secondary Data.

Table 8.4 indicates the regression analysis result of Interest Expense as Percentage to Total Expenses as dependent variable and year as independent variable.

As a result of analysis within **Private Bank** category Interest Expense as Percentage to Total Expenses has been significantly explained by years with R^2 value is 0.009, F-value 0.090 not found to be significant as P-value is 0.771 (P value should be ≤ 0.05) and coefficient of year value is -0.084 which is also not found to be significant (even here P-value is 0.771 which is not ≤0.05).

As a result of analysis within **Public Bank** category Interest Expense as Percentage to Total expenses has been significantly explained by years with R^2 value is 0.438, significant F-value is 7.802 as P-value is 0.019 (P-value should be ≤ 0.05) and significant coefficient of year value is 1.57 (even here P-value is 0.019 which is ≤0.05).

As a result of analysis within **Foreign Bank** category Interest Expense as Percentage to Total Expenses has been significantly explained by years with R^2 value is 0.070, F-value 0.756 not found to be significant as P-value is 0.405 (P-value should be ≤ 0.05) and coefficient of year value is 0.382 which is also not found to be significant (even here P-value is 0.405 which is not ≤0.05).

Table 8.5: Operating Expenses as Percentage to Total Expenditure for the period 2003-04 to 2013-2014

Bank Category	R^2	*F-value*	*p-value*	*Year Coefficient*	*p-value*	*Constant Coefficient*	*p-value*
Private Banks	0.204	2.568	0.140	0.408	0.140	23.156	0.000
Public Banks	0.744	29.059	0.000	-1.114	0.000	31.537	0.000
Foreign Banks	0.001	0.011	0.919	0.032	0.919	35.702	0.000

Source: Computed from Secondary Data.

Table 8.5 indicates the regression analysis result of Operating Expenses as Percentage to Total Expenditure as dependent variable and year as independent variable.

As a result of analysis within **Private Bank** category Operating Expenses as Percentage to Total Expenditure has been significantly explained by years with R^2 value is 0.204, F-value 2.568 not found to be significant as P-value is 0.140 (P-value should be

≤ 0.05) and coefficient of year value is 0.408 which is also not found to be significant (even here P-value is 0.140 which is not ≤0.05).

As a result of analysis within **Public Bank** category Operating Expenses as Percentage to Total Expenditure has been significantly explained by years with R^2 value is 0.744, significant F-value is 29.059 as P-value is 0.000 (P-value should be ≤ 0.05) and significant coefficient of year value is -1.114 (even here P-value is 0.000 which is ≤0.05).

As a result of analysis within **Foreign Bank** category Operating Expenses as Percentage to Total Expenditure has been significantly explained by years with R^2 value is 0.001, F-value 0.011 not found to be significant as P-value is 0.919 (P-value should be ≤ 0.05) and coefficient of year value is 0.032 which is also not found to be significant (even here P-value is 0.919 which is not ≤0.05).

Table 8.6: Spread as Percentage to Total Assets for the period 2003-04 to 2013-2014

Bank Category	*R^2*	*F-value*	*p-value*	*Year*		*Constant*	
				Coefficient	*p-value*	*Coefficient*	*p-value*
Private Banks	0.862	62.519	0.000	0.117	0.000	1.761	0.000
Public Banks	0.182	2.224	0.167	-0.044	0.167	2.857	0.000
Foreign Banks	0.565	5.977	0.005	0.106	0.005	2.734	0.000

Source: Computed from Secondary Data.

Table 8.6 indicates the regression analysis result of Spread as Percentage to Total Asset as dependent variable and year as independent variable.

As a result of analysis within **Private Bank** category spread as Percentage to Total Asset has been significantly explained by years with R^2 value is 0.862, significant F- value is 62.519 as P-value is 0.000 (P-value should be ≤ 0.05) and significant coefficient of year value is 0.117 (even here P-value is 0.000 which is ≤0.05).

As a result of analysis within **Public Bank** category Spread as Percentage to Total Asset has been significantly explained by years with R^2 value is 0.182, F-value 2.224 not found to be significant as P-value is 0.167 (P-value should be ≤ 0.05) and coefficient of year value is -0.044 which is also not found to be significant (even here P-value is 0.167 which is not ≤ 0.05).

As a result of analysis within **Foreign Bank** category Spread as Percentage to Total Asset has been significantly explained by years with R^2 value is 0.565, significant F-value is 5.977 as P-value is 0.005 (P-value should be ≤ 0.05) and significant coefficient of year value is 0.106 (even here P-value is 0.005 which is ≤0.05).

Table 8.7: Interest Income as Percentage to Average Working Fund for the period 2003-04 to 2013-2014

Bank Category	R^2	*F-value*	*p-value*	*Year*		*Constant*	
				Coefficient	*p-value*	*Coefficient*	*p-value*
Private Banks	0.134	1.553	0.241	0.077	0.241	7.844	0.000
Public Banks	0.013	0.59	0.727	-0.019	0.727	8.494	0.000
Foreign Banks	0.018	0.181	0.679	-0.038	0.679	7.618	0.000

Source: Computed from Secondary Data.

This Table indicates the regression analysis result Interest Income as Percentage to Average Working Fund as dependent variable and year as independent variable.

As a result of analysis within **Private Bank** category Interest Income as Percentage to Average Working Fund has been significantly explained by years with R^2 value is 0.134, F-value 1.553 not found to be significant as P-value is 0.241 (P-value should be ≤ 0.05) and coefficient of year value is 0.077 which is also not found to be significant (even here P-value is 0.241 which is not ≤0.05).

As a result of analysis within **Public Bank** category Interest Income as Percentage to Average Working Fund has been significantly explained by years with R^2 value is 0.013, F-value 0.59 not found to be significant as P-value is 0.727 (P-value should be ≤ 0.05) and coefficient of year value is -0.019 which is also not found to be significant (even here P-value is 0.727 which is not ≤0.05).

As a result of analysis within **Foreign Bank** category Interest Income as Percentage to Average Working Fund has been significantly explained by years with R^2 value is 0.018, F-value 0.181 not found to be significant as P-value is 0.679 (P-value should be ≤ 0.05) and coefficient of year value is - 0.038 which is also not found to be significant (even here P-value is 0.679 which is not ≤ 0.05).

Table 8.8: Non-Interest Income as Percentage to Total Average Working Fund for the period 2003-04 to 2013-2014

Bank Category	R^2	*F-value*	*p-value*	*Year*		*Constant*	
				Coefficient	*p-value*	*Coefficient*	*p-value*
Private Banks	0.300	4.287	0.065	-0.033	0.065	2.163	0.000
Public Banks	0.773	34.040	0.000	-0.105	0.000	1.919	0.000
Foreign Banks	0.865	63.985	0.000	-0.571	0.000	8.637	0.000

Source: Computed from Secondary Data.

Table 8.8 depicts the analysis of the Non-Interest Income as Percentage to Total Average Working Fund for the period 2003-04 to 2013-14.

Table 8.8 indicates the regression analysis result of Non-Interest Income as Percentage to Total Average Working Fund as dependent variable and year as independent variable.

As a result of analysis within **Private Bank** category Non-Interest Income as Percentage to Total Average Working Fund has been significantly explained by years with R^2 value is 0.300, F-value 4.287 not found to be significant as P-value is 0.065 (P-value should be ≤ 0.05) and coefficient of year value is -0.033 which is also not found to be significant (even here P-value is 0.065 which is not ≤ 0.05).

As a result of analysis within **Public Bank** category Non-Interest Income as Percentage to Total Average Working Fund has been significantly explained by years with R^2 value is 0.773, significant F-value is 34.04 as P-value is 0.000 (P value should be ≤ 0.05) and significant coefficient of year value is -0.105 (even here P-value is 0.000 which is ≤ 0.05).

As a result of analysis within **Foreign Bank** category Non-Interest Income as Percentage to Total Average Working Fund has been significantly explained by years with R^2 value is 0.865, significant F-value is 63.985 as P-value is 0.000 (P-value should be ≤ 0.05) and significant coefficient of year value is -0.571 (even here P-value is 0.000 which is ≤ 0.05).

Table 8.9: Operating Profit as Percentage to Average Working Funds for the period 2003-04 to 2013-2014

Bank Category	*R^2*	*F-value*	*p-value*	*Year*		*Constant*	
				Coefficient	*p-value*	*Coefficient*	*p-value*
Private Banks	0.000	0.001	0.979	0.000	0.979	2.544	**0.000**
Public Banks	0.580	13.820	0.004	-0.55	0.004	3.014	**0.000**
Foreign Banks	**0.739**	**28.357**	**0.000**	**-0.160**	**0.000**	**8.041**	**0.000**

Source: Computed from Secondary Data.

Table 8.9 depicts the analysis of the Operating Profit as Percentage to Average Working Funds for the period 2003-04 to 2013-14.

Table 8.9 indicates the regression analysis result of Operating Profit as Percentage to Average Working Funds as dependent variable and year as independent variable.

As a result of analysis within **Private Bank** category Operating Profit as Percentage to Average Working Funds has been significantly explained by years with R^2 value is 0.000, F-value 0.001 not found to be significant as P-value is 0.979 (P-value should be ≤ 0.05) and coefficient of year value is 0.000 which is also not found to be significant (even here P-value is 0.979 which is not ≤0.05).

As a result of analysis within **Public Bank** category Operating Profit as Percentage to Average Working Funds has been significantly explained by years with R^2 value is 0.580, significant F-value is 13.820 as P-value is 0.004 (P-value should be ≤ 0.05) and significant coefficient of year value is -0.55 (even here P-value is 0.004 which is ≤ 0.05).

As a result of analysis within **Foreign Bank** category Operating Profit as Percentage to Average Working Funds has been significantly explained by years with R^2 value is 0.739, significant F-value is 28.357 as P-value is 0.000 (P-value should be ≤ 0.05) and significant coefficient of year value is -0.160 (even here P-value is 0.000 which is ≤0.05).

Table 8.10 depicts the analysis of the Return on Assets (PAT/Total ASSETS) Income for the period 2003-04 to 2013-14.

Table 8.10: Return on Assets (PAT /Total assets) for the period 2003-04 to 2013-2014

Bank Category	*R^2*	*F-value*	*p-value*	*Year Coefficient*	*p-value*	*Constant Coefficient*	*p-value*
Private Banks	0.238	3.115	0.108	0.042	0.108	0.968	0.000
Public Banks	0.007	0.071	0.796	-0.004	0.796	0.837	0.000
Foreign Banks	**0.441**	**7.889**	**0.019**	**-0.156**	**0.019**	3.372	0.000

Source: Computed from Secondary Data.

Table 8.10 indicates the regression analysis result Return on Assets (PAT/Total Assets) Income as dependent variable and year as independent variable.

As a result of analysis within **Private Bank** category Return on Assets (PAT /Total assets) Income has been significantly explained by years with R^2 value is 0.238, F-value 3.115 not found to be significant as P- value is 0.108 (P-value should be ≤ 0.05) and coefficient of year value is 0.042 which is also not found to be significant (even here P-value is 0.108 which is not ≤ 0.05).

As a result of analysis within **Public Bank** category Return on Assets (PAT/Total Assets) has been significantly explained by years with R^2 value is 0.007, F-value 0.071 not found to be significant as P-value is 0.796 (P-value should be ≤ 0.05) and coefficient of year value is -0.004 which is also not found to be significant (even here P-value is 0.796 which is not ≤ 0.05).

As a result of analysis within **Foreign Bank** category Return on Assets (PAT /Total Assets) has been significantly explained by years with R^2 value is 0.441, significant F-value is 7.889 as P-value is 0.019 (P-value should be ≤ 0.05) and significant coefficient of year value is -0.156 (even here P-value is 0.019 which is ≤ 0.05).

Table 8.11 depicts the analysis of the Gross NPA as Percentage to Net Advances for the period 2003-04 to 2013-14.

Table 8.11: Gross NPA As Percentage to Net Advances for the period 2003-04 to 2013-2014 using Regression Analysis

Bank Category	*R^2*	*F-value*	*p-value*	*Year*		*Constant*	
				Coefficient	*p-value*	*Coefficient*	*p-value*
Private Banks	0.578	13.671	0.004	-0.343	0.004	5.309	0.000
Public Banks	0.617	16.105	0.002	-0.920	0.002	11.573	0.000
Foreign Banks	0.313	4.566	0.058	-2.098	0.058	23.475	0.009

Source: Computed from Secondary Data.

Table 8.11 indicates the regression analysis result of Gross NPA as Percentage to Net Advances as dependent variable and year as independent variable.

As a result of analysis within **Private Bank** category Gross NPA as Percentage to Net Advances has been significantly explained by years withR^2 value is 0.578, significant F-value is 13.671 as P-value is 0.004 (P-value should be ≤ 0.05) and significant coefficient of year value is -0.343 (even here P-value is 0.004 which is ≤0.05).

As a result of analysis within **Public Bank** Gross NPA as Percentage to Net Advances has been significantly explained by years with R^2 value is 0.617, significant F-value 16.10 as P-value is 0.002 (P-value should be ≤ 0.05) and significant coefficient of year value is -0.920 (even here P-value is 0.002 which is ≤0.05).

As a result of analysis within **Foreign Bank** category Gross NPA as Percentage to Net Advances has been significantly explained by years with R^2 value is 0.313, F-value 4.566 not found to be significant as P-value is 0.058 (P-value should be ≤ 0.05) and coefficient of year value is -2.098 which is also not found to be significant (even here P-value is 0.058 which is not ≤ 0.05).

Table 8.12 depicts the analysis of the Net NPA as Percentage to Net Advances for the period 2003-04 to 2013-14.

Table 8.12: NPA as Percentage to Net Advances for the period 2003-04 to 2013-2014

Bank Category	R^2	*F-value*	*p-value*	*Year*		*Constant*	
				Coefficient	*p-value*	*Coefficient*	*p-value*
Private Banks	0.840	52.399	0.000	-0.148	0.000	2.179	0.000
Public Banks	0.490	9.626	0.011	-0.369	0.011	4.978	0.000
Foreign Banks	**0.104**	**1.156**	**0.308**	**-0.178**	**0.308**	**2.648**	**0.055**

Source: Computed from Secondary Data.

Table 8.12 indicates the regression analysis result of Net NPA as Percentage to Net Advances as dependent variable and year as independent variable.

As a result of analysis within **Private Bank** category Net NPA as Percentage to Net Advances has been significantly explained by years with R^2 value is 0.840, significant F-value is 52.39 as P-value is 0.000 (P-value should be ≤ 0.05) and significant coefficient of year value is -0.148 (even here P-value is 0.000 which is ≤0.05).

As a result of analysis within **Public Bank** Net NPA as Percentage to Net Advances has been significantly explained by years with R^2 value is 0.490, significant F-value is 9.626 as P-value is 0.011 (P value should be ≤ 0.05) and significant coefficient of year value is -0.369 (even here P-value is 0.011 which is ≤0.05).

As a result of analysis within **Foreign Bank** category Net NPA as Percentage to Net Advances has been significantly explained by years with R^2 value is 0.104, F-value 1.15 not found to be significant as P-value is 0.308 (P-value should be ≤ 0.05) and coefficient of year value is -0.178 which is also not found to be significant (even here P-value is 0.308 which is not ≤ 0.05).

Table 8.13 depicts the analysis of the Net Profit (PAT) on Owned Funds for the period 2003-04 to 2013-14.

Table 8.13: Net Profit (PAT) On Owned Funds for the period 2003-04 to 2013-2014

Bank Category	R^2	*F-value*	*p-value*	*Year*		*Constant*	
				Coefficient	*p-value*	*Coefficient*	*p-value*
Private Banks	0.033	0.342	0.572	-0.25	0.572	15.209	0.000
Public Banks	0.008	0.077	0.788	-0.063	0.788	13.388	0.000
Foreign Banks	**0.589**	**14.349**	**0.004**	**-0.824**	**0.004**	**18.016**	**0.000**

Source: Computed from Secondary Data.

Table 8.13 indicates the regression analysis result of Net Profit (PAT) on Owned Funds as dependent variable and year as independent variable.

As a result of analysis within **Private Bank** category Net Profit (PAT) on Owned Funds has been significantly explained by years with R^2 value is 0.033, F-value 0.342 not found to be significant as P-value is 0.572 (P-value should be ≤ 0.05) and coefficient of year value is -0.25 which is also not found to be significant (even here P-value is 0.572 which is not ≤ 0.05).

As a result of analysis within **Public Bank** category Net Profit (PAT) on Owned Funds has been significantly explained by years with R^2 value is 0.008, F- value 0.077 not found to be significant as P-value is 0.788 (P-value should be ≤ 0.05) and coefficient of year value is -0.063 which is also not found to be significant (even here P-value is 0.788 which is not ≤ 0.05).

As a result of analysis within **Foreign Bank** category Net Profit (PAT) on Owned Funds has been significantly explained by years with R^2 value is 0.589, significant F-value is 14.349 as P-value is 0.004 (P-value should be ≤ 0.05) and significant coefficient of year value is -0.824 (even here P-value is 0.004 which is ≤0.05).

Table 8.14 depicts the analysis of the Capital Adequacy Ratio (Tier I plus Tier II) (Under Basel I) for the period 2003-04 to 2013-14.

Table 8.14: Capital Adequacy Ratio (Tier I Plus Tier II) (Under Basel I) for the period 2003-04 to 2013-2014

Bank Category	*R²*	*F-value*	*p-value*	*Year*		*Constant*	
				Coefficient	*p-value*	*Coefficient*	*p-value*
Private Banks	0.057	0.604	0.455	0.53	0.455	11.981	0.000
Public Banks	0.000	0.002	0.964	-0.004	0.964	11.838	0.000
Foreign Banks	**0.447**	**8.083**	**0.017**	**-1.450**	**0.017**	**27.941**	0.000

Source: Computed from Secondary Data.

Table 8.14 indicates the regression analysis result of Capital Adequacy Ratio (Tier I plus Tier II) (Under Basel I) as dependent variable and year as independent variable.

As a result of analysis within **Private Bank** category Capital Adequacy Ratio (Tier I plus Tier II) (Under Basel I) has been significantly explained by years with R^2 value is 0.057, F-value 0.604 not found to be significant as P-value is 0.455 (P-value should be ≤ 0.05) and coefficient of year value is 0.53 which is also not found to be significant (even here P-value is 0.455 which is not ≤0.05).

As a result of analysis within **Public Bank** category Capital Adequacy Ratio (Tier I plus Tier II) (Under Basel I) has been significantly explained by years with R^2 value is 0.000, F-value 0.002 not found to be significant as P-value is 0.964 (P-value should be ≤ 0.05) and coefficient of year value is -0.004 which is also not found to be significant (even here P-value is 0.964 which is not ≤0.05).

As a result of analysis within **Foreign Bank** Capital Adequacy Ratio (Tier I plus Tier II) (Under Basel I) has been significantly explained by years with R^2 value is 0.447, significant F-value is 8.083 as P-value is 0.017 (P-value should be ≤ 0.05) and significant coefficient of year value is -1.450 (even here P-value is 0.017 which is ≤ 0.05).

Findings of the Study

The finding of the study shows that:

- Average Credit Deposit Ratio across all three Bank Categories is different.
- Average Interest Income as Percentage to total income across all three Bank Categories is different.
- Average Non-Interest Income as Percentage to total income across all three Bank Categories is different.
- Average Interest Expense as Percentage to total expenses across all three Bank Categories is different.
- Average Operating Expenses as Percentage to total expenditure across all three Bank Categories is different.
- Average Spread as Percentage to total assets across all three Bank Categories is different.
- Average Interest Income as Percentage to average working fund across all three Bank Categories is different.
- Average Non-Interest Income as Percentage to total average working fund across all three Bank Categories is different.
- Average Operating Profit as Percentage to average working funds across all three Bank Categories is different.
- Average Return on Assets (PAT /Total Assets) across all three Bank Categories is different.
- Average Gross NPA as Percentage to net advances across all three Bank Categories is alike.
- Average Net NPA as Percentage to net advances across all three Bank Categories is alike.

- Average Net Profit (PAT) on owned funds across all three Bank Categories is alike.
- Average Capital Adequacy Ratio (Tier I plus Tier II) (Under Basel I) across all three Bank Categories is different.
- The Comparative performance of Private Sector Banks is better than Public Sector Banks.
- The Comparative performance of Foreign Sector Banks is better than Public Sector.
- The Comparative performance of Foreign Banks is better than Private Sector Banks.
- The Comparative performance of Foreign Sector Banks is better than Private and Public Sector Banks.

Policy Suggestion

- ➢ Public Banks must employ the methods to increase the Average Credit Deposit Ratio by making full use of their resources.
- ➢ Private and Foreign Banks must employ the methods to increase the Average Interest Income as percentage to Total Income.
- ➢ Private Banks and Public Banks must employ the methods to increase the Average Non-Interest Income as percentage to Total Income by increasing the income earned in the form of commission, exchange and brokerages and income from profit on sale of investments and non-banking assets.
- ➢ Private Banks and Public Banks must employ the methods to decrease the Average Interest Expense as percentage to Total Expenses by reducing of the amount of their gross income paying interest on borrowed money.
- ➢ Private Banks and Public Banks must employ the methods to increase the Average Operating Expenses as percentage to Total Expenditure.
- ➢ Private Banks and Public Banks must employ the methods to increase the Average Spread as percentage to Total Assets by earning more from loans and other interest-accruing activities.
- ➢ Foreign Banks must employ the methods to increase the Average Interest Income as percentage to Average Working Fund by improving its ability to leverage its average total resources in enhancing its mainstream operational interest income.
- ➢ Private Banks and Public Banks must employ the methods to increase the Average Non-Interest Income as percentage

to Total Average Working Fund by improving their earning from exchange commission, brokerage, gains on sale and revaluation of investments and fixed assets, and profits from exchange transactions.

- Private Banks and Public Banks must employ the methods to increase the Average Operating Profit as percentage to Average Working Funds. This ratio is a profitability parameter for the performance of a bank.
- Private Banks and Public Banks must employ the methods to increase the Average Return on Assets. It indicates how well the bank's assets are managed to bring profit of asset that has been invested to the bank.
- Public Banks and especially Private Banks must employ the methods to increase the Average Capital Adequacy Ratio. Capital Adequacy is seen as the measure of a bank's strength to absorb credit risks i.e. its strength is to provide for losses that may arise upon its advance going bad. It is expressed as a proportion of capital to assets weighted according to the risk of default attached to them.
- The position of NPAs is improving in India. Though NPAs are having a declining trend over a period of study, but Non-Performing Assets of public sector banks are still higher than private and foreign sector banks. Top management of private and foreign sector banks is more professional, core competent and expertise than public sector banks. So, they are more competent in making plans for recovering funds from borrowers (both individuals and institutional). The public sector banks are required to lend money to weaker sections of the society also, where the chances of recovery is almost negligible. That is why, though the NPAs of public sector banks have sharp declining trend, still it is higher than private and foreign sector banks. Further various steps have been taken by the government to recover and reduce NPAs. Thus, Public Banks need is to have 'Now performing assets' than 'Non-performing assets'.

References

Altunbas Yener, Lynne Evans, Philip Molyneux, "Bank Ownership and Efficiency", Journal of Money, Credit and Banking, Vol. 33, No. 4, November 2001.

Aparna, T, "State Bank of India: Flying High", Chartered Financial Analyst, Vol. 8, Issue 9, September 2002, pp. 60-61.

Bhattacharya, K. and Das, A. (2003), "Dynamics of Market Structure and Competitiveness of the Banking Sector in India and its Impact on Output and Prices of Banking Services", *RBI Occasional Papers,* pp.123-159.

Bhide, MG, Prasad, A, Ghosh, Saibal, "Banking Sector Reforms: A Critical Overview", Economic and Political Weekly, Vol. XXXVII, No. 5, February 2, 2002, pp. 399-408.

Birla Institute of Scientific Research, "Banks Since Nationalization", Economic Research Division, Allied Publishers, New Delhi, 1981.

Garima Chaudhary (2014), Performance Comparison of Private Sector Banks with the Public Sector Banks in India, International Journal of Emerging Research in Management and Technology, Volume 3, Issue 2.

Malhotra, R N, "Banking Enter a New Phase", The Journal of the Institute of Bankers, Special Number: Bank Economists Conference, Vol. 57, No. 2, April-June 1986, pp. 94-103.

Mittal, R K and Dhingra Sanjay, "Assessing the impact of computerization on productivity and profitability of Indian banks- An Application of Data Envelopment Analysis", Delhi Business Review, Vol. 8, No. 1, January- June, 2007.

Nagar, Nirupma and Mishra, Jitendra Kumar, "Non-Performing Assets of Commercial Banks- A Case Study of State Bank of Indore", Madhya Pradesh Journal of Social Sciences, Vol. 7, No.1, 2002, pp. 102-112.

Raju, D N M, "Evaluation of the Performance of State Bank of India with special reference to Non-Performing Assets (NPAs)", Abstract of Doctoral Dissertation, Finance India, Indian Institute of Finance, Vol. XXIII, No. 3, September, 2009, pp. 985-989.

Saha, Gurudas, "Financials of Indian Banking Industry and the Competitive Viability of the Public Sector Banks", The Management Accountant, Vol. 36, No. 5, May 2001, pp. 373-386.

Sahu, Bihari Gagan and Rajasekhar, D, "Banking Sector Reform and Credit Flow to Indian Agriculture", Economic & Political Weekly, Vol. XL, No. 53, Dec-Jan, 2005-06, pp. 5550-5559.

Samanta, Amitava, "Impact of NPA on Working of Commercial Banks in India", Journal of Economic and Social Development, Vol.11, No.1, 2006, pp 87-95.

Reserve Bank of India (1999), Report on Currency and Finance.

Reserve Bank of India (2000), Report on Trend and Progress in Banking.

Reserve Bank of India (1991), "The Committee on Financial Sector Reforms", RBI, Bombay (Chairman M. Narasimham).

Dr Jayanta Kumar Nandi, Performace Evaluation of Selected Banking Companies in India: a Study Submitted in the University of Burdwan, West Bengal, India.

9

Gaps and Limitations of Official Statistical System of India: A Note

Dr Shri Prakash and Sudhi Sharma

Introduction

There is need to clearly define the terms 'statistics' and 'system'.

'Statistics' in one sense refers to that branch of mathematics which deals with the methods of collection and analysis of samples of data used to infer the properties or the unobserved characteristics of the population' (*Oxford Dictionary of Economics*). 'Statistics' in another sense refers to facts or data, which the 'science of statistics' deals with (Yule and Kendall, 1958). System refers to the set of elements which are arranged according to well defined pattern and order. Therefore, statistical system may be defined as the set of ordered and well-arranged data according to a priori determined pattern and classification in and present the same to make it amenable for drawing meaningful inferences from the analysis of the same. The size of the data system may differ between the objectives for the realisation of which data are collected. Data and facts to which data pertain may be scattered or clustered.

Scientific and Non-Scientific Facts

All physical sciences are empirical; hence, scientific research uses facts, which are embodied in scientific data. According to Heady (1981), data may be defined as the *facts that the researcher derives from the environment of research investigation.* Laboratory Experiments constitute the research environment of such sciences as physics, chemistry etc.. But subjects like astronomy economics, psychology, sociology, political science, etc. do not have the facility of laboratory experimentation. Medicine also falls in this category to a large extent. Their research environment is constituted by the movements of planets, changes in economy, society, politics, and human behaviour. These are subject to observation. So observation plays very important role in the derivation of data from the corresponding environment of these subjects.

Scientific facts, and hence, scientific data differ from common facts. But all data or statistics may not be scientific in nature and orientation. However, facts are facts and there is no penumbra of approbation and acclaim around facts. Therefore, data are data and they do not speak for themselves. They are made to speak by research and researchers invest meanings in data or observed facts (Alfred Marshall, 1891). Facts are just the objects of observation and measurement. Incidentally, common facts remain common, and hence, non-scientific as long as these are not used in research. Once the given facts are observed and found to be of interest by some research investigator, all such facts which were dismissed as not important become important and acquire scientific character. Several instances may be cited from real life. Till Mrs Indira Gandhi gave the slogan 'Remove Poverty', poverty remained an unimportant non-scientific fact of Indian economy. Therefore, the line dividing common and scientific facts is very thin (Shri Prakash, 2013).

Data Generating Agencies

Social scientists require extensive data for conducting scientific research. But it is extremely difficult for individual researcher to marshal facts needed for investigation. Therefore, government of practically all the countries of the world have entrusted the task of data collection to designated public agencies.

Economic analysis and Empirical Econometrics use a variety of data. Scientific data are of different types and are collected by different agencies. Government of India and state governments and their agencies are the major sources of data generation. Central Statistical Organisation and National Sample Survey Organisation are the major sources of data for economists. Data collected by these agencies are supplemented by State Directorates of Economics and Statistics and several Ministries and Departments of Government of India such as industry, commerce, rural development and agriculture, and RBI etc.

No doubt, statistical system of India is among the best of the world, yet the official statistical systems are afflicted by several maladies which adversely affect the reliability and quality of data. Limitations of official statistics cause problems in research relating to Indian economy. *Besides, several important data required for research are not available at all.* This paper, however focuses largely on data needed for research in input output framework, though it goes a step beyond I-O.

Important Features of Scientific Data

Following ten are important features of scientific data:

> (i) Abstractness; (ii) Verifiability; (iii) Elusiveness; (iv) Closeness to Reality; (v) Recognition of Need for Research; (vi) Regularity; (vi) Approximation to Conceptual Framework; (vii) Inter-temporal, Inter-spatial and Inter-personal Consistency of Measurement; (viii) Accuracy; (ix) Reliability and (x) Testability of Consistency and Accuracy.

Some of these facets are well known. So only some facets are described hereunder:

Abstractness

As most of the scientific data pertain to ideas, concepts, or hypothesis, abstraction from complex reality is an inevitable requirement; it necessitates reduction of details and simplification of complexity. Even otherwise, **reality is part factual and part perceptual.** Therefore, part of data relates to perception/concept of reality.

Besides, such derived data as growth rates, productivity, capital-labour ratio, labour-output ratio are not directly observable. Therefore, data required for such derivatives have to be made available. This is not the case always with data collected by government agencies. For example, data relating to school education is quite comprehensive, but it is difficult to distinguish between drop-outs and failures from the year on year class-wise enrolments.

Verifiability

Socio-economic data are mostly non-experimental. Therefore, these have to be observable and accessible to all. However, official statistics is now sold at high prices. Besides, several companies have emerged who obtain data from government agencies and sell the same at high prices. Prowess, India-Stat, Amron etc. are examples of this. For example, we procured Census report (Economic Tables) for more than Rs 1 lakh for library; we pay ₹ 60,000 per annum for Prowess. Indian academicians, unlike those of developed countries, do not receive annual research grants from employers. How can, such data be accessed by them for research?

Elusiveness

Elusiveness portrays the efforts required and difficulties encountered to access the data. Most of the **business data are treated as confidential**, and are generally partially retrievable or even totally inaccessible or these are available in forms un-suitable for research.

Inter-Temporal, Inter-Spatial and Inter-Personal Consistency of Measurement

Different agencies use different concepts and/or method of measurement. Even the same agency changes the concepts, classification, method of measurement and classification, which make inter-temporal comparison difficult. If data relate to different spatial units, this difficulty becomes even greater. For example, base year of price index is changed periodically, then, it becomes difficult to obtain data, say from 1950 to 2015 in same base year's constant prices. Changing the base year by individual researchers for their own objective(s) may not be feasible unless data in two base year's constant prices is available. This is not always possible. Now that the approach to determine growth rate of GDP is changed, it becomes difficult to analyse data for inter-temporal comparison.

Classification of CSO's input output tables and NSSO's expenditure classes. Dimensions of CSO's I-O Tables have been increased from 60x60 to 115x115 and then 130x130. What is needed in such cases is to revise and up-date the past periods' tables also to match the current tables based on more detailed classification. But it is much easier to prepare current table first in earlier classification and present it in more aggregative dimensions of classification.

More detailed classification of I-O tables is always welcome, since the input coefficients matrix represents technology in use. So, aggregation conceals technological differentials in the coefficients.

Another problem is posed by the capturing of influence of inflation on prices of inputs and outputs. As all input coefficients, elements of final demand and outputs are expressed in monetary units, while technology *per se* operates as an instrument of transformation of physical inputs into physical output, changes in prices tend to camouflage the technological and monetary change in values of the coefficients.

Besides, bulk purchases of inputs represent **business to business** (B to B) and the prices may differ from sector to sector according to the scale of purchases and sales. This affects the monetary values of the coefficients of different sectors differently. It needs clarification and correction, if necessary. This is important for the determination of the solution of price model which is the dual of Leontief's quantity model of output.

Non-accessibility of information about prices compatible with I-O model makes it extremely difficult to test the validity of Fix-Flex Price input-output model (For example, See, Prakash, Shri, 1981). The problem may be overcome if the twin matrices of sector-wise market and factor prices of inputs and outputs are presented along with transaction matrices. This will also facilitate the updating of I-O tables for changing prices over the years; it will also facilitate inter-temporal comparison of results.

Pure technology effect and price effect may also be separated from each other (For Illustration, See, Prakash-Balakrishnan, 2010). This will also facilitate productivity analysis in I-O framework.

WPI and CPI are not appropriate for deflation of inputs and outputs in I-O models. Far too many commodities are excluded from these indices. For example, 'Educational Inputs' Price Index' (Prakash-Chowdhury, 1997) depicts the non-suitability of WPI/ CPI with price differentials embodied in two approaches. Spatial price differentials are also substantial. Pronounced differential of prices between sectors, space and time in I-O Tables make inter-temporal and inter-spatial comparison difficult.

Non-availability of B-matrix forces the use of static model even for analysing growth. The transaction matrix also presents the distribution of final demand among private and public consumption, investment and net trade. It is obvious that the investment component is the surplus output of its production sector. But how is it allocated among different sectors? Distribution of investible surplus of producing sector among different sectors in proportion to input coefficients embodies unknown error margins. This information needs to be included in order to facilitate construction of B matrix. In the absence of requisite information we do not know margins of errors involved in the preparation of B matrix.

Then, the cost of raising financial capital from different sources remains unknown. So, appropriate interest rate for loan capital is difficult to choose. Banks advance credits to different debtors on different rates. Highest interest rate is charged from individual entrepreneurs and SMEs. Therefore, weighted average of lending rate may be provided, weights may be proportional to amount of loan capital advanced on each rate. What is the appropriate rate to be used as an imputed rate on own capital.

Interest paid is not the only cost of capital. Dividend per annum is also a charge on equity capital. Besides, some expenditure is incurred in raising equity capital from the market or loan capital raised through loan papers or interest paid on fixed deposits collected by corporate houses. It shall be greatly helpful if CSO collect all these data and present the same in a consolidated but comprehensive format.

Labour's contribution is the distinct component of value added. Therefore, this is high time that labour employed in each sector is reported in the transaction table. It will still be better if the education and skill components of work-force employed in different sectors are also shown in transaction matrix. This will be of great help in employment/manpower and educational planning, though privatisation of education has reduced the value of planning. However, release of advance figure may help regulators infixing intake capacities in professional courses. Corresponding wage/salary expenses are an indispensable part of estimation of value added from which **economic value added may also be deduced.**

This will help in proper allocation of resources among different lines of production at micro units. Besides, classification of employment among the organised sectors, SMEs and non-formal activities will help in analysis and explaining of the behaviour of the Indian economy at the given point in time and through time. It will also be of great help, if separate I-O tables for organised and SMEs are prepared and presented separately.

Use-wise classification of competitive and non-competitive imports will serve the purpose of determining the import dependence of production base of Indian economy. Besides, preparation of imported inputs separately from domestically inputs used in production will bring greater degree of precision in analysis and forecasting, it may also help in capturing the gains from inter-regional economic cooperation *a la* P. N. Mathur and Wonnacot. More detailed classification of sectors producing consumer durables is the need of the hours. For example, consumer electronics and other electronics, light electrical goods and heavy electrical/electronic goods etc. need more detailed classification. This holds true for automobiles also. Accessories and parts sector needs separate treatment. This will better reflect the dynamics of development of Indian economy.

Then there is some camouflaging in classification of sectors: wheat and wheat milling, paddy and paddy milling are not the same either in terms of technology or products. It is a fact that the product-mix of agro-based industries causes lot of problems in separation of inputs used for the production of specific products and by-products. Edible oil and paddy milling and wheat milling are examples. Both these use the same machinery and equipment though the basic inputs, material used for packaging oil and rice are different, yet certain chemical inputs are difficult to separate. Use of proportionality approach may result in negative output. This is the data difficulty. But the difficulty is not insurmountable.

Incorporation of sector-wise FDI is another direction of change needed in the currently prepared tables.

Inter and Intra-Regional Transaction Matrices

India is a very vast country in terms of population and geographical area. Neither level nor stage of development nor the pace of economic growth has been uniform across within the states and through time. Consequently, regional and intra-regional inequalities are still highly marked. Therefore, inclusive growth is an important objective of Indian economy and polity.

Spatial units as centres of production and consumption are the platforms of economic activities. Just as sectors of the economy are inter-dependent, spatial; units are also closely inter-woven together by inter-dependence. Just as an economic system is a whirlpool of inter-dependencies, spatial units are also an integrated agglomeration of mutually related activities and variables involved in their operations in a system of inter-dependence between-spatial units. Some of these spatial units may belong to contiguous geographical space. But some of the inter-related spatial units may also be far apart in geographical locations. **But the data collection agencies in general and CSO in particular has been overlooking the inter-dependence of economies of the states and areas within the states. Consequently, these are left out in** the formulation and applications of **input-output models** in empirical applications. The negligence of research of the regional and intra-regional trade and development in input–output framework by researchers is accounted by almost total want of data, especially regional and intra-regional input output tables.

However, several state input-output table were prepared in nineteen sixties by individual researchers. But these tables have not contained data pertaining to inter and intra-regional trade. The use of such tables has remained confined to some limited applications, especially development of specific states.

Inter-temporal Input-Output Growth Models of spatial units in Comparative Static Framework, or Regional/Intra-Regional Dynamic Input-output Growth Models, having **Space as core unit of analysis**, have not been empirically attempted. This is despite the fact that **periphery-centre based theory of regional development** has been in the centre stage of regional analysis/economics, and regional development planning for long. Interestingly, **Research in input-output framework cannot be promoted without generation of data** required for the preparation of

1. Inter-Spatial Transaction Matrix at the levels of states and districts. Such tables will facilitate preparation of inter-sector transactions table at state and district levels.
2. Inter-spatial Transaction Matrix at district level will have both rural and urban spatial units located within the districts. This will be helpful in preparing more comprehensive and meaningful plans of development of the districts and blocks within the districts.
3. Above tables can easily be integrated into one unified table to present inter-sector and inter-spatial units' transactions taking place among the spatial units during the specified period of time. The table will thus display not only the sector from which supply of specific material emanates but it will also portray the spatial location of production/supplier units.

4. Such tables will portray not only development linkages among micro spatial units of the districts but these tables will also highlight the direction and composition of inter and intra-spatial trade.

Availability of such data will help in evolving an input output model for the analysis of the district economy and its constituent parts as an organically unified entity.

Conclusion

All above observation and suggestions are based on long drawn research by authors in the area and the experience gained in the construction of 60x60 input-output table of M.P. for 1965 for the planning department of government of the state by the senior author. The filling up of these data gaps will facilitate in the integration of programmes of inclusive growth in scientific and systematic manner rather than ad hoc mechanisms in operation so far.

References

Black, John, Hashimzade, Nigar and Mykes, Gareth (1997), *Oxford Dictionary of Economics,* Oxford.

Leontief, W.W. (1965), *The Structure of American Economy 1919-1939,* Oxford.

Leontief, W.W. (1965), *Input Output Economics,* Oxford.

Marshall, Alfred (1891), *Principles of Economics,* Macmillan.

Mathur, P. N. and Hashim, S.R. (1967), A Model for Optimum Location and Flows. In?

Mathur, P.N. and Venkatramaiah (Editors), *Economic Analysis in Input Output Framework,* Vol.II, Gokhale Institute of Politics and Economics, Pune.

Prakash, Shri (1981), Cost Based Prices in Indian Economy 1951-1974, *The Malayan Economic Review,* Vol. XXVI. No.1.

Prakash, Shri (2013), *Facts, Science and Theory,* Reading Module, BIMTECH, Greater Noida.

Prakash, Shri and Balakrishnan, Brinda (2010), Input Output Modeling of Labour Productivity and its Human Capital and Technology Components in Indian Economy, *Bulletin of Political Economy,* Vol. 2, No. 2. Athens.

Prakash, Shri and Chowdhury, Sumitra (1997), *Expenditure on Education, Theory, Growth and Models,* NIEPA, New Delhi.

Yule, Y.A. and Kendall, M.G. (1958), *Introduction to Theory of Statistics,* Macmillan.

Part – II

AGRICULTURE, ENVIRONMENT AND LABOUR

10

Political Economy of Climate Change: Debates, Contestations and Issues in India/Karnataka

Professor Muzaffar Assadi

1. Introduction

Climatic change has become a buzz word in recent past both for academics as well as for public policy makers. It is now known as planetary crisis, crisis of the globe, crisis of the science, crisis of the nature and crisis of the political economy. At the same time it is no more seen as a concern of environment alone rather a "biggest developmental challenge or concern".[1] It is also seen as "biggest man made global problem". It is also an issue of how the relation between society and science are established in the years to come. The different debates in the context of climate change such as the one on the need for reworking the issues of governance, issues of development, issues of sustainability etc (Devid Held *et al* 2011). Thomas George *et.al*, (2011), Albrecht Ansohn, Boris Pleskovic (2010) have percolated down to the domain of policy making too. This is because of the inherent problem in addressing the climate change issue from the perspective of governance. Further it is also due to the belief that climate change is the result of increasing commercialisation or commodification of nature both by the individual as well as corporate sector. Incidentally UNESCO argues that "humans are altering the climate"[2], thereby bringing back the human beings as the centrality of and for crisis. At the same time it is argued that climate change ultimately

[1] UNDP, Ckunate change, Perspectives from Indiam 2009, http://www.undp.org.in/content/pub/ClimateChange/UNDP_Climate_Change.pdf

[2] Catherine P. McMullen, Clinate Chanage, Science Compendium 2009, UNESCO, http://www.unep.org/pdf/ccScienceCompendium2009/cc_ScienceCompendium2009_full_en.pdf

affect the poor more than anybody and thereby any policy-making should take into cognisance of its large socio-economic consequence than just revolving around environmental one. It is here the issues of governance become all the more important. It is in this context it is argued that governance should take into cognisance four important questions: one, how to combat the climate change through the mediation of different public policy two, will the paradigm shift in the governance help in mitigating climate change? Three, what would be the socio-economic cost of climatic change? And finally, what would be the nature of governance emerging in the context of climate change. It is in this background different governments both at the regional as well as national level have taken up the issues much more seriously in recent past.

In fact, climate change governance poses different challenges for the contemporary political systems.[3] This is because of the fact that climate change effects not only everyday life practices but also the fact that it has larger political consequences too: series of dislocation of population, rehabilitation of displaced population, increasing cost of mitigating the climate change, recurring drought in due course, etc. would eventually affect political system to tackle the issues judiciously. This is the reason why the political system ultimately has to take cognisance of the problems afflicting the system. This calls for the paradigm shift in the public policy vis-à-vis the governance. Nonetheless, the governance faces four important problems vis-à-vis the climate change in years to come: They are (a) Problem of Societal Reach, (b) Problem of Equity and Distribution, (c) Problem of addressing the issues judiciously and (d) Problem of adaptability. Nonetheless climate change governance has three requirements (James Meadcroft, 2010): Adaptation Mitigation, paradigm shift in public policy: governance in this context believes in introducing such policies which will take care of the effect of climate change on human activity and politics.

II. Myths and Climate Change

It is in this context one can understand the kind of myths that have been perpetuated in recent past. One of the myths is that the democratic countries are not adequately prepared to mitigate the climate change due to the political intricacies as well

---

[3] James Meadcroft,Climate Change Governacne, The World Bank, 2010.

political manoeuvring. This particular argument does not hold good to countries like India, including its units such as Karnataka. There are sufficient proof to say that democratic country are inadequately prepared to face the climate change. This is apparent in the way the pattern of governance shifted from immediate needs to mitigate the problems of future.

Second, myth is that developing countries lack holistic picture vis-à-vis the climate change. In fact, the developing countries like India looks at the issues both from larger political perspective but also from socio-economic perspective. In India, such issues as poverty, loss of energy, degradation of land, social life style, recurring drought and employment opportunities etc taken along with climate change.

Third, important myth is that developing countries are not sufficiently debating the issues. It is true that in countries like India climate change has become a major concern, even more than the Western world. This does not mean that the debate is uniformly spread across the country. In some states there are concerns however issues have been addressed without much debate.

Fourthly, the myth also combined in the discreet "amnesia". This is particularly reflected in the case of the role of Global capital or the MNCs – their contribution to global climate change and the transformation of natural resources into commodities. It is a fact that MNCs power has increased phenomenally in recent past, including the fact that their total capital some time surpasses the GDP of many developing countries. In fact MNCs have been accused of damaging the environment in many developing countries. In In May 2002, the United Nations Environment Program (UNEP) reported that released "there was a growing gap between the efforts to reduce the impact of business and industry on nature and the worsening state of the planet".[4] There are many example for the environmental degradation that the MNCs have made, the best example is the oil extraction in Nigeria.

III. Debates and Perspectives

There are different perspectives vis-à-vis the climate change. One perspective tries to look at the issues by linking it to the larger issues of economic growth and prosperity. Sunita Narain, for example, argues that, "the more prosperous country's economy is

---

[4] http://www.globalissues.org/article/55/corporations-and-the-environment

higher is its fossil fuel consumption, resulting in higher greenhouse gas emission".[5] Adding to this the second argument tries to locate the reason for changing climate change in the over consumption of rich countries than by the poor countries. It is argued that, "the unsustainable consumption pattern of rich industrialised nations are responsible for the threat of climate change, argues Kirtith Parikh (2002)".[6] It is further argued that, "Only 25 per cent of the global population lives in these countries, but they emit more than 70 per cent of the total global CO emissions and consume 75 to 80 per cent of many of the other resources of the world.

Thirdly, it is also seen as changing the patterns of consumption and distribution also. This calls for a paradigm shift from the key industry to low carbon emission economy- in other word climate change is seen as part of changing political economy of development. It requires what is called development of new technologies and doing away with the traditional one.

IV. Effects, Political Contestation and Climate Change

All these have made to find out whether issues of climate change is a political one? Given the controversy in recent past centring around the issues of cap on carbon omission, historical role played by the industrialised countries in sharpening green house, role of developing countries in addressing the larger issues of survival etc., have contributed to the fact that climate change has become highly contested political issue. This is because of the following reasons:

1. Highly developed or the western world tries to blame the developing world including India for the larger climate crisis. International PP argues that climate change effects LDCs more than the DC (Developing countries) - it is because it effects food security, health, economic growth, degradation of land etc. It is said that Africa over the last couple of decades has

[5] Sunita Narain, A Just climatie Change agreement: The Framework for an effective global deal" in Catherine P. McMullen, Clinate Chanage, Science Compendium 2009, p 10. See. UNESCO.,http://www.unep.org/pdf/ccScienceCompendium2009/cc_ScienceCompendium2009_full_en.pdf

[6] Jyothi K Parikh and Kirit Parikh, Climate Change: India's Perceptions, Positions, Policies and Possibilitiess, IGIDR< Mumbai, 2002 p.2.

witnessed the highest number of droughts (254) followed by Asia and Latin America. Quite contrary is the case of flood. Asia has witnessed highest number (737) followed by Latin America and Africa. Incidentally Asia also the victim of windstorms (726), "followed by North America and Europe, with Latin America".

2. Western world is not prepared to take up the resultant effect of climate change- such as dislocation, migration, ecological degradation, sea erosion etc.
3. Event during the time of negotiations western world is trying to bully the third world to accept its terms on the ground that the latter's contribution to the climate crisis is considerable.
4. There are instances such as the case of Africa-6,000 instances of social conflict over 20 years—the Social Conflict in Africa Database (SCAD) argued that there is a direct co-relation between the climate change and political conflict – it has led to different forms of conflict[7] including civil war, political unrest.
5. It is also a fact that climate change may affect the peace process such as the case of Israel and Palestine case for the water sharing. Hence water issues may become a political and potential issue in the context of conflictual situation.
6. It is also argued that the food scarcity due to the climate change would definitely create two conditions : conditions for and of social conflict leading to food riots and two, would help in global capital/ western capitalist to dump food to the developing countries under the grab of "aid" or assistance. This would finally leads to trapping of developing world into neo-colonial framework.
7. In countries like Kenya it has led to organised crime and clashes.
8. Climate change has also led to what is called "climate change induced migration. There are examples of environmental migration leading to conflict. Best case is the case of Bangladeshi migrants who are called environmental migrants, migrated to India, numbering around 12 to 17 million over the past couple of decade, resulting in ethnic conflict in northern parts of India.
9. Rafael Reuveny in his study (2012) argues that between 1975-2001 "droughts affected about 1.1 billion people in Asia, 222 million in Africa, 48 million in Latin America, 9 million in Oceania, 6 million in Europe, and 30,000 people in North

[7] Nils Petter Gledisch, Whither the weather? Climate change and conflict, Journal of Peace Studies, Vol.49, No. 3,2012.

America. Floods affected about 2.1 billion people in Asia, followed by Latin America (40 million), Africa (29 million), Europe (8 million), North America (800,000), and Oceania (500,000). Windstorms affected about 416 million people in Asia, followed by Latin America (22 million), Africa (9 million), Europe (8 million), Oceania (6 million), and North America (3 million).[8]

V. Debate and Public Policy Governance on Climate Change in India

In India, debate requires to be seen at three level: one, at the level of its effect on the everyday life practices and two, the debate on the public policy and the third, is how to address the issues at the global level. In the first case the issue has taken a political form with degradation of land or forest. It has led to agitational politics to radical politics in India. This is apparent in the case of Himalayan region, Western Ghat region as well as in the western parts of India, these parts of have seen series of agitations including radical politics. This has created the serious concern about the Indian Political system vis-à-vis the land degradation denuding of forest, loss of agricultural land, increasing greenhouse gas emission. Secondly, this politics has also given rise to the larger debate on (1) how to contain the migration of Bangladeshis (2) how to contain the communal conflict in the context of influx of migration of Bangladeshis, (3) it also led to interstate dispute between two or three riparian states on river water (classic case is of between Karnataka and Tamil Nadu).

On the contrary, in India, the public policy concern centred around the issues of reduction in the productivity of agriculture, increase in drought and flood frequency, increase in sea level water and frequency of extreme events. That does not mean that there wasn't other concerns too. In fact, in India, the concern also expressed on the social categories who contributed towards climate change. It was found that in India the large amount of contribution to climate change came from urbanite, rich including the fact that it is centred around some sectors such as power energy = 48 per cent of emissions, followed by road transport (10 per cent), iron

8. Rafael Reuveny, Climate change-induced migration and violent conflict Political geography, Vol. 26, 2007, pp. 656-673.

and steel (10 per cent) The class/ sectoral nature of the climate change is apparent in the followed:

Table 10.1: Per Capita Annual Energy Use (Direct and Indirect) 1989–90*

Income Group	*Coal (kg)*	*Oil (kg)*	*Elec (Kwh)*	*Carbon (t)*
		RURAL		
Bottom (50%)	74	22.5	95	054
Middle (40%)	127	39.7	152	093
Top (10%)	262	89.8	284	204
		URBAN		
Bottom (50%)	130	45.6	164	101
Middle (40%)	302	118.6	366	246
Top (10%)	765	332.3	858	656

In India, other concern is that it would adversely affect the sustainable development. In fact, the climate change is not viewed in isolation but rather linked to the larger issues of science and technology, economy and trade, diplomacy and politics.

It is in this context Central Government has come out with a National Action Plan for Climate Change. This action plan combined the issues of sustainable development with climate change. It has had couple of guiding principles: Protection of poor and vulnerable groups through what is called "inclusive and climate change sensitive development", secondly, "achieving growth through sustainable development", thirdly, "integration of demand side of management for the purpose of saving resources", fourthly, 'adaptation of appropriate technologies, engineering of new technologies, sustainable development." Its mission centred around seven important issues. They include energy security with emphasis on solar energy and its decentralisation, two, energy efficiency which include green projects, captive generation, three sustainable Habitat which include development of energy efficient building, and waste management, fourthly, water management – this include establishment of water data base for the purpose of its utilisation in the public domain, promotion of judicious management of water. In fact, most important is the Green India Project. This project include Enhancing Carbon Sink potentials to bring down greenhouse gases, enhancing resilience of species and eco-systems to reduce vulnerability," enabling adaptation of forest dependent local people in the context of climatic vulnerability", other two issues are Sustainable Agriculture and Strategic Knowledge. In the former case, the stress is on increasing the share of dry and rain-fed agriculture, enhancement of farm productivity and risk management and in the latter case, establishment of Central Knowledge system and increasing the capacity building of people and institutions. Interestingly all these things have remained at the rhetorical level.

Thirdly, India's concern at the global level is to push the principle of equity which called for western world to cut their carbon emission in a timely manner including the fact that it demanded incremental cost to be beared by the developing world. All these politics have beared little fruit given the fact that India is slowly but literally emerging as a country with "potential for disturbing climate at the global level".

VI. Debate in Karnataka

Karnataka is slowly but steadily witnessing climate issue as political one-Growing concern for river water, increasing migration of population from north Karnataka, suicides of thousands of farmers, depleting forest areas, increasing pressure on the coastal belt by the industrialisation, recurring drought situation etc., all have contributed towards larger debate on climate change – at the same time the debates have centred around the political implication of climate change on the body politics too- will the state able to contain the recurring drought situation, will it be able to contain the migration of people to metropolitan areas ? Will it be able to delink the development from the larger loss of livelihood? Will the climate change is the gift of science? What would be the larger implication of climate change? Are some of the major debates taking place in Karnataka? Most of the time the issues of climate change is viewed as problem of science, and urbanisation and industrialisation rather than the issues of increased commodification of nature in Karnataka.

Projection and Concerns of Climate Change in Karnataka

Karnataka is of the first states in India to initiate steps on climatic change. This is because of the fact that after Rajasthan, Karnataka is said to be the second most vulnerable state in India for climate change in the years to come.[9] Incidentally, recent study conducted by Indian Institute of Science stated that not all the

---

9 Deccan Herald, Change to avoid climate change, December 23, 2010.

districts in Karnataka will be uniformly affected by climate change rather five districts of North Karnataka would be badly affected by it by 2030. These five districts include Bidar, Gulbarga, Raichur, Bellary and Bijapur. These districts will witness an increase of 2 to 3°C in temperature, and at the same time they witness reduction of 5 to 10 per cent in rainfall. They would witness extremity in weather condition. It is said that northern districts will witness an increase of 2°C by the year of 2030. It is further argued that by 2030 state would be witnessing a warming of 1.8 to 2.2°C.

Many studies (CSST: 2010, ISEC: 2010, EMPRI: 2010) have predicted that Karnataka will emerge as one of the driest places as well as it will witness depletion of rain fall in the years to come. It is believed that it will increase the drought by thirty per cent.

Further it is argued that climate change would affect the green cover in the Karnataka, particularly the Western Ghat regions. – It is predicted that by 2035 Karnataka will loose not less than 4/2 million sq km of forest area = which is approximately 38 per cent of the current forest areas/ this has led to the growth of areas of concerns.

There are other concerns too. One of the major concerns is in the area of land – the increasing use of fertiliser, pesticide and also the degradation of land has led to the thinking of preserving the land, the most important concern is apparent in the sphere of agriculture. Poverty and economic status. It is argued that the climate change will deplete agricultural production particularly maize and pulses[10] and thereby increases the vulnerability of peasants or farmers to the vagaries of larger market.

VII. Green House Inventory[11] of Karnataka: Who Contributes to Climate Change in Karnataka?

There has been a raging controversy with regard to the green-house inventory. Who literally contributes for the greenhouse effect in Karnataka is one major question quite often asked.

Karnataka is one of the fast developing states in India, and therefore it is easy to link the issues of climate change and the development. In fact, Karnataka is now witnessing two path of development: Aggressive Path of Capitalist Path and Non-Aggressive Path of development. However, not all the sectors

---

[10] The Hindu, " Climate change to hit north Karnataka hard," March 28, 2011.

[11] http://www.cstep.in/node/260

are contributing the Green House effect – It is found that the contribution of power is highest amounting to 35.90 per cent followed by agriculture 20.2 per cent. Iron and steel is the third sector which affects the climate change in Karnataka, (10.73 per cent) followed by transport 10.48 per cent, and cement (9, 5 per cent), this is obvious from the following chart.

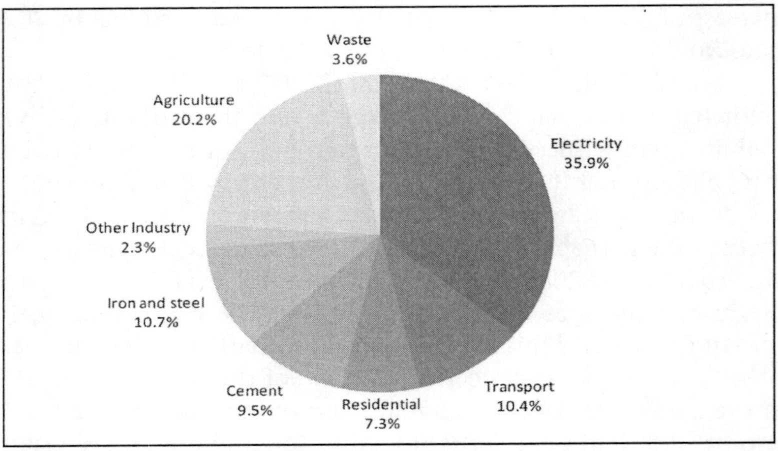

Figure 10.1: Karnataka: GHG Emissions by Sector.

Interestingly the electricity generation constitute the main culprit of green house effect in Karnataka. During 2008-09 they contributed nearly 28 per cent towards carbond emission in Karnataka.

Table 10.2: Karnataka: Industrial Emissions, 2008-2009

Industry		*Production (Million Tons)*	*CO_2 Emissions (Tons)*	*Total CO_2 Emisions (Millions Tons)*
ALUMINIUM		0.11	1.65	0.180
IRON	PIG IRON	0.23	1.46	0.330
&	SALEABLE STEEL	0.14	0.70	0.098
STEEL	STEEL INGOTS	0.15	0.08	0.012
PAPER		0.37	1.05	0.384
SUGAR		3.40	0.241	0.819
AMMONIA		0.24	0.82	0.197
CEMENT		12.10	0.63	7.642
IRON ORE		36.39	0.008	0.291
TOTAL				9.954

Table 10.3: Karnataka: Summary Of Greenhouse Gas (Ghg) Inventory*

	Particulars	*Quantity/ Production/ Area*	*Production (Units)*	*CO_2 Emissions (In Million Tonnes)*	*CH_4 Emissions (In Million Tonnes)*	*N_2O Emissions (In Million Tonnes)*	*CO_2 Equivalence (In Million-Tonnes)*
ENERGY	Electricity Generation (2009-2010)	11,495	*MW*	28.76	-	-	28.76
	Transport (2007-08)	-	-	8.35	-	-	8.35
	Residential {2007-08J	-	-	3.57	0.0900	0.0012	5.84
INDUSTRY (2008-2009)	Cement Production	120.97	*Lakh tonnes*	7.64	-	-	7.64
	Iron & Steel Production	115.4	*Lakh tonnes*	S.S9	-	-	8.59
	Ammonia Production	2.36	*Lakh tonnes*	0.19	-	-	0.19
	Aluminium Production	1.09	*Lakh tonnes*	0.180	-	-	0.18
	Iron Ore	423.14	*Lakh tonnes*	0.291	-	-	0.29
	Pulp and Paper	3.65	*Lakh tonnes*	0.38	-	-	0.38
	Sugar	33.97	*Lakh tonnes*	0.82	-	-	0.82
AGRICULTURE	Enteric Fermentation (2003)	2,56,17,000	*Animals*	-	0.50	-	10.54
	Livestock Manure Management (2003)	2,56,17,000	*Animals*	-	0.04	0.00654	2.93
	Rice Cultivation (2007)	1.40	*Million hectare*	-	0.13	-	2.75
WASTE		-	-	-	0.126	0.00079	2.89
TOTAL							**80.16**

* It has to be pointed out again that the data for the same period was unavailable for all sectors. All attempts were made to get the most recent data for each of the sector. Hence it is likely that the total emissions will be higher than the 80 million tonnes given above. One could have fixed a particular year and projected the emissions of sectors where data was unavailable. However, this would introduce more errors as several assumptions had to be made in the projection. Going forward the government should take concerted efforts to collect annual data.

The Green House Effect or Climate Change has effected different sectors as well as categories. The state of environment report of 2003 for example has identified, that, vehicular pollution effects public health much more. The Degradation of forest due to the construction of thermal plants has affected the biodiversity , "vulnerable groups", and critical eco system. It also caused productivity loss too.

Table 10.4:

Problem	*Public Health*	*Loss of biodiversity*	*Impact on vulnerable groups*	*Productivity Loss*	*Critical Ecosystem*	*Irreversibility*	*Urgency*	*Total*
Degradation of forests due to firewood extraction	3	5	5	5	3	5	5	31
Loss of forest areas due to power plants	1	5	3	3	5	5	1	23
Air pollution due to thermal plants	3	1	3	1	1	3	3	15
Air pollution due to vehicles plants	5	1	5	3	1	5	3	23
Air pollution due to captive power plants	3	1	5	1	1	5	3	19
Soil pollution due to thermal plants	3	1	3	1	1	3	3	15
Unequal distribution of energy	1	1	5	5	1	1	5	19
Energy shortage	3	1	5	5	1	1	5	21
Low energy Efficiencies	5	5	5	5	1	5	5	31

VIII. Paradigm Shift

The shift in the governance is apparent when state government came out with different policy measures including establishing Climate Hub in Institute of Social and Economic Change. It is also planning to have a task force to deal with the issues of climate change. More than that it has come out with a draft policy on climate change. In the former case mode of the governance has shifted over the past one decade towards insisting on rain water harvesting, water conservation, community based tank management, priority to organic farming, use of solar energy afforestation programmes etc.

In fact, paradigm shift is apparent in the following major concerns:

(a) **Concern about environment:** Karnataka is one of the first states to come out with "State Environmental Report". Along with a draft bill on climate change state government has come out with a action plan, covering such issues as Green House Gas inventory, Climate variability and climate change projections, Impact on Forests, Agricultural Sector, Water Resources, Socio-economic Vulnerability and Adaptive Capacity Assessment and Mitigation options in energy sector.

(b) **Energy:** Karnataka government has come out with Karnataka Renewable Energy Policy of 2009-14 which aims at massively increasing the renewable energy, it has come out with Eco-friendly resorts, and it has made mandatory the use of certain energy saving appliance for certain uses. And energy efficient motor pump sets, power. Further, it has gone in for regeneration of degraded forest and protection of old trees through the participation of local population. It has undertaken massive greenery programme in the cities and also it has identified what is called "lung spaces in the urban areas". It has come out with what is called Bhoo-Chetana programme meant for promoting dry land farming. It aims at increasing the yield at 44 per cent and aims at covering 12.5 lakh hectares of fifteen districts Energy policy envisages the establishment of series of mini hydel projects in the Western Ghats under private-public partnership or Build Operate Own or BOOT scheme. To mitigate the air pollution, the government has established Task Force, appointed a steering committee on Development of Bio-Fuel.

(c) **Land:** Third important concern as well as paradigm shift is obvious in the case of land. The degradation of land including the agricultural as well as forest land has been the other major concerns of the Karnataka government. One thing is clear that the increasing use of chemical fertilisers and pesticides have affected the environment. The increasing use of chemical fertilisers has contaminated the water and soil. This is obvious with the fact that the use of chemical fertiliser has increased from 1.11 million tonnes in 1996-7 to 1.29 million tonnes 2001-02. In this context couple of districts have been identified as the hotspots of excessive use of chemical fertilisers (Shimoga, Mandya, Bellary and Raichur). Excessive pesticide use (Gulbarga, Raichur and Bijapur), hotspot of soil erosion (all northern plain districts) and hotspot of water erosion (coastal and western ghat region). Under the National Watershed Development Programme it has initiated to reclaim the alkine lands and resorted to for massive reforestation.

Paradigm Shift and Initiatives of The Government

Other than the above, the Karnataka government has come out with series of programmes to combat climate change this is obvious in the following:

- Fiscal incentives for voluntary reduction of emission.
- Kannada Ganga: A new scheme to supply safe drinking water.
- Rejuvenation of 36,000 tanks in different parts of Karnataka.
- Establishment of Bio Fuel Board.
- Capacity building of local and urban bodies.
- Establishment of Waste Energy Project in Karnataka.
- Ground water harvesting.
- Starting Jalasiri Programme to establish two lakh check dams to increase the underground water level.
- Development of Lakes in Metropolitan areas such as in Bengaluru (twenty five lakes have been rejuvenated till date).
- Establishment of Western Ghat Task Force as the latter is said to be hot spot of four thousand five hundred varieties of species.
- Establishment of Village Forest Committees to protect the forest cover/ (Till date fifty thousand such committees have been established in different villages.
- Planting trees in more than 80,000 hectares per annum.
- Establishment of 3377 Bio-diversity Management Committees.
- Supporting organic farming. (Till date 52,300 farmers covering 70,000 hectares of land have adopted organic farming).

IX. Conclusions

Although it is true that Karnataka as a state has prepared itself for the climate change however not all the states have prepared themselves to face the larger socio-political implication of climate change. This issue is not simply an issue of environment but an issue of science and society- can people continue to live with unrestricted exploitation of natural resources? Can people live under the perpetual threat of extinction in the context of climate change? Will it not translate into larger political crisis? All these questions required to confront in due course. However, it is definite and clear-cut that climate change is the child of science, and its implication on politics is much larger than what is anticipated. Although states might have come out with different public policies, however question remains as to the possibilities of facing the climate change in the years to come. It is true that States as well as societies will not survive unless and until "capitalism is not disciplined, commoditisation of environment is not contained, and consumption is not restricted".

Appendix

Sl. No.	*District*	*Increase projected in T_{avg} (in °C)*	*Increase projected in T_{min} (in °C)*	*Increase projected in T_{max} (in °C)*
1	Yadgir	2.21	2.34	2.10
2	Bijapur	2.20	2.32	2.11
3	Raichur	2.20	2.31	2.12
4	Gulbarga	2.19	2.33	2.04
5	Bagalkote	2.15	2.25	2.10
6	Koppal	2.14	2.21	2.09
7	Bidar	2.12	2.30	1.93
8	Bellary	2.08	2.16	2.03
9	Gadag	2.08	2.15	2.05
10	Belgaum	2.01	2.11	1.98
11	Chitradurga	2.00	2.07	1.97
12	Dharwad	2.00	2.08	1.97
13	Mandya	1.99	2.03	2.00
14	Tumkur	1.99	2.06	1.96
15	Chikballapur	1.98	2.06	1.91
16	Davangere	1.98	2.05	1.98
17	Bangalore Rural	1.97	2.06	1.91
18	Haveri	1.97	2.04	1.97
19	Ramanagar	1.97	2.05	1.92
20	Bangalore Urban	1.96	2.06	1.88
21	Chamarajanagar	1.96	2.03	1.94
22	Kolar	1.96	2.06	1.87
23	Mysore	1.95	1.99	1.98
24	Hassan	1.92	1.96	1.95
25	Shimoga	1.88	1.95	1.91
26	Uttarakannada	1.87	1.96	1.86
27	Chikmagalur	1.86	1.93	1.89
28	Kodagu	1.79	1.86	1.81
29	Dakshina Kannada	1.72	1.81	1.71
30	Udupi	1.71	1.78	1.72

11

Economy, Environment and Sustainable Development—Concepts and Concerns

Professor S Rajendran

1. Introduction

There is a spurt in the academic literature that the concept of Sustainable Development emerged as leading mantra. Research studies cutting across boundaries have been flooded in the domain of Sustainable Development. Though everyone stakes claim over this, it is more appropriate in Development Economics as it is related to all spheres of human activity. Development planners and policy-makers have often emphasised the need for Sustainable Development in the long run. Any development programme should sustain shocks, though larger sometimes, and ultimately deliver the goods in a judicial manner. The concept, Sustainable Development is more and closely related to resource use as the resource has to be meticulously used for attaining Sustainable Development. Unfortunately due to increasing wants such resources - mainly nonrenewable -are non-judiciously used. This has forced the planners and policy-makers to think over Sustainable Development. This has been seriously put to debate and action ever since the earths submit held in 1991 at Brazil.

There is a clear distinction between the developed and developing regions in terms of resource use, production frontiers and consumption patterns. In other words while the developed countries consume more developing countries suffer to meet both ends. Even within developing countries, the affluent consumes more and the poor suffers, a lot. This cannot be avoided in a pluralistic politically diverse ideological set up in countries like India. But the gap has to be bridged for a balanced, equitable, faster, inclusive and sustainable development.

Against this backdrop the present study makes a moderate attempt to explore the Sustainable Development with regard to India. During the course of discussion on Sustainable Development as is largely related with agriculture sector obviously for the best known reason, agriculture sustainability is taken into account. As is known resource use is a complex and serious issue in agriculture. Hence it is appropriate to relate the Sustainable Development with agriculture and environment.

Indian Economy

There has been a drastic change in the composition of Indian Economy ever since political Independence of 1947. After a long spell of political slavery India virtually had many issues to tackle immediately with the domestic front. There was series of famines, starvation deaths, poor sanitation, and political unrest in some regions, alarming birth rate and so on, which came as stumbling block in the development works.

Available data indicate that more than 80 per cent of active population depended on agriculture. It also initially contributed substantially to the Gross Domestic Product (GDP). Literally manufacturing and service sector were inactive in those days. Even in agriculture sector, the performance was far from satisfactory and sometimes disguising. Hence there was a huge investment in agriculture sector especially for irrigation projects, research and development during the initial phases of planning.

In the course of development planning attention has been paid for other sectors as well. Consequently, there has been a considerable shift in the contribution of GDP from manufacturing and services sectors. Now the agriculture sector contributes less to GDP and other economic sectors - manufacturing and service – give maximum share. Nevertheless, the population depends on agriculture sector continues to over 50 per cent, which is a challenging task for the planners to reduce it. Simultaneously new technological packages in the form of green revolution have been launched to increase food production. Modern inputs, which induce yield in select crops with back up of rural credit delivery the food grain production increased considerably. There are arguments that such technology has helped and concentrated on a specific crop groups like cereals leaving others like minor millets, oilseeds and pulses to mercy. Dismally, is a telling truth that such farm technology has rendered adverse impact on the economy and environment in general and agriculture in particular?

In tune with this, industrial sector too got attention to boost the manufacturing sector. The Nehruvian Model of 'Mixed Economy' has helped the industrial sector to grow both horizontally and vertically. Till the arrival of information technology the service sector was showing a lukewarm response. Now this sector superseded others and gives a flip to Indian Economy. Nonetheless, it is to be remembered that industrial development resulted in environmental damage through dumping and excessive fossil energy use.

Unfortunately the balance of payments crisis in early 1990s forced the government to introduce economic reform policies on a determined way. Since then there has been a complete change in the composition of Indian Economy with varying degrees of sustainability. Political instability, social tension and intrusion of terrorism have often hampered the development where the phrase of sustainability is at stake. Now there is a situation that the Indian Economy is growing comfortably rather than rapidly. Many left wing thinkers foresee that the decent economic growth will not sustain in the present scenario. This is what the agriculture sector is witnessing now, where distress is mounting, resource use becomes absolute and environment collapsed. Consequently, there has been severe distress on the rural segment in general and farm community in particular. There is a complete policy shift in Indian Diaspora. While the market-based economic policies come to play, the agriculture sector got back seat. A number of unpleasant developments including distress and suicides have been surfaced and intriguing arguments have been cited for this distress situation. One group of Think-Tank argues that the 'technology fatigue, in agriculture is responsible for the present crisis. On the other, there is an argument that 'Policy fatigue' resulted in the present agrarian distress. Hence there is a serious doubt about the agriculture sustainability in the coming years.

A cursory look at the sectoral growth of economy shows that during 1980's GDP grow at 5.6 per cent and the same continued during 1990's. However, the agriculture sector exhibited a dealing trend. Industrial sector too showed a slight decrease. The service sector, depicted a significant increase of 8.1 per cent in 1990s as compared to 2.39 per cent during 1980. This kind of skewed growth pattern is undesirable for countries like India. Also this would not sustain in the long run as it is seen for the past couple of years.

II. Agriculture and Indian Economy

The largest portion of the natural resources of India consists of land and by far the largest number of its inhabitants is engaged in agriculture for their survival. Therefore, in any scheme of economic development of the country, agriculture holds a position of basic importance. Although Indian agriculture is way back compared to the levels in developed countries, some notable developments have occurred over the years since independence in 1947. Large areas which suffered from repeated failure of rainfall have received irrigation; new crops have come to occupy a significant position in the country's production and trade; the agricultural and the industrial economies in the country now exert a powerful influence on one another; problems of rural indebtedness and the exploitative practices of the village money lender are much less, and finally there is already in the countryside an awakening and a desire for raising standards of living.

Now agricultural sector occupies a key position in the India economy. It provides employment to about 55 per cent of the working population of India. Around one-fifth of India's national income originates from the agriculture sector. It is imperative that the problems of farmers are addressed with a sense of urgency. Agriculture being a State subject, the bulk of public investment in agriculture takes place at the level of State and the Union Government supports the State as a catalyst agency.

Agriculture development has been compounded with a number of issues including 'sustainability'. Sustainability is a complex and contested concept. To some it implies persistence and capacity of something to continue for a long time. To others, it implies resilience and the ability to bounce back after unexpected difficulties. Regarding environment it implies not damaging or degrading natural resources.

Definitions of sustainable agriculture are generally concerned with the need for food, to meet the need for agricultural practices to be economically viable, to meet human needs for food, to be environmentally positive, and to be concerned with quality of life. Since these objectives can be achieved in a number of ways, sustainable agriculture is not linked to any particular technological practice. Nor is sustainable agriculture is the exclusive domain of organic farming. Rather sustainable agriculture is thought in terms of adaptability and flexibility over time to respond to the demands for food and fiber (both high and low), its demand on natural resources for productivity and its ability to protect the soil and the resources for production. This goal requires an efficient use of technology in a manner conducive to sustainability in the long run.

In a sense the sustainability is measured in term of the elasticity, i.e. the time taken for output return to trend values after a significant shock. Some empirical studies show that wheat showed an elasticity of 4-7 years or more, while oats had a much lower elasticity and hence higher sustainability at 1-5 years. Overall, Pretty (1990) concludes, the manorial system (utilisation of labour intensive technique) was a low productivity system, a highly equitable system and a sustainable system.

This is an interesting reflection on sustainable development generally since it offers some evidence for the concern that future-oriented system may be at the expense of well being now. In this connection the concept of sustainability did not depend on single factor. Conversely, it depends on various factors.

The next factor of unsustainability relates to diversity or complexity. It has been argued that diversity may be linked to stability and to resilience (Sustainability). But the links between diversity and stability have been strongly disputed in ecology and there is no consensus. Elton (1958) suggested that diversity is a cause of stability, but May (1973) showed that the more complex a system is the less stable it is in the context of general mathematical models. That is, the diversity-stability, link seems far less researched, however. Arguments in favour of conserving diversity, as opposed to the stock of biological resources diversity, have been advanced in terms of ethics, aesthetics and economics (Wilson, 1998). It is widely argued, however, that biodiversity conservation is required for insurance purpose: i.e., for sustaining output, particularly agricultural output, in the face of risk to the genetic base of existing output. If so, then diversity does have a link to sustainable development.

There is a theoretical argument that as the country moves towards economic development in with high growth in manufacturing sector agriculture would lose its significance (Timmer, 2005). Unfortunately, in India the proportion of population depends on agriculture is decreasing slowly. Contradictory to this the share of agriculture to total GDP is decreasing very fast and it is well behind 19 per cent in India. This kind of distorted growth pattern will not sustain in the long run.

III. Environmental Pollution and Natural Resources

Probably the most vocal the critics of our development strategy are the environmentalists. This is not surprising as the concern for environment compels one to take a holistic and long-term view. If the present trend continues, the environmentalists warn us, our cities would soon begin to cross the critical level of pollution, the land and water resources would get irreparably damaged and processes of human development, which are already slow, rather than promote it. How do the environmentalists look at the agricultural scenario over the coming critical decades?

All over the world the environmental pollution is posing a serious problem to living organisms. Air, water, land and habitations are falling prey to the increasing environmental concerns. Increased use of plastic and other harmful substances results in environmental pollution, which would have a serious repercussion to the sustainable development. The US Environmental Protection Agency estimated that e-waste will increase at the rate of 5-10 per cent globally. The e-waste, a recent but deadly pollutant would (1962) harm soil and human health.

Solid waste emerges from habitation is another challenging task. While India produces 25 million tonnes, the USA generates 11 billion tonnes of solid waste every day. The Citizens Reports on Environment, published by the Centre for Science and Environment warned the growth of solid waste and its harmful effects on environment.

The chief cause of concern about agriculture is the use of chemicals. The silent spring by R. Carson (1962) brought to fore a number of adverse effects of agro-chemicals. In fact, application of agro-chemicals was very low in the early stages of adopting green revolution technologies. It was negligible in those years, while today it is probably around 80 kgs per hectare. This is by no means a high level of application but the problem of pollution has already appeared on the sense and is spreading. The prevailing fertiliser use in India has three aspects calling for policy attention. Firstly, an imbalance is emerging between the use of organic and chemical fertilisers. When modernisation invades agriculture, traditional practices lose out including some which are as important and relevant today as in the past. Secondly, application of chemicals in an unscientific manner would lead to human cost. Thirdly, irrecoverable damage would be done to beneficial organisations that are present in the environment.

Table 11.1: Health Disorders in Padre Village

Health Disorders	*No. of Cases*
Cancer	49
Mental Retardation	23
Congenital Anomalies	09
Psychiatric Cases	43
Epilepsy	23
Suicides	09
Total	**156**

Source: Rajendran (2002).

A case pertinent to this group is environmental terrorism unleashed on Padre village in Kasargod. The state institution - Karnataka Cashew Plantation Corporation (KCPC) – itself aerial sprayed endosulphan to prevent caterpillar pest in cashew plantation. Ultimately the entire eco-system has been affected. Many children became crippled and a few have been affected with dreaded diseases. While the civil societies contested this, the state supported machineries supported.

There are a number of environmental problems, affect the natural resources in general. The important are as follows:

- Contamination of water by pesticides and fertilisers.
- Overuse of natural resources causing depletion of ground water, water logging and increased salinity and alkalinity, leading to deterioration in productivity of soil and quality of farm products.
- Of the country's total geographical area of 329 million hectare, about 188 million hectare (57 per cent) is degraded due to various reasons such as overuse and non-judicial use of fertiliser in some pockets. Wind and water erosion due to removal of vegetative cover in potential regions.
- Contamination of food and fodder by residues of pesticides nitrates and antibiotics.
- Damage to farm and natural resources by pesticides, causing harm to farm workers and public, disruption of ecosystem and harm to wild life.
- Pesticide – induced pest resistance and resurgence.

- Removal of habitats of wise predators.
- New health hazards for workers in agro-chemical and food processing industries.

Table 11.2: Endoasulphan Residues in Kasargod District

Sample	*Detected value of Endosulpahn*	*Maximum Residue Limited—MRL*	*No. of Times values Exceeds MRL*
Water	9.9	0.18	51
Butter	14.0	NA	NA
Cows skin/fat	49.99	0.1	500
Vegetables	31.24	0.4-2.0	78-16
Human milk	22.40	NA	NA
Human blood	196.47	NA	NA
Live frog	10.35	NA	NA
Cashew	3.74	NA	NA
Spices	212.28	NA	NA
Fish	22.24	NA	NA
Soil	35.16	0.09	391
Cash leaves	6.52	NA	NA

Source: Rajendran, 2002, *Note*: All figures parts per million (ppm).

There are possibilities for carrying out farm operations without using chemicals. Therefore, the present conventional farming, which is capital intensive and energy consuming system, needs to be modified or changed. Hence of three major farming systems, organic in focused as advantageous.

Table 11.3: Features of Different Farming System

Issues	*Traditional*	*Conventional*	*Organic*
Productivity	Low	High	Low
Sustainability	Moderate	Low	High
Farm Complexity	Complex	Simple	Complex
Environment diversity	Diverse	Uniform	Diverse
Production orientation	Subsistence	Market	Subsistence/Market
Input – Seeds	Local	HYVs	Improved/Local
Synthetic inputs	Low	High	Nil

Farming can be classified based on various issues. However, for a layman's understanding, it is classified only three as traditional, conventional and organic. Each system has its own merits over others. But it is unfortunate that there is no clear methodology, which has been developed for measuring sustainable development. Some economists like M.V. Nadkarni, Monteith and Partha Das

Gupta have been ventured towards this direction without much useful result.

IV. Sustainable Development

A number of individuals and organisation has defined Sustainable Development in many ways. As it was outlined already, it is a contention for a few and others it is a challenging task. The environmentalists, economists and policy-makers have been attempting to develop a model for sustainable index. A bird's eye view of the Sustainable Development is given below.

Niu *et al* (1993) have developed a framework for sustainable development that builds on the basic definition of sustainability development. They suggested employing a spatial systems approach, with each spatial system comprising five systems as Richness of the resource, Strength of the economy, Stability of society; Tolerability of the environment and Soundness of decision. Sustainability indicators are then selected to gauge each of these.

Montieth (1990) proposed determining sustainability from a contingency table of trends of inputs and outputs. This is a simple indicator as presented below.

Table 11.4: Linkage Between Inputs and Outputs

Outputs	*Inputs*		
	Decreasing	*Constant*	*Increasing*
Decreasing	In determinant	Unsustainable	Unsustainable
Constant	Sustainable	Sustainable	Unsustainable
Increasing	Sustainable	Sustainable	In determinant

Although a single sustainability indicator may be relatively easy to interpret provided one has clear reference point, the interpretation of a suite of sustainability indicators may be problematic. What does one conclude if some are within the reference limits and some are not? Does one take an all or nothing point of view (the 'binary' view of sustainability – either a system is sustainable or not), or can one conceive of gradations of sustainability (van Pelt *et al*, 1995)? However, a few notable definition of Sustainable Development is given below:

"Sustainable development that meets the needs of the current generations without compromising the ability of the future generations to meet their needs and aspirations" (WCED, 1987).

The Technical Advisory Committee of the Consultative Group on International Agricultural Research (TAC/CGIAR,1988) states that *Sustainable Agriculture is the successfully management of resources for agriculture to satisfy changing human needs while maintaining or enhancing the quality of the environment and conserving natural resources. The location specific appropriate technologies are to be evolved to develop economically viable, ecologically sound, socially acceptable, culturally adaptable and humane which take care of the soil and thus sustain agricultural production.*

Sustainable development that improves the quality of human life while living within the carrying capacity of the supporting ecosystems (IUCN,1991).

Development is sustainable if the increase in living standards or the processes by which development occurs can be maintained without the continual injection of outside resources (Graforth, 1993).

Indicators of Unsustainable Agricultural Development

- Practices using soil to erode those which conserve soil.
- Removal of habitats of insect predators or kill them directly, and those that conserve predators.
- Decrease in soil fertility, crop loss due to increased pest and disease incidence, loss of crop diversification, increased use of external inputs, and loss of potentially economic flora/ fauna- all indicators of unsustainability.
- Nevertheless, as outlined for Sustainability measurement here too there are methodological difficulties. The above variables are to either modified or changed as per the need for measuring unsustainability.

V. Conditions For Sustainability Agriculture

Sustainable agriculture needs more than new technologies and practices. It needs agricultural professionals willing and able to learn from farmers. It needs local groups and institutions capable of managing resources effectively and more important, it needs agricultural policies that support these features.

- In the diverse, complex and complex 'resource-poor' lands of the third world, farmers adopting regenerative technologies have doubled crop yields. Often with little or no use of external inputs;

- In the high input and generally irrigated lands, farms adopting regenerative technologies have maintained yields while sustainability reducing inputs;
- In the industrialised agricultural systems, a transition to sustainable agriculture could mean a fall in per hectare yields of 10-20 per cent in the short-term, but with buffer levels of financial returns to farmers.
- Using indigenous knowledge with local resources.
- Identify, propagate and manage appropriate, sustainable techniques and technologies for overall development.

Strategies of Sustainable Agriculture development

Sustainable agricultural development mainly depends on the following three essential steps. They should also be viable, appropriate, feasible and adoptable to the society.

A. Appropriate System
B. Appropriate technologies, and
C. Institutional arrangement.

With slight modification, appropriate technological system may be developed, tested and put to use. Again periodical evaluation has to be made with appropriate institutional arrangements for attaining Sustainable Development.

In the union budget 2016-2017, there has been announcement to promote sustainable farm practices. Both the union government and other state governments should join hands for pushing this crucial issue in the interest of overall and sustainable agriculture development. There have been academic debates in the forums that both policy fatigue and technological fatigue led to distress in farm sector. It clearly shows that both the policymakers and the scientists shall work towards promoting agriculture development. For this organic farming is not only sustainable but also feasible to adopt in the long run.

Against this backdrop, time has come to look into various economic and environmental issues besides food security in view. Because during the transition from modern farming to sustainable farming system, it is possible that the yield and production will be lower. This needs to be considered in the context of ensuring food security for a large country like India.

VI. Concluding Observations

Undeniably the sustainability argument is attracted in all disciplines of academia. This is particularly pertinent to Economic Development as it is directly related to welfare of the people. While there are serious flaw in production, distribution and consumption patterns of goods and services across developed and developing countries sustainable development needs to be carefully and critically looked into many ways and India is not an exception to this. Hence the whole question of sustainable development has to be viewed carefully. This is very much on the focus after the launching of new economic policies in this subcontinent.

There has been a considerable shift in the sectoral contribution to national economy. Unfortunately due to various challenging factors, the development is unsustainable in the long run. The classic example is agriculture development during 1970s and 1980s and the glamour for information technology during the last two decades. Now due to recession in major economies the future of Information Technology sector is in gloom.

Due to the non-judicial use of inputs in agriculture the resource management and environment became debatable issues. Unfortunately there is no clear methodology to explore further in the academic arena. This has forced the researchers to comfort and deliberate on the whole issues of sustainable development on a holistic manner. It is high time that the research fraternity shall seriously attempts towards this direction for attaining equitable, feasible, adoptable and sustainable development.

The union government has given some attention the recent budget to promote sustainable organic farming system in India. However, it (the success) depends upon the active support of both state governments and the union government.

References

1. CGIAR (1988), "Sustainable Agriculture Production: Implication for International Agricultural Research", *Report of the Technical Advisory Committee, Consultative Group on International Agricultural Research"*, Rome, Italy, FAO.
2. Elton, C.S. (1958), "The Ecology of Invasions by Animals and Plants", London, Menthuen.
3. Graforth, Chris (1993), "Sustainable Extension for Sustainable Agriculture", Rural Extension Bulletin.

4. IUCN, (International Union for Conservation of Nature, 1991), "Caring for the Earth: A Strategy for Sustainable Living", *IUCN,* Gland, Switzerland.
5. May, R.M. (1973), "Stability and Complexity in Model Ecosystems", Princeton, New Jersey: Princeton University Press.
6. Niu, W- lu, J J and Khan, A.A., (1993), "Spatial System Approach to Sustainable Development: A Conceptual Framework", *Environmental Management,* 17(2): 179-186.
7. Pretty, J (1990), "Sustainable Agriculture in Asia – Farmers Level Initiatives in India", *ANGOC Resource Book Series,* Philippines.
8. Rajendran, S. (2002), "Pesticides Spraying in Kerala - Human Cost and Environment Loss", *Economics and Political Weekly,* June 8, pp. 2206-2207.
9. ------------ (2008), "Environment Challenges of 21st Century" *Conference Proceedings,* Department of Economics, Periyar University, Salem.
10. Timmer, PC (2005), "Agriculture and Pro-Poor Growth an Asia Perspective", *Centre for Global Development,* Washington, DC.
11. Wilson, E.O. (1988), "Biodiversity", *National Academy Press,* Washington DC.
12. WCED (World Commission on Environment and Development, 1987), Our Common Future, *Oxford University Press,* Oxford.

12

Economic Viability of Rainfed Sericulture vis-à-vis the Competing Crops – An Economic Analysis

Professor D.V. Gopalappa

I. Introduction

There is a substantial evidence that the sericulture (mulberry cultivation and silk worm rearing) activity generates better income and employment to the subsistence marginal and small farmers in the villages (Gopalappa, 2000), and therefore, this activity was introduced as one of the income-employment enhancing poverty alleviation programmes during the Sixth Plan period (GOI, 1980). For the farmers, silk cocoon is the final product and silk reeling is being practiced by the weaker sections, in semi-urban areas, whose livelihood depends on reeling activity (Inbanathan and Gopalappa, 1998).

There are three silk reeling technologies, viz., charka, cottage basin and filature. In India, only, the first two technologies are used to reel the silk cocoons as there are number of deficiencies to go for filature reeling. The other operations like twisting silk, de-gumming, warping, weaving, dyeing, colouring, etc., are the forward linkages in sericulture for generating employment for huge number of labourers. Altogether about 62.69 lakhs of labourers are involved in the activity and per ha., about 13 man years of employment generation is taking place per agricultural year. Out of a rupee, which is generated by the sericulture activity, the cocoon producer gets about ₹ 0.33, reeler takes about ₹ 0.07, all the other processors of silk get about ₹ 0.17 and the traders are getting the major share of about ₹ 0.43 (Gopalappa, 1997). Even then, many studies proved that sericulture is a profitable venture for the farming community. Therefore, a significant progress was achieved in this sector during the decades of eighties and nineties with the assistance of World Bank and other financial agencies. However, the recent trend is quite disturbing for the development of sericulture as most of the farmers are uprooting mulberry plants and shifting towards horticultural crops due to continuous drought from 1999-2000 to 2003-04.

The above trend is visible in all the southern states like Karnataka, Andhra Pradesh and Tamil Nadu. According to a rough estimation by Gopalappa (2002), about 40 per cent of the area under mulberry has come down and mostly the medium and large farmers either they have downsized the area under mulberry or they have totally uprooted the same. Despite this a large number of marginal and small farmers in these states continued to earn their livelihood through rainfed sericulture under the support of whatever little rain that was available. However, there have been drastic changes in the thinking of the policy-makers, R and D as well as extension mechanisms in the State and Central Government agencies towards promoting productivity intensive technologies and practices generally in agriculture but more particularly in sericulture. This intensive promotion has side-lined a large number of the marginal and small farmers and their basic needs. They were left with no relevant technologies or messages specially addressing the needs and constraints of these sections of sericulturists who are following the rainfed sericulture.

All this resulted in a situation where in spite of being a drought resistant plant by nature, mulberry is now generally seen as a high water consuming plant. Farmers as well as the extension officials now believe that mulberry cannot be grown/sustained in the absence of intensive irrigation. Yet, large areas still remain under rainfed conditions, even though the returns appear to be low compared to the irrigated sericulture. Ironically in the official statistics rainfed sericulturists are not even acknowledged, thus denying these farmers any attention or support from the formal agencies whatsoever in the form of appropriate research/extension or credit. Another spin-off of such neglect is the gradual disappearance of cost effective and locally evolved, sustainable sericulture practices in the last two generations, just as it is in the case of small-scale agriculturists. All these lead to the following questions:

- Is rainfed sericulture still relevant for the poor as a livelihood option?
- If so, what are the elements, which contribute to its financial viability and long-term sustainability?

- If not, why do the poor farmers in the southern states continue to depend on rainfed sericulture?

II. Research Method

To understand the importance of rainfed sericulture, field level data was collected through a field survey in the villages where Swiss Agency for Development and Cooperation (SDC) has funded for the promotion of rainfed sericulture. The steps involved in the process of data collection are:

- The primary survey was conducted in Tumkur and Dharwad districts of Karnataka State and Dharmapuri district of Tamil Nadu State.
- The locations were selected purposively as the SDC supported action research in rainfed sericulture was going on through Non-Government Organisations (NGOs) in the specified areas.
- To understand the profitability of rainfed sericulture vis-à-vis agricultural crops the method followed by Bhardwaj (1974) has been considered. In this method, three different cost concepts have been used. Cost 'A' is the cash and kind expenses actually incurred in hiring human labour, for the purchase of seeds, manure and other inputs; for payment of land revenue and irrigation and other cesses; depreciation charges on fixed assets and interest on crop loans, if any assuming that the holding is operated by an owner-operator. Cost 'B' is Cost 'A' + the imputed rent on owned land and imputed interest on owned capital (implements and buildings). Cost 'C' consists of Cost 'B' + the imputed value of labour of the farm operator and his family.
- The interpretations of the returns computed on the basis of these cost concepts are - a owner operator would be concerned with gross income minus Cost 'A' if he were guided by the return to the expenses actually incurred. This is called 'Farm Business Income' (FBI) and constitutes returns to the farm operator's and his family's labour together with that of owned capital and on owned land. Gross Income minus Cost 'B' is considered as 'Family Labour Income' (FLI). It is the return to the farm operator's and his family's labour. Profit or loss is defined as gross income minus Cost 'C'. In a fully monetised and capitalist economy it is this last concept of return as Net Income (NI) that would be relevant. In this study all the cost concepts have been taken into account to observe various types of returns.

III. Village Profiles

Two villages (Thammadihalli and Baluvaneralu) in Tumkur district are dominated largely by *Lingayats* and Scheduled Castes (SCs). Majority of the Households (HHs) constitute marginal and small categories of farmers. Agriculture and agriculture-based labour are the major livelihood activities of the HHs in these villages. The major crops grown in the villages are ragi, coconut, pulses, etc. A few HHs have taken up petty business activities to lead their life. The dairy sector is slowly picking up and there is a greater scope for its expansion and development. The villages are situated about 18 kms away from the taluk headquarters and the transport facility is not quite frequent. However, marketing their produce and purchase basic necessities have to be in the taluk headquarters only. In such villages, Rainfed sericulture was introduced in 2003 by the BAIF Institute of Rural Development. This was one of the major anti-poverty programmes of the NGO.

Bagadagere of Kalgatagi taluk in Dharwad district is a remote village, which is about 30 kms. away from the semi-urban centre. This village is also dominated by mostly Lingayats and SCs. The families belonging to other castes are limited. Most of the farmers in this village are either marginal or small farmers. However, the extent of dry land seems to be little high and it is not fertile, and as a result the productivity per acre is low. The major sources of livelihood in the village were agriculture and agriculture labour. The dairy sector is picking up in the village as the families have been trying to own the milch animals. The major crops cultivated in the village were jowar, soybean, cotton, maize and other minor crops. It is a remote village, where even for bus service the people have to walk about 1.5 kms. Therefore, buying the basic necessities and selling their produce becomes difficult. The awareness about new technologies and development is quite low as the literacy rate and communication facilities are limited. Such a village had an opportunity to take up mulberry cultivation and silkworm rearing with the support of BAIF Institute of Rural Development an NGO working in the region.

The villages in Dharmapuri are well connected to the urban centres, awareness is quite high though the literacy level is low. The transport system and other communication facilities are better in the villages. These villages are dominated by the castes *Reddys* and SCs in terms of the number of families. Otherwise, the Reddys are the dominant caste in terms of owning land and having economic and political power. Most of the farmers were cultivating ragi, vegetables, pulses, etc., and also the horticulture crops were tried as they had sufficient irrigation facilities. However, currently the water table has gone down and therefore, they are finding it difficult to grow horticultural crops, paddy and mulberry. The informants in the village reveal that the farmers had mulberry in most of the irrigated area. Few farmers used to cultivate the extent of about five acres of mulberry at a stretch. Currently they do not have mulberry as the irrigation facilities either through wells or bore-wells are not available. Most of the wells and bore-wells are dried. Such villages had an opportunity to introduce rainfed sericulture with the help of OUTREACH an NGO funded by SDC. The NGO has been trying to help the farmers to undertake rainfed sericulture through awareness programmes by forming 'Self-Help groups' and providing finance and extension services.

IV. Socio-Economic Characteristics of the Farm HHs

The profile of the sample HHs has been presented in Table 12.1 In all the three study places the sample HHs are backward and the literacy is low[1], and they are marginal holdings and hardly any irrigated area available for cultivation. However, there is an exception that the literacy level of the beneficiaries Tumkur is better as the awareness among the people to have better education is quite high. One more exception is that the average HH operated area and the per capita operated area in Dharwad district is quite high compared to the other two places. However, the land is not that fertile. It is interesting to observe from the same table that the beneficiaries hardly have any irrigated land.

Table 12.1: Socio-Economic Characteristics of the Sample HHs

Particulars	Dharwad	Dharmapuri	Tumkur
Avg. family size	5.18	6.25	4.6
Avg. no. of adults	3.29	4.67	3.45
Avg. no. of children	1.88	1.59	1.15
Literary level in per cent	34.29	16.67	65.00
Avg. HH owned area in acres	5.74	2.08	2.64
Avg. HH operated area in acres	4.35	1.81	2.60
Per capita operated area in acres	0.84	0.29	0.57

(Contd.)

[1] The beneficiaries belong to down trodden women, therefore, literacy rate is much low in Dharmapuri.

Proportion of non-operated area	24.10	13.00	1.65
Proportion of wetlands to total operated area	Nil	Nil	1.89
No. of sample households	16	12	18

V. Cropping Pattern in The Study Regions

The Table 12.2 presents that in Dharmapuri and Tumkur, the cropping pattern is not diversified when compared to Dharwad. This is mainly due to the small size of land holdings. The ragi crop has taken the major share of the total operated area in Dharmapuri and Tumkur. The next major crop is mulberry constituting 33.33 and 19.23 per cent respectively in Dharmapuri and Tumkur. Soybean, a commercial crop has dominated in terms of area cultivated in Dharwad followed by jowar - the major food crop. The mulberry area has taken the fourth place in terms of land cultivated as the support was given to only half an acre of land.[2]

Table 12.2: Per HH Average Land Cultivated for Each Crop

Crops	*Dharwad*	*Dharmapuri*	*Tumkur*
Mulberry	0.50	0.60	0.50
Ragi	Nil	0.92	1.33
Jowar	1.32	Nil	0.18
Maize	0.76	Nil	Nil
Soybean	1.38	Nil	Nil
Cotton	0.47	Nil	Nil
Pulses	Nil	Nil	0.40
Others	0.21	0.21	0.20

Note: There may be no data in certain rows columns as the cropping pattern differs from district to district.

VI. Profitability of Sericulture Activity vis-à-vis Other Crops

The analysis is presented in two parts. In the first part, the structure of rainfed sericulture holdings, costs, returns and yield per acre have been examined. In the second part, the comparative advantages and disadvantages of sericulture development as an activity vis-à-vis other crops have been presented. The silk industry, in general, has two phases; one relating to the production

[2] Swiss Development Cooperation on trial basis has assisted local NGOs to support the farmers to take up rainfed mulberry in half an acre of land.

of mulberry leaf and cocoons and two, the production of raw silk and utilisation of its by-products. Silkworm rearing forms the first stage consisting of mulberry cultivation and silkworm rearing and ends with the marketing of cocoons. Reeling is the second stage of the silk industry. Silkworm rearing and reeling together form the raw silk industry. In this study only the first part has been attempted as it is intended to study the rainfed sericulture as a source of livelihood for the poor farmers.

Before going into actual costs and returns, an attempt has been made to understand the number of crops grown, number of Diseased Free Layings (DFLs)[3] brushed per year, average yield of cocoons per 100 DFLs and the total cocoon production per acre and per year. At the first instance, details about costs and returns from sericulture activity have been analysed and later, it has been compared with other agricultural crops.

It is interesting to observe from the Table 12.3 that in 2004-05 all the other crops, except mulberry, are cultivated only once. Whereas mulberry, just for nine months (it is only nine months because the beneficiaries started silkworm rearing from the month of September 2004) have taken 3.20 crops and the farmers have expressed that there is a possibility to take one more cocoon crop. The data reveals that the beneficiaries have taken only a single agricultural crop due to lack of sufficient rain and the irrigation facilities. Whereas sericulture/ mulberry is a drought resistant and if it rains twice in a month the farmers get leaf and can take up silkworm rearing. Though the scale is low the farmers were able to get some cash income, which is bleak in case of other agricultural crops.

Table 12.3: Average No. of Crops Grown for each Operational Holding in a Year

Crops cultivated	*Dharwad*	*Dharmapuri*	*Tumkur*
Mulberry	3.18	3.17	3.22
Ragi	Nil	1.00	1.00
Jowar	1.00	Nil	1.00
Maize	1.00	Nil	Nil
Soybean	1.00	Nil	Nil

(Contd.)

[3] Diseased Free Layings are the silkworm eggs produced by the grainages of the Department of Sericulture, GOK, Central Silk Baord, GOI the private licensed seed preparers. They are called DFLs mainly because, before they are released for commercial purpose they are tested for various diseases.

Cotton	1.00	Nil	Nil
Pulses	Nil	Nil	1.00
Others	1.00	1.00	1.00

Production details of sericulture activity are presented in Table 12.4. It is visible from the table that the scale of operation is much high in Dharmapuri study area. This can be seen in terms of DFLs brushed or cocoons produced per family/per acre. In Dharmapuri, per family, around 164 DFLs are brushed when compared to 63 DFLs in Tumkur and only 34 DFLs in Dharwad. The difference is mainly due to the quality of land, which was used for rainfed sericulture. Most fertile land was used for rainfed mulberry in Dharmapuri, therefore, the leaf yield is much higher in these gardens. Where as in other two places, the beneficiaries are new to the rainfed sericulture activity, their gardens are developed from the barren lands, which was used for grazing bovine. However, interestingly, in terms of yield per 100 DFLs Dharwad stands second place. This was mainly due to the loss of worms in Tumkur as the worms were eaten away by the reptiles like lizards, snake, rat, etc., and moreover the huzi menace was also high. The NGO (BAIF) has provided the low cost rearing shed and it could not control the enemies and also in most of the cases the sheds were brought down by the wind. The NGO had provided about ₹ 6,000 to build the sheds and the farmers have built it by using the same amount and they have not contributed any other material. Therefore, the quality was poor and we didn't find any structure with most of the beneficiaries.

Table 12.4: No of DFLs Brushed and Quantum of Cocoon Production Per Acre

Study areas	*Total area under mulberry*	*Avg. area under mulberry*	*Ttl. No. of DFLs brushed*	*Avg. no. of DFLs brushed per family*	*Per acre DFLs brushed*	*Total cocoons produced in Kgs.*	*Avg. yield per 100 DFLs in kgs.*	*Avg. no. of kgs of cocoons per family*	*Per acre Ttl. Cocoon Production*
Dharwad	8.00	0.50	550	34.38	68.75	308	56.00	19.25	38.50
Dharmapuri	7.25	0.60	1965	163.75	271.03	1371	68.00	114.25	189.10
Tumkur	9.00	0.50	1130	62.78	125.56	524	46.37	29.11	58.22

The gross returns per family and per acre are illustrated in Table 12.5. As expected, gross income per family is much higher for the Dharmapuri farmers when compared to the other two places. However, the gross return is high for the beneficiaries in Tumkur though the yield rate is high in Dharwad. This is mainly because the beneficiaries in Tumkur have brushed around 126 layings per acre when compared to the Dharwad, where it was only around 69 layings per acre.

Table 12.5 Total Gross Returns from Sericulture Activity

Study areas	*Ttl. Gross income of the sample HHs*	*Gross income per family*	*Gross income per acre*
Dharwad	38,956	2435	4,870
Dharmapuri	1,69,621	14,135	23,327
Tumkur	56,419	3,134	6,269

Followed by this the cost of the establishment of mulberry garden in the study areas is given in Table 12.6. The total cost incurred by the farmers in the study areas is around ₹ 932. However, in Dharmapuri, farmers have spent little higher constituting about ₹ 1,072 compared to the other two study areas, who have spent more or less the same amount. This is mainly because, the sericulturists in Dharmapuri region have purchased the water to keep their gardens alive. Whereas in the other two study areas, water was not available nearer to their gardens.

Table 12.6: Cost of the Establishment of Mulberry Garden (Rs Per acre)

Various Costs incurred	*Dharwad*	*Dharmapuri*	*Tumkur*
Total Cost 'A'	16600	15450	16600
Total Cost 'B'	16900	20950	17000
Total Cost 'C'	17140	21430	17360
Effective Cost per year **	857	1072	868

Note: ** As mulberry is a perennial crop, and cultivated under pit system, it lasts about 20 years. And therefore, by using 'straight line method' the effective cost of mulberry establishment is worked out.

Mulberry is a peculiar crop, because its cultivation is not the end, as the farmers can take about five crops in a year and after every crop the farmers have to carry out some intercultural activities to raise the next crop. Therefore, there is a cost involved, which is called maintenance cost, and details are furnished in Table 12.7. Even the mulberry maintenance cost reveals that Dharmapuri farmers spend more when compared to the other two study areas. This is mainly because, the scale of operation, which is much higher in Dharmapuri and further labour cost adds to this. The wage rate is much higher, which ranges from ₹ 50 to

₹ 100 based on the demand for labour in various seasons. The second place taken by Tumkur farmers as their scale of operation is higher compared to Dharwad.

Table 12.7: Cost of the Maintenance of Mulberry Garden (Rs Per Acre/Year)

Various costs	*Dharwad*	*Dharmapuri*	*Tumkur*
Total Cost 'A'	1260	2180	1520
Total Cost 'B'	1560	7680	1920
Total Cost 'C'	1910	8330	2410

Note: ** As mulberry is a perennial crop, and cultivated under pit system, it lasts about 20 years. And therefore, by using 'straight line method' the effective cost of mulberry establishment is worked out.

The next issue is to analyse the cost of silkworm rearing and Table 12.8, presents the total cost of silkworm rearing per acre. As it is observed in the case of mulberry maintenance cost, even in case of the cost of silkworm rearing also the same trend is noticed. The farmers in Dharmapuri incurred about ₹ 11,400 per acre, which is much higher than the other two study areas for the obvious reasons which are already explained. Dharwad is much lower constituting not even 50 per cent of the total cost of Dharmapuri farmers.

Table 12.8: Cost of Silkworm Rearing (in Rs Per Acre)

Various costs	*Dharwad*	*Dharmapuri*	*Tumkur*
Total Cost 'A'	972	3036	1487
Total Cost 'B'	972	3036	1487
Total Cost 'C'	5042	11405	6639

A consolidated picture of various costs of mulberry cultivation, maintenance and silkworm rearing have been presented in Table 12.9. The cost on mulberry cultivation, maintenance and silkworm rearing reveals that the cost 'A' the real cost is much lower in all the study areas. However, when the interest on owned capital and the rent on owned land and the imputed cost on family labour is considered the cost is more than double in Dharwad and Tumkur and it is more than three times of cost 'A' in Dharmapuri. Therefore, it will be interesting to study the impact of these various costs on the total returns of the beneficiaries in all the three study areas.

Table 12.9: Cost of Mulberry Establishment, Maintenance and Silkworm Rearing Per Acre (in Rs)

Various costs	*Dharwad*	*Dharmapuri*	*Tumkur*
Total Cost 'A'	3062	5989	3837
Total Cost 'B'	3377	11764	4257
Total Cost 'C'	7809	20807	9917

Before getting into the returns from sericulture the production details of the agricultural crops (competing crops) are presented. The Table 12.10 reveals various crops cultivated in all the three study areas. Interestingly in all the selected regions, the number of crops taken in a year is only one and therefore, the cropping intensity is just one, in case of the agricultural crops. The major crops cultivated are ragi in Dharmapuri and jowar in Dharwad, whereas in Tumkur both ragi and jowar are cultivated. Therefore, jowar and ragi are the major competing crops for mulberry. The other crops cultivated are maize, soybean, cotton and pulses. However, coconut and vegetable crops are cultivated in smaller area.

Table 12.10: Production Details of the Competing Crops

Crops	*Dharwad*			*Dharmapuri*			*Tumkur*		
	No. of crops grown	*Avg. Qty. Produced in Qtl.*	*Avg. price per Qtl.*	*No. of crops grown*	*Avg. Qty. produced in Qtl.*	*Avg. price per Qtl.*	*No. of crops grown*	*Avg. Qty. produced in Qtl.*	*Avg. price per Qtl.*
Ragi	----	----	----	01	2.40	415	01	2.35	405
Jowar	01	2.78	520	----	----	----	01	3.12	545
Maize	01	2.92	625	----	----	----	----	----	----
Soybean	01	2.54	1200	----	----	----	----	----	----
Cotton	01	1.46	1659	----	----	----	----	----	----
Pulses	---	----	----	----	----	----	01	0.76	1680

Note: To work out the profitability, other crops (minor crops) are not taken into account as the area under these crops is much low. However, the returns from these crops is considered for the total HH income.

In Dharwad, about four types of crops are cultivated and of these, the highest cost per acre seems to be for the cultivation of Soybean (Table 12.11). The cost is high for this particular crop because the farmers apply chemical fertilisers. The jowar is the lowest in terms of cost as the application of chemical fertilisers is much low. Coming to Dharmapuri, ragi is the only major crop and the area under other crops is negligible, therefore, only ragi is taken into account for analysis. The cost of ragi cultivation is about ₹ 3,766, which is little higher when compared to Tumkur as the farmers in Dharmapuri have been cultivating the hybrid ragi and they use sufficient organic manure. For all the crops, in all the study areas, the imputed cost of family labour is low as the operations of these crops have to be done at a time in a particular season and therefore, the farmers have to hire labour to a large extent.

Table 12.11: Average Cost per Acre of Agricultural Crops

Crops	*Dharwad*			*Dharmapuri*			*Tumkur*		
	Cost A	*Cost B*	*Cost 'C'*	*Cost A*	*Cost B*	*Cost 'C'*	*Cost A*	*Cost B*	*Cost 'C'*
Ragi	----	----	-----	1610	3138	3766	1585	2635	3220
Jowar	1488	2952	3514	----	----	-----	1384	2726	3242
Maize	1712	3326	3994	----	----	-----	----	----	-----
Soybean	1886	3568	4242	----	----	-----	----	----	-----
Cotton	1644	3209	3847	----	----	-----	----	----	-----
Pulses	----	----	-----	----	----	-----	658	2110	2326

Per acre gross income by crops and size classes has been presented in Table 12.12 the gross income from rainfed sericulture activity has been much higher when compared to the agricultural crops in all the study areas. Across the three study areas Dharmapuri stands first followed by Tumkur. This clearly reveals that whatever the scale, as of now, in all the study areas rainfed sericulture stands first. Again one should not forget that the economics of rainfed sericulture is not for the entire year and it is only for about nine months. Hence, sericulture has to be encouraged even as a rainfed crop as it is clearly proved that it is remunerative.

Table 12.12: Per Acre Gross Income by Crops and Size Classes (in Rs)

Crops	*Dharwad*			*Dharmapuri*			*Tumkur*		
	Main product	*By-Product*	*Total*	*Main product*	*By-Product*	*Total*	*Main product*	*By-Product*	*Total*
Mulberry	4870	620	5490	23327	856	24183	6269	684	6953
Ragi	-----	-----	------	996	1100	2096	952	1100	2052
Jowar	1446	1350	2796	-----	-----	------	1700	1415	3115
Maize	1825	1250	3075	-----	-----	------	-----	-----	------
Soybean	3048	----	3048	-----	-----	------	-----	-----	------
Cotton	2422	---	2422	-----	-----	------	-----	-----	------
Pulses	-----	-----	------	-----	-----	------	1277	650	1927

The Farm Business Income (FBI) presented in Table 12.13 is much more in case of rainfed sericulture activity when compared to agricultural crops. As mentioned already the FBI is the income, which constitutes returns to the farm operator's and his family's labour together with that on owned capital and on owned land. Actually the farmer considers this as the income from the crop, which they cultivate. Since the FBI is much more for mulberry than the agricultural crops the farmers can be motivated to go for rainfed sericulture.

Table 12.13: Farm Business Income Per Year (GI-Cost 'A' in Rs)

Crops Cultivated	*Dharwad*	*Dharmapuri*	*Tumkur*
Mulberry	2428	18194	3116
Jowar	----	486	467
Ragi	1308	----	----
Maize	1363	----	----
Soybean	1162	----	----
Cotton	778	----	----
Pulses	----	----	1269

Gross income minus Cost 'B' is considered as Family Labour Income (FLI). It is the return to the farm operator's and his family's labour. It is interesting to observe from the Table 12.14 that even the FLI is higher for rainfed sericulture compared to the agricultural crops and from almost all the agricultural crops the income is negative when one considers the interest on owned capital and the rent on owned land. Therefore, from the analysis it can be concluded that the agriculture is not at all attractive in all the three study areas. Hence, rainfed sericulture is the better crop and option compared to the agricultural crops.

Table-12.14: Family Labour Income Per Acre/Year (GI - Cost 'B' in Rs)

Crops cultivated	*Dharwad*	*Dharmapuri*	*Tumkur*
Mulberry	2113	12419	2696
Jowar	----	-1042	-674
Ragi	-156	----	----
Maize	-251	----	----
Soybean	-528	----	----
Cotton	-787	----	----
Pulses	----	----	-183

Profit or loss is defined as gross income minus Cost 'C'. In a fully monetised and capitalistic economy it is this last concept of return as Net Income (NI) that would be relevant. The Table 12.15 presents the NI from various crops cultivated in the study regions. It is clear from the table that the NI from all the crops is negative including from rainfed sericulture, this is mainly because of two reasons. First, as mentioned elsewhere, in case of rainfed sericulture the potential has not been utilised and also the crop is taken into account for nine months only. Second, the imputed cost of family labour. In all the three study areas, almost all the beneficiaries were getting wages from the agriculture labour. However, after taking up rainfed sericulture they are working in their own HH activity. Therefore, the imputed cost of family labour is quite high. But it is also fact that the beneficiaries are proud of working in their own house instead of hiring out their labour and sending their women to the fields of rich farmers. However, in Dharmapuri, even the NI is positive and Dharmapuri, is a model as the farmers are trying their level best to utilise the potential. Hence, the paper strongly recommends that the sericulture can be promoted even in the rainfed areas to protect the interests of the subsistence farmers.

Table 12.15: Net Income Per Acre/Year (GI - Cost 'C' in Rs)

Crops cultivated	*Dharwad*	*Dharmapuri*	*Tumkur*
Mulberry	-2319	3376	-2964
Jowar	----	-1670	-1168
Ragi	-718	----	----
Maize	-919	----	----
Soybean	-1194	----	----
Cotton	-1425	----	----
Pulses	----	----	-399

The foregone discussion demonstrates that the sericulture is viable and also adoptable depending upon the geophysical condition of a given region. Other issue like commitment to a particular economic activity also contributes for successfully carrying out crop cultivation like that of rainfed sericulture.

VII. Rainfed Sericulture and its Impact on the Beneficiaries

It is difficult to estimate the impact of rainfed sericulture on the socio-economic status of the farmers as it is too early to comment. However, sericulture can be acknowledged for the same as the beneficiaries pointed out that rainfed sericulture has helped them, to some extent, to improve their standard of living. To start with employment generation - As everyone knows that the villagers have been suffering from un-employment and under employment problems. Therefore, an effort is made to estimate the extent of employment generated in an acre of rainfed sericulture. Table 12.16 presents the employment generation across various crops cultivated in the study regions. In a year, in all the study areas, the employment generation has been much high from rainfed sericulture compared to the agricultural crops cultivated. In Dharwad district, 75.58 per cent of the labour constitutes only family labour. Similar to Dharwad, in Dharmapuri and Tumkur also the family labour constitutes more or less in the same magnitude (75.68 and 74.01 per cent respectively). This strongly suggests that rainfed sericulture is a labour intensive crop and the marginal and small farmers can take it up as they totally involve in the activity.

Table 12.16: Employment Generation Across Crops (Man-days per acre)

Crops	*Dharwad*			*Dharmapuri*			*Tumkur*		
	Family	*Hired*	*Total*	*Family*	*Hired*	*Total*	*Family*	*Hired*	*Total*
Mulberry	132	42	174	168	54	222	131	46	177
Ragi	----	----	----	19	22	41	18	18	36
Jowar	16	18	34	----	----	----	----	----	----
Maize	21	24	45	----	----	----	----	----	----
Soybean	24	28	52	----	----	----	----	----	----
Cotton	22	25	47	----	----	----	----	----	----
Pulses	----	----	----	----	----	----	16	19	35

Household annual income generated from various sources has been presented in Table 12.17. The table reveals that there was no income from rainfed sericulture before 2002-03. However, in the year 2004-05, the income from rainfed sericulture was ₹ 1,214. Whereas agricultural income was only ₹ 121 in Dharwad district, which declined at the rate of 34.59 per cent per year from 2002-03 to 2004-05. Interestingly the beneficiaries used to earn their livelihood by getting wages from agricultural labour constituting ₹ 5,760 per annum, which has come down to ₹ 4,541 showing 21.16 per cent decline per annum. The decline in the wage income is due to rainfed sericulture activity taken up by the beneficiaries. The HH income from dairying is most important. Before two years, the income from dairy activity was only ₹ 678, which is increased to ₹ 1,282 showing an increase of about 89.09 per cent. Hence, it can be concluded that the income from labour has gone down and from dairy it has gone up. This is a positive trend because rainfed sericulture has been responsible to make the farmers to work in their own fields and also generating nutritious fodder for the milch animals, which helped the farmers to increase the livestock, resulted in increase in income. Similar trend can be noticed from the other two study areas as well. Hence, it can be concluded that sericulture is an important activity in the rainfed areas to earn the farmers' livelihood.

Table 12.17: Change in HH Annual Income (Before and After Taking up Rainfed Sericulture Activity (in Rs)

Income sources	*Dharwad*			*Dharmapuri*			*Tumkur*		
	Before	*After*	*% Change*	*Before*	*After*	*% Change*	*Before*	*After*	*% Change*
Sericulture	----	1214	100	---	13707	100	----	3289	100
Agriculture	185	121	-34.59	2976	1928	-35.22	5986	4428	-26.03
Agri-labour	5760	4541	-21.16	7200	4541	-36.93	6800	4358	-35.91
Dairy	678	1282	89.09	842	1816	115.68	6570	8287	26.13
Service*	1765	1767	0.11	Nil	Nil	----	Nil	Nil	Nil
Trade**	2118	2355	11.19	3388	3974	17.30	2746	3246	18.21
Total	10506	11280	7.37	14406	25986	80.38	22102	23608	6.81

Note: * Only one beneficiary has got some job, ** One beneficiary doing petty-business.

There has been change in the level of HH income of the farmers after taking up rainfed sericulture. According to the well-established economic theory, when there is a change in income, there will be change in expenditure of the households. Therefore, an effort is made to understand the expenditure level of the sample HHs and the details are presented in Table 12.18. The table reveals that there is an increase in consumption expenditure of the HHs in all the three study areas. The percentage increase in expenditure on medicine, entertainment, pan/tobacco, transport, vegetables and meat is quite high starting from 17.15 per cent to 70.18 per cent in Dharwad, in Dharmapuri, the expenditure on education, medicine, vegetable, fish/meat, edible oil, pan/tobacco and entertainment is higher ranging from 18.63 to 35.26 per cent. In Tumkur, the expenditure on pan/tobacco, medicine and education is quite high ranging from 16.33 to 20.83 per cent. In all the three study areas the expenditure has gone up by about 10.08, 14.19 and 10.13 respectively. Therefore, this enables us to conclude that the standard of living of the beneficiaries, who belong to downtrodden, has gone up as they are spending on education, medicine, vegetables, meat, edible oil and entertainment.

Table 12.18: Average HH Expenditure at 2002-03 prices (Rs per year)

Items of expenditure	*Dharwad*			*Dharmapuri*			*Tumkur*		
	Before	*After*	*% Change*	*Before*	*After*	*% Change*	*Before*	*After*	*% Change*
Cereals	2068	2258	9.18	2494	2684	7.62	2282	2512	10.08
Pulses	584	642	9.93	648	722	11.42	624	662	6.09
Vegetables	312	368	17.95	402	509	26.62	384	414	7.81
Fish/Meat	618	724	17.15	728	910	25.00	714	764	7.42
Edible oil	452	488	7.96	512	622	21.48	496	548	10.48
Sugar/Jagary	168	168	00	172	172	00	172	172	00
Transport	358	486	35.75	462	526	13.85	438	492	12.33
Medicine	228	388	70.18	314	424	35.03	312	372	19.23
Entertainment	304	412	35.53	408	484	18.63	392	428	9.18
Pan/Tobacco	314	411	30.89	402	478	18.91	384	464	20.83
Clothes	2425	2700	11.34	2956	3258	10.22	2788	3050	9.40
Education & Others	228	242	6.14	312	422	35.26	294	342	16.33
Total	8063	8876	10.08	9818	11211	14.19	9280	10220	10.13

Many studies have highlighted that silk and milk go together and therefore, the status of the stock of livestock in the two time periods is worked out to observe any change in the stock of milch animals due to rainfed sericulture. Table 12.19 presents the status of livestock in to two time periods (i.e., before and after sericulture) over a period of two years. It can be clearly understood from the table that there is a greater change in the case of the stock of milching cows and buffaloes in all the three study areas. Any way the change in livestock need not be directly attributed to the income from rainfed sericulture activity alone. However, the fodder, which is generated from rainfed sericulture, induced the beneficiaries to go for buying rearing milch animals (Gopalappa, 1996).

Table 12.19: Distribution of Livestock (Two Different Time Periods in No. per HH)

Livestock	*Dharwad*			*Dharmapuri*			*Tumkur*		
	Before	*After*	*% Change*	*Before*	*After*	*% Change*	*Before*	*After*	*% Change*
Bullocks	14	14	----	03	05	33.33	04	04	---
Cows	05	08	30.00	05	08	30.00	03	05	33.33
Buffaloes	05	08	30.00	---	01	100.00	---	---	---
Sheep/Goat	---	03	100.00	---	---	----	13	15	7.69

(Contd.)

Conclusions

Rainfed sericulture in all the three study locations proved to be profitable as their Farm Business Income and Farm Labour Income has been high. The Net Income is not positive in two study areas because of three reasons. First, in these locations, the farmers are relatively new to rainfed sericulture and mulberry is cultivated only on barren land used for grazing bovine, which has been developed over a period of one and half years. Therefore, there is every possibility to increase the mulberry leaf yield and also increase in DFLs brushings. In turn it is expected that there will be increase in total production as well as income. Second, since the rearing sheds were constructed by using local material, the reptiles could not be prevented. These reptiles have eaten away the silkworms to some extent. If one can take care of these problems, there is a scope to increase the productivity. Last, the potential period of another three months, in a year has not been fully utilised. It is during this period farmers can take an additional crop, which will influence the total returns.

The most important point is when compared to other seasonal crops, in all respects, rainfed sericulture proved to be remunerative as the income and employment generation is more. This has resulted in the improvement of the standard of living of the rainfed sericulturists. More than these the rainfed sericulturists stopped/reduced hiring out their labour (especially female labour) as they have got gainful employment in their own HHs. The men, in these HHs, say that their social status has gone up due to rainfed sericulture, as they are not sending their women to other HHs and they themselves are not hiring out their labour. Hence, rainfed sericulture is strongly recommended to be introduced in the vast rainfed regions of Andhra Pradesh, Tamil Nadu and Karnataka States in India. This also helps to compete with China, who is producing the highest silk constituting about 71 per cent of the total raw silk production in the world and dumping in the Indian silk market (CSB, 2008). As of now India produces only 17 per cent of the total world silk production.

References

Central Silk Board (2008). *Statistical Biannual,* Ministry of Textiles, Government of India, Bengaluru.

Gopalappa, D.V. (1996). Crop Diversification and Income Levels in Karimnagar District of Andhra Pradesh. *Indian Journal of Agricultural Economics,* 51(3): 381-8.

Gopalappa, D.V. (1997). Challenges in Silk Reeling Industry. *Productivity,* 37(4): 704-11.

Gopalappa, D.V. (2000). Small Farmers and Sericulture – A Study of Rayalaseema Region in Andhra Pradesh. A Ph.D. Thesis Submitted and awarded from the Bengaluru University, Bengaluru.

Gopalappa, D.V. (2002). Sericulture Industry and Liberalisation Regime. *The Asian Economic Review,* 44(3): 503-11.

Government of India (1980). *The Sixth Five Year Plan.* Planning Commission, New Delhi.

Inbanathan Anand and D.V. Gopalappa (1998). Health and Sericulture. Unpublished Project Report. *Institute for Social and Economic Change,* Bengaluru.

13

International Labour Migration and India

Professor H.R. Uma and Madhu. S

I. Introduction

According to The International Migration Report 2015 the number of international migrants worldwide has continued to grow rapidly over the past fifteen years reaching 244 million in 2015, up from 222 million in 2010 and 173 million in 2000. Nearly two-thirds of all international migrants live in Europe (76 million) or Asia (75 million). Northern America hosted the third largest number of international migrants (54 million), followed by Africa (21 million), Latin America and the Caribbean (9 million) and Oceania (8 million). In 2015, two-thirds (67 per cent) of all international migrants were living in just twenty countries. The largest number of international migrants (47 million) resided in the United States of America, equal to about a fifth (19 per cent) of the world's total. Germany and the Russian Federation hosted the second and third largest numbers of migrants worldwide (12 million each), followed by Saudi Arabia (10 million).

Migration is a global phenomenon, deeply affecting the lives of millions of migrants around the globe and also the lives of those connected to them, in particular those left behind in the countries of origin. Migration is a multi-faceted experience that encompasses opportunities for personal, social and economic development and also includes risks of violence, abuse and exploitation for men and women alike.

According to a report published by Global Commission on International Migration, more than 60 per cent of global migrants are in developed countries and remaining 40 per cent are in developing countries. The report recognises that nearly one out of every 10 persons living in developed countries is a migrant. The highly developed regions receive each year around 2.3 million migrants.

Globalisation has actually opened up national boundaries for human mobility across borders, even though it includes all strategies to let capital and commodities flows across them. Globalisation and post-reform play an important role in international migration and they are responsible for an increase in the international flow from developing countries. They are not only driven international labour flow but also considered as an important consequences of this. There is deep divergence in demographic trends in developed and developing countries leading to a high demand for labourers in developed countries and supply of labourers in developing countries along with this changing trends in consumerism, advancement in transport and telecommunication are become the key factors to stimulate large scale labour migration. With this background the paper analyses recent trends in the international labour migration with specific reference to migration from India. The paper for its data source is dependent on different rounds of NSSO, World Bank Data Bank and Ministry of External Affairs, Government of India.

II. Labour Migration Corridors Across the World

India is one of the labour abundant countries. With improvement in education and skill, India is considered as a country with a huge reservoir of both skilled and semi-skilled labour force. This has improved the status of India at international level as it is considered as one of the major contributors to contemporary labour flows. Since 1990 the liberalised India has registered an impressive growth of labour migration not only with its traditional destinations like United States of America (USA), the United Kingdom (UK), and Canada and Arab countries, but also diversified and expanded its migrant destinations to Germany, France, Belgium, Australia, New Zealand, Japan (East Asia) and Singapore, Malaysia (South East Asia). This has led to drastic increase in the proportion of Indian migrants to other countries in recent decades. In 2015, of the 244 million international migrants worldwide, 104 million (43 per cent), were born in Asia. In 2015, India had the largest "diaspora" in the world with 16 million.

Table 13.1: Top 10 Labour Migration Corridors in the World

Migration Corridors	*Number of Migrants*
Mexico-USA	11,635,995
Russian FED-Ukraine	3,684,217
Ukraine-Russian FED	3,647,234
Bangladesh-India	3,299,268

Turkey-Germany	2,733,109
Kazakhstan-Russian FED	2,648,315
Russian FED-Kazakhstan	2,226,706
China-Hong Kong	2,224,503
India-United Arab Emirates	2,185,919
China-USA	1,736,314

Source: World Bank Data Bank.

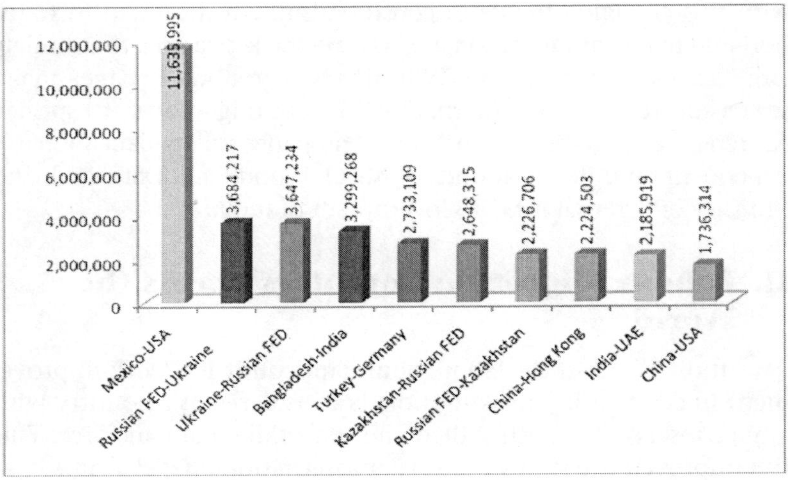

Fig 13.1: Top 10 Labour Migration Corridors in the World.

The above Table 13.1 shows the top 10 labour migration corridors in the world. India has two major labour migration corridors in the top 10; one corridor belongs to the immigration and one belongs to the emigration. Bangladesh to India takes fourth place in the table as immigration. Bangladesh is the major labour sending country to India. There is 3,299,268 Bangladesh migrants stock in India. It is fourth highest migration flow in the world. Indian highest number of skilled, semi-skilled and unskilled labourers is migrating to United Arab Emirates. This is another major migration corridor in the world. It takes ninth place in the list of top ten migration corridors in the world with migrants 2,185,919. Mexico to USA is in the first place with 11,635,995. It is highest migrants flow from one country to another particular country in the world. Russia to Ukraine and vice versa is another major migration corridor in the world. 3,684,217 Russian migrants are residing in Ukraine and 3,647,234 Ukraine migrants residing in Russia. Kazakhstan-Russian FED and vice versa is another major labour exchange corridor. 2,648,315 Kazakhstan labourers in Russian federation and 2,226,706. Russian federation labourers are residing in Kazakhstan. It is in sixth and seventh place respectively. China to Hong Kong and China to USA are other major migration corridors in the top 10 migration corridor. Many of the push and pull factors determine the migration flows in the above corridor.

Table 13.2: Top Migration Corridors With Reference to India

Top Migration Corridors with Reference to India	*Number of migrants*
Bangladesh-India	3,299,268
India-United Arab Emirates	2,185,919
India-USA	1,654,272
India-Saudi Arabia	1,452,927
Pakistan-India	1,150,952
India-Bangladesh	1,052,775
India-Nepal	831,432
India-United Kingdom	657,792
Nepal-India	564,906
India-Canada	516,508
India-Oman	447,824
India-Kuwait	393,210

Source: World Bank Data Bank.

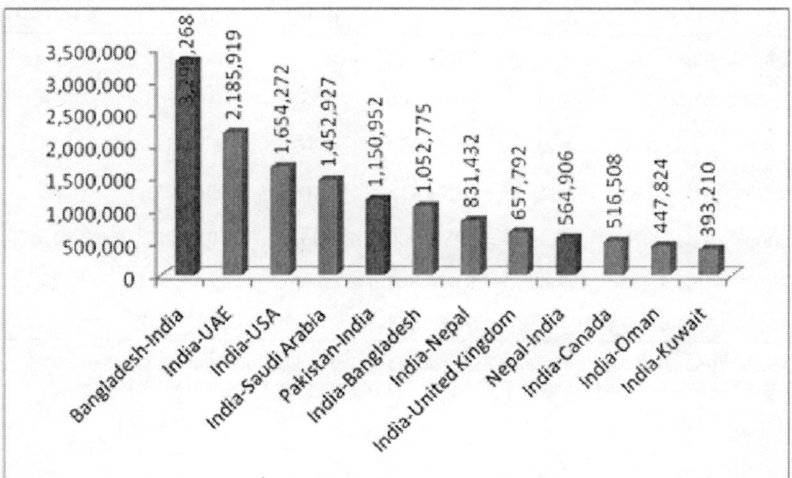

Fig 13.2: Top Migration Corridors with reference to India.

Above Table 13.2 shows the international labour migration corridors with reference to India. Bangladesh is the highest immigrants sending country to India; Bangladesh is one of the neighbouring countries. For shorter distances between Indian and Bangladesh, environmental and socio-economic reasons Bangladesh immigrants enter India for livelihood and safety. Pakistan and Nepal labourers are also immigrating to India. Some of the reasons are distance, religious, economic and political reasons. Pakistan labourers immigrate to India; Nepal labourers are immigrating to India for livelihood and better employment compare to their origin country. Indian semi and unskilled labourers emigration to UAE, Saudi Arabia, Omen, Kuwait for higher remuneration and employment. On the other side, skilled and semi-skilled labourers are emigrating to USA, UK and Canada for higher wages for their qualification, skill, higher living standard, good working environment and professional development. India receives the immigrants mainly from Asia and neighbour countries. Indian emigration mainly to Arab countries and developing countries for above mentioned reasons. Figure 3.B is showing the major origin and destination with reference to India.

Table 13.3: Indian Emigration Stock in Other Asian Countries and SAARC

Year	*Emigration from India*	*Decadal Growth Rate*	*Asian Total*	*Decadal Growth Rate*	*SAARC*	*Decadal Growth Rate*
1960	90,81,856		75,55,722		72,87,696	
1970	82,60,671	-9.04	64,03,888	-15.24	60,04,951	-17.60
1980	75,82,075	-8.21	59,07,053	-7.76	55,76,517	-7.13
1990	81,76,570	7.84	54,71,415	-7.37	48,65,051	-12.76
2000	95,16,805	16.39	58,36,080	6.66	44,35,027	-8.84
2010	1,34,25,336	41.07	93,76,305	60.66	26,28, 651	-40.73
2013	1,41,65,774		98,86,328		26,17 ,187	

Source: 1960-2000 data from World Bank data bank Global Bilateral Migration Database, 2010 and 2013 data from UN population division, department of economic and social affairs.

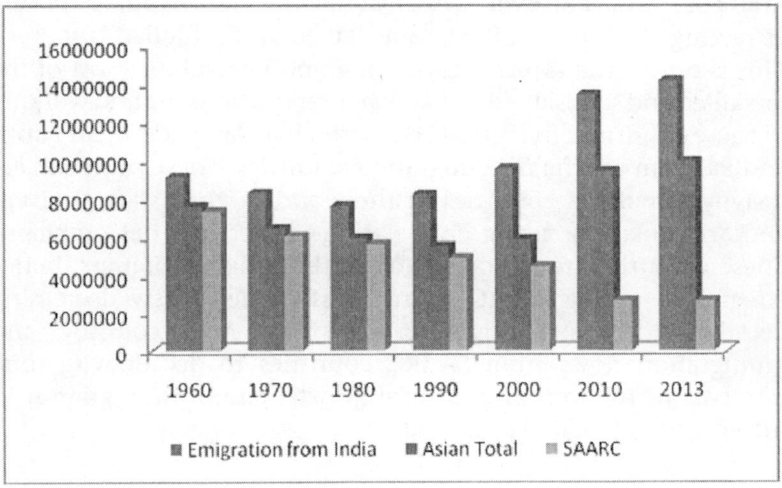

Fig 13.3: Indian Emigration Stock in Asian Countries and SAARC.

Table and Figure 13.3 shows the emigration. flows from India. Total emigration stock of India is 90,81,856 in 1960, it decreases to 75,82,075 in 1980, total emigration stock increases to 81,76,570, decade by decade emigration increases and it is 1,34,25,336 in 2010. Emigration from Asia is also follow the same trend of total emigration flow from India, but emigration to SAARC countries is decreasing continuously, emigration to SAARC countries is 72,87,696 in 1960, it decreases to 48,65,051 in 1990 and 26,28,651 in 2010. Decadal growth rate shows the decade-wise change in emigration flow. Emigration from India is -9.04 per cent and -8.21 per cent in 1970 and 1980 respectively. Decadal growth rate of emigration is 7.84 per cent in 1990. This percentage sharply increased to 16.39 per cent and 41.07 per cent in 2000 and 2010 respectively, 2000 to 2010 decadal growth of emigration is tremendously increased. The decadal growth rate of emigration to Asian countries is -15.24 per cent in 1970, it is -7.37 per cent in 1990, 6.66 per cent in 2000, sharp increase of 66.6 per cent between 2000 to 2010, on the other side decadal growth rate of emigration stock in SAARC countries is -17.60 per cent between 1960 to 1970, -8 84 per cent between 1990-2000 and -40.73 per cent between 2000 to 2010. It shows the continuous decrease in the Indian Emigration stock in SAARC countries. Emigration to Asian countries is increasing and emigration to SAARC countries in decreasing. Emigration to Asian countries from India mainly to

Arab countries is likely to UAE, Qatar, Omen and Saudi Arabia are attracting the Indian skilled, semi-skilled and unskilled labourers. This is one of the top ten labour migration corridors. Most of the unskilled and semiskilled Indian labourers are residing and working in these countries, but SAARC countries like Bangladesh, Sri Lanka and Pakistan are the net emigrating countries. These countries are heavily populated countries in the world. Afghanistan, Pakistan and Sri Lanka are facing civil war and other internal problems. These countries are failing to attract the Indian labourers, hence emigration to the SRRAC countries is tremendously decreasing decade by decade. Immigration flows from Asian countries and immigration flows from SAARC countries to decade-wise total numbers in millions and decadal growth rate of immigration in the year of 1960-2010 and 2013.

Table 13.4: Trends In International Labour Migration From Selected Indian States

State /Year	*2005*	*2010*	*2012*
Andhra Pradesh	48 498 (8.8)	72 220 (11.3)	92 803 (12.4)
Bihar	9336 (1.7)	60 531 (9.4)	84078 (11.3)
Karnataka	75 384 (13.7)	17 295 (2.7)	17960 (2.4)
Kerala	125 075 (22.8)	104 101 (16.2)	98 178 (13.1)
Maharashtra	29 289 (5.3)	18 123 (2.8)	19 259 (2.6)
Punjab	24 088 (4.4)	30 974 (4.8)	37 472 (5.0)
Rajasthan	21 899 (4.0)	47 803 (7.5)	50 295 (6.7)
Tamil Nadu	117 050 (21.3)	84 510 (13.2)	78 185 (10.5)
Uttar Pradesh	22 558 (4.1)	140 826 (22.0)	191 341 (25.6)
West Bengal	5 102 (0.9)	28 900 (4.5)	36 988 (5.0)
All India	548 853	641 356	747 041

Note: Figures in brackets reflect the percentage to total.
Source: MOIA, 2010 and 2013.

The annual level of recorded low-skilled labour migration to GCC countries (estimated at 600,000– 800,000 workers) is a small proportion of India's labour force (estimated at nearly 485 million);

yet, in comparison with the annual addition to the labour force in the past two decades (at an average of seven million to eight million workers per year), the figure for the labour outflow is quite significant and has had a crucial role as a safety valve for the labour market. In view of the long-term changes in demographic composition and ageing of populations in most of the industrialised world and the persisting demand for migrant labour in the developing and developed countries, international migration from India will continue to be an important instrument for leveraging India's demographic dividend.

III. Stagnant Employment Growth

A major challenge for the Indian economy is the generation of adequate employment; employment growth during the current decade has been much lower than the rates recorded during the two previous decades (Table). Such deceleration in employment growth is visible across spatial and gender differentials.

Table 13.5: Growth Of Employment, By Rural Or Urban Location And Sex (In per cent)

Years	*Rural*			*Urban*			*Total*		
	Male	*Female*	*Total*	*Male*	*Female*	*Total*	*Male*	*Female*	*Total*
1983–1994	1.9	1.4	1.7	3.1	3.4	3.2	2.2	1.6	2
1994–2005	1.4	1.6	1.5	3.1	3.3	3.1	1.9	1.8	1.8
1983–2005	1.7	1.5	1.6	3.1	3.3	3.2	2	1.7	1.9
2005–2012	1.1	-2.8	-0.2	2.5	1.1	2.2	1.5	-2	0.4

Note: Usual principal and subsidiary status employment.
Source: NSSO, various years.

One of the major concerns regarding the Indian labour market is the relatively high youth unemployment rate, as indicated in the Table. While the open unemployment rate (for all age groups) in India has been relatively low, the rate of unemployment among youth has been almost double the overall rate.

Table 13.6: Unemployment Rate (Current Daily Status), By Age Cohort And Sex (In per cent)

Age	*Male*	*Female*	*Total*
1993–94			
15–24	11.4	10.8	11.2
25–34	6.5	6.7	6.6

(Contd.)

35 and older	3.0	4.0	3.3
Total	**5.9**	**6.3**	**6.0**
	2004–05		
15–24	14.5	15.7	14.8
25–34	7.8	10.4	8.5
35 and older	4.9	6.1	5.3
Total	**7.8**	**9.2**	**8.3**
	2011–12		
15–24	12.9	14.7	13.3
25–34	5.4	7.4	5.9
35 and older	2.9	3.8	3.1
Total	**5.3**	**6.6**	**5.6**

Source: NSSO rounds of various years.

The magnitude of the problem becomes all the more evident when the unemployment rate among educated youth is factored in. The demographic composition of the population, while providing a window of opportunity, could become a serious issue if jobs of adequate quality are not made available to the increasingly educated young entrants to the labour market.

It is clear from the above table that the provision of quality employment to the increasingly youthful population is emerging as a prominent challenge in India. Although the generation of quality employment within the country is the surest means to enable sustainable livelihoods to the vast majority of the low-income and low-skilled population, it is also important to consider the role of overseas migration in reducing the pressure on domestic employment. This is particularly compelling because, unlike in most industrialised countries, the level of unemployment rates in India has a direct correlation with educational attainment. In this context, it is critical to recognise the importance of improving the skill base of the labour force in order to respond to the changing skill demand in destination countries.

TABLE 13.7: SHARE OF EMPLOYMENT, BY MAJOR SECTORS (In per cent)

Sectors/ Year	*1993–94*	*2004–05*	*2011–12*
Agriculture and allied activities	64.8	58.5	48.9
Mining and quarrying	0.7	0.6	0.5
Manufacturing	10.5	11.7	12.8

(Contd.)

Electricity, gas and water supply	0.4	0.3	0.4
Construction	3.1	5.6	10.6
Trade, hotels and restaurants	7.4	10.2	11.4
Transport, storage and communication	2.8	3.8	4.4
Financing, real estate and business services	0.9	1.5	2.6
Community, social and personal services	9.4	7.7	8.2

Source: NSSO, various years.

In the case of emigration, there is a demand for more workers (including those previously in the agriculture sector) to migrate to other countries, particularly developed and GCC countries, to work in various occupational categories, both low-skilled (such as construction, the low-end service sector and domestic work) and medium-skilled (such as healthcare workers and high-end service activities). The destination countries study (which this report draws from) sheds some light on the emerging sector-specific demand for migrant workers in the GCC countries and highly skilled migrants in developed countries.

The GCC countries are the major destinations for South Asian migrants during the 1970s and has remained the number one destination due to massive development brought about by the oil boom. Nowadays GCC countries (except Saudi Arabia) has a small native population relation to their total population size amount of natural resources and the need for human resources to meet the demands of their growth sectors. On the other hand developed countries and some of the European countries are facing a shortage of highly skilled labourers. Foreign labour made up nearly 99 per cent of the private sector's labour force in Qatar (2012); 93 per cent in Kuwait (2013) and 89 per cent in Saudi Arabia (2011). The GIZ/ILO study (2015). Most of the GCC and other destination countries will continue facing demand pressure to keep up with their growth, causing the demand for low-skilled and semi-skilled workers from India (as well as other countries in Asia and Africa) to persist in the short to medium terms. The extent of the pressure will depend on the demographic and policy shifts in those countries. Nationalisation policies combined with the increasing workforce participation of indigenous women are likely to result in labour-substitution effects as native workers take up positions occupied previously by labour migrants, reducing the demand for foreigners.

IV. Conclusion

Migration is an emerging global issue affecting most of the nations, particularly developing ones. Since it is linked to employment and income generation it has developed a bond to an overall development to the economy. The contribution of the migrants in terms of remittance to their home countries is not only significant but is also rising. The labour migration not only bringing economic benefits to the developing countries, productive labour to the ageing developed countries but also leading to socio-cultural interrelations. When supported by appropriate policies, migration can contribute to inclusive and sustainable economic growth and development in both home and host communities. The 2030 Agenda for Sustainable Development recognises the positive contribution of migrants for inclusive growth and sustainable development. It further recognises that international migration is a multi-dimensional reality of major relevance for the development of countries of origin, transit and destination, which requires coherent and comprehensive responses. International cooperation is critical to ensure safe, orderly and regular migration involving full respect for human rights and the humane treatment of migrants and refugees.

References

Chiswick, B., and Hatton, T. J. (2003). International migration and the integration of labour markets. In *Globalization in historical perspective* (pp. 65-120). University of Chicago Press.

Docquier, F., and Rapoport, H. (2008). Skilled migration: the perspective of developing countries.

Hatton, T. J., and Williamson, J. G. (2005). *What fundamentals drive world migration?* (pp. 15-38). Palgrave Macmillan, UK.

Kritz, M. M. (1992). *International migration.* John Wiley and Sons, Ltd.

Nayyar, D. (1989). International labour migration from India: a macro-economic analysis. *To the Gulf and Back Migration: Studies on the Economic Impact of Asian Labour migration, edited by Rashid Amjad,* 95-142.

Nayyar, D. (1994). Migration remittances and capital flows: the Indian experience.

Page, J., and Plaza, S. (2006). Migration remittances and development: A review of global evidence. *Journal of African Economies, 15*(suppl 2), 245-336.

Sasikumar, S.K., and Thimothy Rakkee (2015). From India to the Gulf region: Exploring links between labour markets, skills and the migration cycle, *the International Labour Organisation (ILO)*.ISBN: 978-92-2-129939-4, and 978-92-2-129940-0.

Skeldon, R. (2006). Interlinkages between internal and international migration and development in the Asian region. *Population, space and place, 12*(1), 15-30.

Prof. Manjappa D. Hosamane: A Bibliography

ARTICLES, PROJECTS AND CHAPTERS IN BOOKS

- Impact of FDI on Growth Performance of Corporate Manufacturing Sector in India- An Empirical Analysis, (With Sadhana) **Journal of Regional Disparities and Socio-economic Changes**, KARENG 04154, Vol.1, ISSUE 1, January 2011, ISSN-2231-0533.
- FDI and Output Growth in Top Six FDI Received Indian Industries- An Empirical Analysis, (with Sadhana) **International Journal of Social and Economic Research** (ISSN Web/Online Journal), Vol.1, No.1, Issue 1, January - June 2011.
- Financial Liberalisation, Development and Industry growth (with Niranjan R) in **Business Perspectives**, Volume 12, No.1, 2011.
- Determinants of Investment Pattern in Indian Manufacturing Industries, (with Niranjan R) **Indian Journal of Economics and Business**, Vol. 9, No. 1, March 2010.
- Industrial Growth and Policies in Karnataka, **FKCC Journal**, Vol. XXX, Issue 12, December 2009.
- Entrepreneurship and Higher Education: The Relationship between Management and SSIs Performance in Iran, (with Y A Vakil), **Indian Journal of Adult Education**, Vol. 70, No. 4 October-December 2009.
- Management of Retail Assets in Banking Credit Migration and Default Correlation, **International Journal of Economic Issues**, (Co-Author with Dinabandhu Bag) Vol. 2, No.1, June 2009.
- Iran Small Scale Industries and Export Decision Making: Selection of Preference Order, (Co-Author with Y A Vakil) **Asian Profile**, Vol. 37, No. 2, April 2009.
- Entrepreneurship and Development of Small-Scale Industries in Iran: Strategic Management Tools and Business Performance Assessment, (with A Y Vakil) *The ICFAI University Journal of Entrepreneurship Development*, Vol. VI, No. 1, pp. 27-40, March 2009.

- Entrepreneurial Innovation: Theories and Policies in Some Countries (with Y A Vakil) **Asian Journal of Development Matters**, Vol. 3. No1. January 2009.
- Entrepreneurship and Higher Education: The Relationship between Management and SSIs Performance in Iran, **Review Journal of Philosophy and Social Science**, Vol. xxxiv, No. 1 and 2 January, 2009.
- Management of Retail Assets in Banking Comparison of Internal Model over Basel, **International Journal of Rural Development and Management, (Co-Author with Dinabandhu Bag)**, Vol. 2, No. 2 December 2008.
- Telecom Market Structure, Regulation and Pricing in India - An Empirical Study, **The ICFAI University Journal of Infrastructure**,(Co-author with Farahani T**)** *The ICFAI University Journal of Infrastructure,* Vol. VI, No. 4, pp. 65-73, December 2008.
- Productivity Performance of Selected Capital-Intensive and Labour-Intensive Industries in India During Reform Period – An Empirical Analysis, (Co-Author with Mahesh M) **The ICFAI University Journal of Industrial Economics**, Vol. V, No. 4, pp. 57-65, November 2008.
- Dynamic Gains from Foreign Trade –Measurement and Empirical Evidence from **Indian Journal of Development and Social Change**, Vol. 5, No. 3 and 4, April to June 2008 and July – September, 2008.
- Measurement of Productivity Growth, Efficiency change and Technical Progress of Selected Capital-Intensive and Labour-Intensive Industries during Reform Period in India, **(**Co-author, Mahesh**) Indian Journal of Economics and Business**, Vol.7, No. 1, June 2008.
- Estimating Consumer Welfare in Indian Mobile Telecommunications Market: An Empirical Study, (Co-author, T Farahani) **Business Perspectives**, BIMT, New Delhi Vol. 10, No. 1, January-June 2008.
- Substitutability between Wireless and Wire Line: An Empirical Study of Indian Telecom Sector, (Co-author, T Farahani), **Business Perspectives**, BIMT, New Delhi, Vol. 9, No. 1; January-June 2007.
- Export Performance of India during Post-reform Period: **Constant Market Share Analysis, Indian Journal of Economics and Business**, Vol. 5, No. 1, June 2006.

- Dairy Cooperatives: Vital Role in Rural Economy, (with Vinay M R), **Kurukshetra**, A Journal of Rural Development, Vol. 52, No. 12, October, 2004.
- Money Supply, National Income and Foreign Trade: Empirical Explorations of Indian Economy, **The Asian Economic Review**, Vol. 46, No. 2, August 2004.
- Impact of United Kingdom Membership to European Community on Indian Exports' **Indian Development Review**, Vol. 2, no. 2, December 2004.
- Import-led Growth-led Export: A Trade -Development Model for Developing Countries, **The Indian Economic Journal**, (with I V Hegde) Vol. 45, no. 3, Jan-Mar. 1997 - 98 (Econlit).
- Cost-Benefit Analysis of Priority Sector Lending in India - An Empirical Study, **Finance India**, Vol. XI, No. 2, June 1997.
- Impact of Export Financing on Inter-Industrial Output of Indian Economy: An Empirical Study, **Journal of Foreign Exchange and International Finance**, Vol. 9 (3), Oct-Nov.1995.
- The Budgetary Deficit and the External Trade Account in India: An Empirical Study, **Foreign Trade Review**, Vol. 30 (1), April-June, 1995.
- Urban Growth in India- the Context of Developing Countries Urbanisation, **Asian Journal of Economics and Social Studies**,Vol.13,(2), April, 1994.
- Cost-Benefit Analysis of Concessional Export Financing in India, **Journal of Foreign Exchange and International Finance**, July-Sept, 1993.
- Export Finance in India: An Empirical Study, **Pigmy Economic Review**, Syndicate Bank, Manipal, April 1991.
- Economics of Bio-Gas Technology in India, **The Indian Economic Journal**, April-June, 1990. **(Econlit)**.
- Changing Scenario of International Bank-scope, problems and prospects for Indian Banks, **The Banker**, December 1989.
- Export Credit - Medium and Long Term Finance, **The Economic Time**; October 17, 1986.
- Exim Bank and Export Promotion, **The Economic Time**; July, 17, 1985.
- Mathematical Models in Development Planning, **Economic Affairs**, July-Sept. **(Econlit)**, 1981.

- Recent Trends of Trade of Less Developed Countries, **Eastern Economist**, July 1981.

EDITED BOOKS

- Dairy Cooperatives: Vital Role in Rural Economy, **Better Quality of Rural Life**, Edited Vol. 1 edited by Sawalia Bihari Verma, Murali Krishna Sharma and Niraj Kumar Sharma. Sarup & Sons, New Delhi, 2008.
- Government Policy, Technology Inflow and Industrial Behavior – A Case of India Automobile Industry, **WTO and Indian Economy**, Edited Vol, M N Jugale, (with Vinay M R), Serials Publications, 2004.
- Financing of Foreign Trade in the Post – W T O Period, **W.T.O. and Banking Sector in India**, Edited by G V Joshi, Mangalore University, 2004.
- Globalisation and Consumer Behaviour: A Case Study of Automobile Industry, in edited volume on **Globalisation, Growth and Poverty** edited by V B Jugale, (with Vinay M R) Serial Publication, 2003, New Delhi.
- Department of Studies in Economics and Cooperation : Achievement and Prospects, **Legacy of Learning**, edited by V G Talawar and B S Kiranagi, Mysore University, 2002.
- Impact of Commercial Banking Institution on Some of Macro-Variables of Indian Economy, **Econometric Studies of Economic Reforms in India**, Edited by V V Somayalu, 2000, Academic Foundation.
- "Sectoral Resource Allocation and Asset Management for Improving Profitability", **Banking Better Profitability**, McMillan India, 1982.

BOOKS REVIEWED

- Workforce Development Networks in Rural Areas: Building the High Road, Gary Paul Green, Edward Elgar Publishing, 2007, Journal of Social and Economic Development, Jan-June-2008,Vol. 10, No.1.
- Econometrics and Data Analysis for Developing Countries by Chandan Mukherjee, Howard White and Marc Wuyts Published by Routledge London for Data Archive Bulletin, May,1998.

RESEARCH PROJECTS

- Theoretical Models Applied to Explain the Growth Path of Indian Economy: An Empirical Investigation, 2009.
- Performance, Constraints and Prospects Analysis of Small Scale Industries in Karnataka, 2007.
- Evaluation of Minor Irrigation Scheme, Replacement of Oil Engine by Electric Motors – Gujarat, 1983 (Sponsored by NABARD).
- Inland Fisheries Development Scheme in Dur – Rajnandgaon District, Madhya Pradesh, 1986, (Sponsored by NABARD).
- Evaluation of Scheme for the development of Sericulture in Bangalore District, Karnataka State, 1985, (Sponsored by NABARD).
- Evaluation of Scheme of Financing of Family – Size Gobar Gas Plant in Surat and Valsad District, Gujarat, 1984, (Sponsored by NABARD).
- Concurrent Evaluation Study of Institutional Finance for the Development of Women Entrepreneurs, Bangalore District, Karnataka State, 1989, (Reserve Bank of India).

Index